当代国外语言学与应用语言学文库

U0687265

Discourse Analysis
话语分析

Gillian Brown and George Yule 著

罗选民　导读

外语教学与研究出版社
剑桥大学出版社

京权图字：01-2000-0162

图书在版编目（CIP）数据

话语分析 ＝ Discourse Analysis ／（英）布朗（Brown, G.）著. — 北京：外语教学与研究出版社，2000.8（2022.10 重印）
（当代国外语言学与应用语言学文库）
ISBN 978−7−5600−2006−8

Ⅰ. 话… Ⅱ. 布… Ⅲ. 话语语言学 Ⅳ. H0

中国版本图书馆 CIP 数据核字 (2000) 第 68148 号

出 版 人　王　芳
责任编辑　彭举鸿　刘相东
封面设计　诸中英
出版发行　外语教学与研究出版社
社　　址　北京市西三环北路 19 号（100089）
网　　址　http://www.fltrp.com
印　　刷　北京虎彩文化传播有限公司
开　　本　650×980　1/16
印　　张　20.25
版　　次　2000 年 8 月第 1 版 2022 年 10 月第 15 次印刷
书　　号　ISBN 978-7-5600-2006-8
定　　价　36.90 元

购书咨询：（010）88819926　电子邮箱：club@fltrp.com
外研书店：https://waiyants.tmall.com
凡印刷、装订质量问题，请联系我社印制部
联系电话：（010）61207896　电子邮箱：zhijian@fltrp.com
凡侵权、盗版书籍线索，请联系我社法律事务部
举报电话：（010）88817519　电子邮箱：banquan@fltrp.com
物料号：120060101

记载人类文明
沟通世界文化
www.fltrp.com

当代国外语言学与应用语言学文库

CONTENTS

Contents

Preface by Halliday

Foreign Language Teaching & Research Press is to be congratulated on its initiative in making these publications in linguistics available to foreign language teachers and postgraduate students of linguistics in China.

The books are a representative selection of up-to-date writings on the most important branches of linguistic studies, by scholars who are recognized as leading authorities in their fields.

The availability of such a broad range of materials in linguistics will greatly help individual teachers and students to build up their own knowledge and understanding of the subject. At the same time, it will also contribute to the development of linguistics as a discipline in Chinese universities and colleges, helping to overcome the divisions into "English linguistics", "Chinese linguistics" and so on which hinder the progress of linguistics as a unified science.

The series is to be highly commended for what it offers to all those wanting to gain insight into the nature of language, whether from a theoretical point of view or in application to their professional activities as language teachers. It is being launched at a time when there are increasing opportunities in China for pursuing linguistic studies, and I am confident that it will succeed in meeting these new requirements.

M. A. K. Halliday
Emeritus Professor
University of Sydney

王宗炎序

　　近年来，国际交往日益频繁，国际贸易急速发展，出现了一种前所未有的现象：学外语、教外语、用外语的人多了；研究语言学和应用语言学的人多了；开设这方面专业的高校也多了，语言学硕士生和博士生也多了。就是不以此为专业，学习语言学和应用语言学的也不乏其人。为了给从事这个专业的师生提供便利，同时又帮助一般外语教师、涉外工作者以及汉语研究者开阔思路，扩大视野，提高效率，我们献上这套内容崭新而丰富的丛书——英文版《当代国外语言学与应用语言学文库》。

　　文库首批推出 54 部外国英文原著，它覆盖了语言学与应用语言学 26 个分支学科。这批书是我们与各地有关专家教授反复研究之后精选出来的。出版这样大规模的语言学与应用语言学丛书，这在我国语言学界和外语教学界是破天荒第一次。

　　我们这样做，抱着什么希望呢？总的说来，是遵循教育部关于加强一级学科教育的指示，在世纪之交，推出一套书来给中国的外语教育领航，同时也给一般外语工作者和汉语研究者提供信息，拓宽思路。

　　我们希望这个文库能成为进一步带动外语教学改革和科研的发动机；我们希望它能成为运载当代外国语言学理论、语言研究方法和语言教学方法来到中国的特快列车；我们希望，有了这套书，语言学与应用语言学专业师生就能顺利地进行工作；我们希望，通过读这套书，青年外语教师和外语、汉语研究者能迅速把能力提高，把队伍不断扩大。

　　以上是我们的愿望，可是从广大读者看来，这个文库是否真的有出台的必要呢？我们想，只要大家看一下今天的客观情况，就知道这套书有填空补缺的作用，是让大家更上一层楼的扶梯。

我们跟许多人一样，认为国内的外语教学和语言学与应用语言学研究是成绩斐然的，但是某些不足之处也无庸讳言。

在语言研究方面，有大量工作还等着大家去做。汉语语法研究，过去由于结构主义的启示，已经成绩卓著，可是现在虽则引进了功能主义，还看不出什么出色的成果。语料语言学是新兴学科，在我国刚刚起步，机器翻译从50年代就有人搞，然而其进展至今不能令人满意。

在语言理论方面，我们不时听到一些片面的、所见不全的论调。有人说，1957年前西方根本没有什么理论语言学，其创始者是Chomsky；也有人说，语言纯属社会文化范畴；还有人说，搞语言研究只有量化方法才是科学方法，定性方法不值得一提。

谈到外语教学，某些看法做法是分明不值得赞许的。有人以为交际教学只管听说，不管读写，也有人以为教精读课就是教阅读，不管口语。在分析课文时老师满堂灌，学生开口不得，是常见的；教听力课时老师只管放录音，对学生不给半点提示点拨，也并非罕有现象。

上述这些缺点，我们早有所知，现在我们更加明白，必须力图改进，再也不能安于现状了。为了改进，我们就得参考国外的先进理论，借鉴国外的有效措施。眼前这个文库，就是我们上下求索的结果。

在编辑这个文库时，我们在两方面下了功夫。

一方面，在选书时，我们求全，求新，求有代表性和前瞻性。我们不偏爱一家之言，也不只收一家外国出版社之书。语言学与应用语言学的主干学科固然受到了应有的重视，分支学科可也不忽视。语料语言学、语言统计学是新兴学科，我们收入了专著；句法学、语义学久已有人研究，我们也找到了有关的最新著作。

另一方面，我们邀请了国内知名的博士生导师、硕士生导师为各书撰文导读，为读者铺平道路。语言学和应用语言学专著包罗宏富，初学者读起来可能觉得茫无头绪。为了助他们一臂之力，本文库中每一种书我们都请专家写了一万字左右的导读材料。哪怕书中内容比较陌生，谁只要在读书前看一下导读材料，读书后把材料再看一遍，一定能弄清脉络，掌握要点。

在结束本文时，我们想向爱好泛读的人们提个建议。语言和社会生活息息相关；我们靠语言与他人协作；通过语言继承传统文化，接受外国先进思想和科学知识；利用语言来教育下一代，帮助他们创造美好的未来；语言又反过来表达着我们的个性和我们充当的各种角色。学一点语言学和应用语言学，有助于增强我们的语言意识，对我们的工作和生活都是有利的。我们不妨把此事作为一个项目，列入自己的日程。持之以恒，必有所获。

王宗炎

中山大学教授
博士生导师

导　读

自 80 年代以来，出现了不少有关话语分析的著作，如 Michael Stubbs（1982）的《话语分析：自然语言的社会语言学分析》（*Discourse Analysis：A Social Linguistic Analysis on Natural Language*）；Malcolm Coulthard（1985）的《话语分析导论》（*Introduction to Discourse Analysis*）；van Dijk（1985）主编的《话语与文学》（*Discourse and Literature*）；Buy Cook（1989）的《话语》（*Discourse*）；Michael McCarthy（1991）的《话语分析教学参考书》（*Disocurse Analysis for Lanaguage Teacher*）；Evelyn Hatch（1992）的《话语和语言教育》（*Discourse and Language Education*）；Jamaes Paul Gee（1999）的《话语分析入门：理论与方法》（*An Introduction to Discourse Analysis：Theory and Method*）。这些著作大大地推动了话语研究向前发展。

我们现在导读的《话语分析》（*Discourse Analysis*）一书，1983 年由剑桥大学出版，作者 Gillian Brown 为剑桥大学英语教授，George Yule 为路易斯安那州立大学语言学教授。虽然这是出版最早的有关话语分析的论著之一，但至今仍然具有它的权威性。它与前面介绍的话语分析类著作的不同之处在于它全面地介绍了话语分析的不同理论与方法，系统地论述了语言是如何在实际生活中得到应用的，语料涉及谈话录音、通知、书信、小说、报刊文摘等。它有利于学习者全面掌握话语分析这门学科并在今后进行深入的学习和研究，堪称话语分析领域的经典之作。

为了方便读者，现将各章节导读如下。

第一章　引言

本章着重探讨了语言的形式与功能，区分了语言的两种功能：信息性（transactional）功能和互动性（interactional）功能。前者用来表达命题和传达信息，后者用于建立和维持社会关系。作者进而探讨了口语和笔语产生的方式及它们之间的区别与联系等等。

当交际双方都在场时，说话人可以充分利用面部表情、体态和情境等语言外部因素来进行交际。他必须时时观察对方，并根据对方的反应来调整自己的发话，必要时可用语调和音色来加强感情色彩。同说话人不一样，笔语作者在书写时，不必担心有第二者来打断，他可以停顿，可以参阅前面的话，可以从容地修改，但他无法得到及时的反馈。笔语与口语在功能上也存在差异。Goody（1977）认为，笔语有两个主要功能：1）使超越时空的交际成为可能的贮存功能；2）让词语在脱离原始语境的情况下仍能得到分析和研究的转换功能。但就传递具体信息而言，说话人的优势显而易见。口语与笔语最大的差别仍在于一个是传递的，一个是永久的。口语不会象笔语那样得到严密的组织，它可能是松散的，信息也不会那么密集，但口语载有许多互动的标记，而这些标记恰恰是话语分析者最感兴趣的。

作者继而讨论了句子（sentence）与语句（utterance）。简单地说，句子是写出来的，语句是说出来的。传统的语法分析与话语分析的根本不同在于：语法的分析对象是句子，而话语分析的对象是语句。语法分析把句子视为语言系统的抽象的单位，故脱离语境来分析句子的意义，分析往往停留在句子的层面，而且素材常常是由语言学家凭直感和经验编造的，不过是静态的成品而已；而话语分析把言语视为语言的具体的运用单位，在语境中分析语句的意义，这种分析常常是超出句子的平面进行的，语言的素材处于动态的过程之中。更重要的区分还在于，语法分析追求的是语言的规则性和正确性，研究的是形成句子的产品；而话语分析追求的是语言的规律性和概率性，研究的是形成语句的过程。

第二章　语境的作用

语用学着重研究语言使用的环境，在这一点上话语分析接近语用学，因为话语的一切分析活动都是在语境的基础上展开的。理解语境的几个基本方法有所指（reference）、预设（presupposition）、会话含义（implicature）和推理（inference）。所指的本质就是说话者通过某种合适的方式所指的东西，它通过所指的行为来研究所指的表达方式（见 Lyons 1977）。所指的行为不是由一个表达构成的，它是人们能用某种表达来进行所指的东西。如在 "My uncle's coming

home from Canada on Sunday +，he's due in +"句中，he 所指的是
my uncle。预设指说话者用来假设会话参与者共有的知识，如参与者
针对上一个英语句子问"How long has he been away for or has he just
been away?"则表示在说话者预设有一个叔叔后，听话者接受了这个
预设，所以他所用的 he 指向上一个句子中的 uncle。会话含义是由
Grice 用来说明说话者的言语表面下所具有的暗示、建议、意味等功
用。简言之，就是说话者的"言外之意"。Grice 还用四个会话原则
来说明这一点，即量的准则、质的准则、关系准则和方式准则。同
时，话语分析者如同听众一样，无法直接从话语发出者的言语中得
出他的真正意图，只有依靠推理的过程来理解。如甲和乙都知道某
某品质不好，但当甲说"他是大好人"时，就违背了质的准则，其
会话含义为"他是个坏蛋"。此时话语分析者可从一些知识、概念或
判断出发，作出假设或形成新概念。

　　本章还着重分析了情景语境，所谓情景语境就是语篇产生的环
境。Hymes（1964）对语境特征作了如下分类：(1)发话者；(2)受话
者；(3)话题；(4)背景(setting)，即言语事件发生的时间与地点；(5)交
际渠道，指人与人之间传递信息的途径与方法，除言语和文字外，还有
击鼓、鸣号、放烟、摇旗等；(6)语码(code)，即用了什么样的语言、方言
或使用了什么样的语体风格；(7)交际形式(message form)，如聊天、辩
论、布道、十四行诗、情书等等；(8)事件。Lewis(1972)的分析不同于
Hymes 的分析，他从人类学的角度出发，提出了一个带有人类图象文
字(ethnographic) 特征的名单和与之相对应的语境的特征。例如用可
能的世界(possible-world)来确定可能存在的某种情形和状况；时间用
来确定句子的时态，以及诸如今天和下一周之类的状语；地点用来帮
助理解"就在这里"一类的句子；发话者(speaker)可帮助理解含有第一
人称的"I, my, me, we, our, us"的句子；同样，受话者(audience)则解
释含有"you, yours, yourself"等代词的句子。以上探讨的都是话语的
客观语境。

　　本章中还讨论了话语的上下文（co-text），人们有时用 linguistic
context, environment 等来替代 co-text。它指在话语中位于某个单项
前的语音、词或短语。如果我们说"李明是个好学生，他连续三年
获甲等奖学金"，第二个小句的"他"则指第一句的"李明"。有些
词的用法很灵活，但我们可以通过上下文来确定它们，如在宾馆说
"这里很舒服"，那么"这里"指的是房间；如说"这里天气很好"，

"这里"则指谈话者所在的地方。除上下文外，作者还讨论了扩展语境（the expanding context）。

为帮助理解上述语境，作者给出了两条原则：就近理解（local interpretation）原则和类推（analogy）原则。就近理解原则要求听话人根据语境而不是超出语境来理解句子。作者举了例句加以说明：

> 一个男人和一个女人坐在起居室……那男人心里很烦，走到窗前，向外望去……然后就出去了，+ 去了，去了俱乐部 + 喝上酒并与酒吧老板交谈起来。

在这一例中，窗子是起居室的窗子，男人前后都是指同一人。喝酒也是在俱乐部喝，这些都可以根据上下文得出来。

又如这么两个句子：a) The baby cried（婴儿哭了）；b) The mommy picked it up（母亲把他抱起来）。它们之间并不连贯，但读者能根据类推的原理和就近理解的原则，推断第二个行为与第一个行为构成一个系列，并能对一些语言线索进行解释，如 it 指前面的 baby，母亲则是婴儿的母亲，而不是其他人的母亲。

第三章　话题与话语内容的表现

话语分析的语料常常指一个话语的片断，话语分析者通过它来决定其开头和结尾。有些话语的分界十分明显，如"从前…… 他们从此就非常幸福地生活着"，"我告诉你我上一周发生的事没有？"但我们遇到的语料常常不会这么清晰，这时就要依靠话题来判断，如交谈者停止了关于"钱"的讨论而进入到"性"的讨论时，就表明了话题的转换。话题可分为句子话题和话语话题。前者在句子结构分析中是一个用来区分一个特有的句子成份的术语，在话语分析中它被用来描写在不同的语言中标明句子的"话语成份"的不同的功能，而不应看作是一种语法分析的成份。话语话题用来描述话语中的句子的信息结构的表达。谈话者、交谈双方会从不同的角度去判断话题，但确定一句话或一个话语的主题往往需要凭直觉，至今尚未有一套切实可行的规则。所以，一些语言学家，如 Bransford、Johnson 等认为任何一个话语都可能有一些不同的话题，从而一个"话题"可以通过不同的形式来表达。所以，作者接着提出了话题框架（topic framework）这一概念。而直接在话语中反映语境以及那些需要用来阐释话语各种成份关系的方面被称之为语境的激化特征

（activated features of context），是话题得以构成的框架。这一框架如一个共知信息库，普遍常识、语言环境、话语内容等均包括在其中。在讨论预设的基础上，作者又提出了预设集（presupposition pools）的概念，预设集包含从普遍知识、从话语的情景语境、从话语的整体部分摄取而构成的信息。话语的参与者尤其是彼此相互了解的参与者所共同享有的预设集中的话语主题的数量非常之多。作者讨论了句子的话题与预设集、关联与话题性等。既然限定主题有困难，我们可以从主题变化（topic shift）入手，这就是话题的界限标记（topic boundary markers），如段落常用来作主题变化，副词短语和小句等也是如此。不同的文体会有不同的主题变化，如小说、说明书等等。口语的话题标记常常有停顿、高音、表情、体态等。

关于话题和话语内容的表现方面，van Dijk 有关话语语义表征的研究很有参考价值。在他看来，一个话题可以看作是一个复杂的命题（preposition），这一命题又被话语后面的句子中所表达的一群命题所包含。Van Dijk 是从话语的潜在的语义表现而不是从一系列句序构成的话语基础上进行研究的。作者还分析了其他几位语言学家如 Bransford 和 Franks、Kinstsch 和 Keenar 等的研究方法，但认为他们的研究方法都存在着缺陷，需要改进。

在谈到话语内容的记忆—故事语法时，作者分析了 Thorndyke（1977）的模式。这是为叙事话语而设计的一套有层次有组织的分析模式，是在 Rumelhart 的简单故事的分析基础上发展形成的，其规则概括如下：

(1) 故事→背景＋主题＋情节＋结局

(2) 背景→人物＋地点＋时间

(3) 主题→（事件）＋

(4) 情节→插曲

(5) 插曲→次目标＋行动＋结果

(6) 行动→ { 事件 / 插曲 }

(7) 结果→ { 事件 / 状态 }

(8) 结局→ { 事件 / 状态 }

(9) { 次目的 / 目的 } 理想状态

$$(10) \quad \left.\begin{array}{l}\text{时间}\\\text{地点}\end{array}\right\}\text{状态}$$

其实，这一图示与 Rumelhart 和 Thorndyke 所使用的话语内容并无专门的联系，相反，它倒是强调了读者在理解和记忆中再现叙述话语的故事构思图式（Schema）的存在。在话语分析者看来，一定存在某些故事语法的应用。

作者最后对 de Deaugrande 关于火箭发射一例加以分析，说明作为网络而表现的话语内容。其实，de Beaugrande 在探讨这一网式表现时，还想借此说明长程记忆与短程记忆对话语的形成和重构所产生的影响。有关这一点，可以参考 de Beaugrande 和 Dressler 于 1981年合著的《话语语言学导论》第五章。

第四章　视角与话语结构的表现

话语的表达呈线性排列，话语发出者在交际时必须选择一个起点，这个起点继而会影响听者或读者对话语的理解，如下面 a、b 两句：

a. I can't stand Sally Binns. She's tall and thin and walks like a crane.

b. I do admire Sally Binns, she's tall and thin and walks like a crane.

a 的第二句意指 Sally Binns 丑陋、笨拙，而 b 句中的第二句，同样的词句，却意指一种幽雅和风度。所以，句子的排列可以影响受话者或读者对其会话含义的判断。视角（staging）必然要涉及发话人的观察角度，于是人们以主位（theme）来表示说话的出发点，代表已知信息，是处于句子最左边的成分；而述位则表示主位以外的发话者所说的其他一切成分。视角是一个比主位化（thematisation）涵义更广、更概括的术语。

主题有时也可用来指一系列句子的语法主语，如 Katz（1982）就说过："话语的话题指的是前面句子的一个共同的主位"。Perfetti 和 Goldman（1974）说得更明白："我们说的主位化指的是一个话语过程，在这个过程中，一个所指被发展成为该话语的中心主语"。他们做了一系列实验，以证明对句子的回忆是如何通过指向主位化的话语的关键词来达到的。主位不等同于主语，其充当的成分可以是名词、地点状语、时间状语等等。在侦探小说中，时间状语常充当主位；在旅游手册中地点状语常充当主位；在百科全书中，所释词条为主位；在讣告中，死者和时间状语常充当主位。标题常常起到主位化的作用，如 "A Prisoner Plans His Escape"，"A Wrestler in a Tignt Corner"。标题可以影响整个语篇的成构，作者举例证明，同一段文字使用了不同的标题后，可以使读者产生不同的理解。主位结构在一些语篇中结构很清晰，但在另外一些语篇中又可能比较模糊。如新闻题材经常是结构松散的，如果把主位化放到即兴发言中去，问题可能会更复杂一些。人们探讨主位的推进，使得话语有一个与其主要目的相关并影响后来语句的结构框架。视角常常涉及到自然顺序和视点（point of view）。自然顺序包括了时间顺序和感知顺序（perceptual salience）。事件的描述常以时间先后为序，不遵守这一顺序则表明话语的发出者想藉此产生某种特殊的效果，如悬念、惊奇等。对状态的描述则常用感知的顺序，由一般到个别，由整体到局部，由大到小，由外到内，如不遵守这些规则，则表明话语发出者另有意图，也能产生某种特殊的效果。视点指讲话人的爱和憎、同情与厌恶等，它可以影响词汇的选择，如在 "a) Mary, Queen of Scots, was executed by the English Queen；b) Mary, Queen of Scots, was assassinated by the English Queen；c) Mary, Queen of Scots, was murdered by her cousin, Elizabeth" 三句中，a 句用 executed 一词，表明一个法律程序；b 句用 assassinated 一词，是作为一种非法和政治行为而报导的；C 句用 murdered 一词，是作为一种非法的犯罪行为而报导的，三个词代表了三种观点。

第五章　信息结构

本章主要讨论话语结构中最小的语言单位：短语和小句层次的小结构单位，讨论信息是如何通过这些小结构而得到包装的；对说话者或作者而言，他们能够通过什么渠道来向话语的接受者表明被引入话语的信息的状况。

作者首先介绍了布拉格学派的 "功能句子观"（Functional Sentence Perspective），探讨了构成句子的被称之为 "交际动态" 的语言成份。这一原理在 Halliday 的研究中得到充分的发展。1967 年，Halliday 发表了一篇极有影响的论文——"关于及物性及英语的主题的几点意见"（Notes on Transitivity and Theme in English）。在该文中，他详尽地探讨并发展了布拉格学派的观点，这些观点与他对话语结构的研究兴趣相符。他尤其欣赏布拉格学派关于"新信息"（new information）与"已知信息"（old information）的观点。一般来说，已知信息在前，新信息在后，前一句的新信息又可以成为下一句的已知信息。Halliday 的研究与英语口语的信息结构十分相关，这种信息结构直接关系到音位和音调的实现。Halliday 认为，说话者通常将已知信息置于新信息之前，信息结构的这种"无标记"的秩序就是已知→新。在 Halliday 看来，英语口语由调群（tone group）构成。从语法上讲，一个调群就是一个信息单位，信息单位必须有一个新信息部分，也可再带上一个已知信息部分。新信息指发话人要受话人格外留心注意的信息，它可能以前没被提到过，或可能同预想的不符，或需要对它加以强调。通过分析各信息结构的新信息部分，便可以把握整个话语的要旨。每个调群都会有一个调节（tonic syllable），这是调群的区分特征，调群的新信息便具备了调节的功能。

说话中常常有停顿，Halliday 认为这些停顿颇似文章的标点，有长短之分，他用了一个图示来表示停顿：

```
0      0.5     1     1.5     2     2.5     3
|————————————|     |—————————|     |—————————|
   短暂停              长暂停            加长暂停
```

此外，音调也常常用来表示某种信息。在讲话中，新信息常用较高的音调，而已知信息常用较低的音调。当然，例外也常有之。如高音调也常用来表示发话人更换话题或新的话题开始，还可表示强调或对比，低音调也可用来表示听话人可以忽略的东西。一个信息单位不一定由一个高音调来实现，可以是两个甚至更多。而且，非限定表达形式也并不像 Halliday 所说的那样总表示一个新信息，如在 draw a triangle + a triangle in red 之中，句子形式本身不能决定哪些是已知信息或新信息，信息结构并不取决于语篇结构，而取决于发话人，而发话人并没有一成不变的规则来指导自己组织信息结构。这些概率的发现只有通过对话语的语境的分析以及深入研究大量的自然语言材料方能得到。

第六章　话语和语篇中的指称性质

如果说第五章着重讨论了小块语料，尤其是名词短语的结构，探讨了语言形式与特定的信息联系的方法，那么，第六章的研究对象则指向了大块语料的成构，讨论它们是怎样被解读而成为连贯的语篇的，重点仍然是话语的指称这一中心问题。

　　作者认为语篇（text）就是交际事件的文字记录。要研究话语，就不可避免要回答如下两个问题：话语的衔接原则是什么？如何理解语篇的衔接关系？对此，作者引用了 Halliday 和 Hasan 的观点。Halliday 和 Hasan 认为一个句群是否构成语篇的关键在于句内各成分之间以及句与句之间的衔接关系，衔接关系使话语具有语篇性。换言之，话语内部的衔接关系主要是由于"语篇中某些语言单位的解释需要借助于其它语言单位的解释"而造成的。如他们对"Wash and core six cooking apples. Put them into a fireproof dish."作了这样的解释：很明显，第二句中的 them 指的是前一句中的 six cooking apples，them 的前指功能把这两句话衔接起来了，所以，我们把这两句话看作是一个整体。把上下文连接在一起的话语的衔接关系可以有形式标记，Halliday 和 Hasan 把表连接关系的标记词作了分类，如表递进的有 and, or, furthermore, similarly, in addition；表转折的有 but, however, on the other hand, nevertheless；表因果关系的有 so, consequently, for this reason, it follows from this；表时间的有 then, after that, an hour later, finally, at last，等等。在连词中 and 的使用频率最高，它可以表达不同的意思，如增加（additive）、相反（adversative）、原因（causal）和时间序列（temporal sequence）。同样常用的词还有 but, so 和 then，它们常常是转换话题的标志，从这一意义上来说，与其把它们看作是连词，不如把它们看作是话语标记。当然，Halliday 和 Hasan 的观点受到了质疑，两个主要问题是：（1）这些衔接是构成语篇所必须的条件吗？（2）这些衔接足以保证语篇的形成吗？因为当 Halliday 和 Hasan 强调语篇性（即衔接标记是区别其它非语篇的东西）时，说明他们讨论的是有形的、具体的词法成分，而不是无形的、深层的语义关系。

　　本章第二节探讨了话语的指称。传统的语义指称性观点认为在一个语篇中词语与客观世界的事物之间存在指称关系，一个语篇中的不同部分的词语之间有共指关系。过去，言及某一事物的词语在描述这一事物时必须是真实的这一点很重要，被称之为正确的指代，但在话语分析中，人们更感兴趣的是成功的指代，即说话者相信他使用的那个词语可以让听话者辩识出他叙说事物的意图。我们要区别开世界存在的实体与个人表述世界实体时心中的表征，后者被称之为个人表征或世界模型。这一心中表征在一定程度上和更为广泛的世界表征连为一体。如在 "There is a pineapple on the table. So I ate it" 一句中，it 明显地回指 pineapple 而不是 table，尽管它更靠近 table，这是我们共有的世界表征在起作用。当某一特定表征从某一个特定话语中产生时，我们称之为个人的话语表征（discourse representations）。

最后作者讨论了话语中的代词。代词是发话者用来指代"给定"项目的。由于代词缺乏具体内容，所以它们也就成了任何有关所指理论必须首要解决的问题。在考虑话语中代词的现存观点时，最重要的是要能够对话语中的代词作充分的解释和描述。如对 "I have just had my hair curled and it looks windblown all the time" 一句中 it 的分析不仅要包括先行名词，而且要包括其伴随的谓语。我们可以这样来表示上句："My hair which I've just had curled looks windblown all the time"。从位置上看，代词可作为先行代词、先行谓语。

那么受话人在什么基础上来理解话语的代词所指呢？作者认为他可以使用他所具有的如下的知识：(1)先行代词的表达（an antecedent nominal expression），(2)先行谓语的表达（an antecedent predicate expression），(3)暗含先行表谓（an implicit antecedent predicate），(4)先行代词的表达"角色"（the 'roles' of antecedent nominal expressions），(5)依附代词的"新"表谓（the 'new' predicates attached to the pronoun）。

第七章　话语理解中的连贯

第七章首先讨论了话语的连贯。在日常言语交际中，我们常常依靠句法结构和语言信息中的词项进行理解，但我们不能认为缺乏这些文字形式上的输入我们就达不到理解。有时，我们可以从作家写出的语法十分规范的句子中得出其字面意义，但实际上我们并未全部理解它，因为我们还需要更多语言之外的信息。此时，我们无法以完整的句法形式来讨论这些语言信息。有时一个句子不一定在表现形式上有连贯，但通过一些原则，我们可以推断出它们是连贯的。请看下面两句对话：

A: Can you go to Edinburg tomorrow?

B：B.E.A. pilots are on strike.

根据 Widdowson，B 的回答是消极的，他希望以这样的回答来说明他不能飞到爱丁堡去。我们可以用言语行为理论来说明语言即使在没有表示接应手段时句子之间的关系仍能得到理解。言语行为理论认为，说话不仅陈述某个事情，而且完成一种社会行为。Austin 指出，我们平时打招呼、命令、警告、邀请等，都是通过说话而完成的社会行为。Austin 把言语行为分为三种：言内行为（locutionary act）、言外行为（illocutionary act）和言后行为（perlocutionary act）。Searle 后来发展了这一理论，他研究了言语的命题内容和语言功能的指示手段，在此基础上，区分了直接言语行为和间接言语行为。对后者的理解取决于对一个具体语境中的言语的成事性效果的认识，也就是说，语句在听者方面产生的效果十分重要。如"I am hungry"这一个句子，其命题意义是生理状态的，其施为作用是说话者所期待产生的效果。

言语行为理论未能产生一种理想的方法让话语分析者能够判断在一个具体的对话环境中言语成分如何能得到正确的理解。在这一点上，作者认为使用世界知识（knowledge of the world）很重要。De Beaugrande 认为，人们对话语中发生了什么的理解与他们对世界上发生什么一样的理解是相同的，是一种特别的现象。所以正如第二章中所说：人们具有的世界认识和推理能力，对理解话语的连贯起着十分重要的作用。

作者继而讨论了"自上而下认识"（top-down processing）和"自下而上认识"（bottom-up processing）。这是心理语言学家、认知心理学和信息处理研究者将人们在理解和学习过程中所运用的方法进行的分类，前者指人们利用先前已有的知识来分析处理所接受的信息，后者指人们理解事物不是依靠先前拥有的知识，而是主要利用刚得到的信息中的单词、句子等材料。这些研究与人工智能有密切的联系。人工智能在很大程度上要靠背景知识来支持，如记忆中的知识的组织就需与框架（frames）和事物摹本（script）相联系，这两个概念对于如何理解话语有十分重要的作用，从而吸引了包括 Wilks、Winston、Findler、Metzing 等在内的研究者。人们常常把 frame 和 script 交换使用，用它们指一些意义单位，其中包括与某些特别环境有关的一系列事件或活动，如机场事物摹本可以包括如下知识：机场是乘飞机的地方，人们到机场要支付机场建设费，要验票后登机等等。Schema（构思图式）在这里再一次被提到（我们前面在讲故事语法时也提到），它指语篇和语法的潜在结构。不同种类的文章和话语（如故事、描述文、信件等）之所以有区别，是因为其话题（topic）、命题（proposition）以及其他内容相互联系，构成了一个宏观的结构。如果一篇文章或一个话语中的构思图式的宏观结构安排得好，那么，该话语的连贯性（coherence）就一定强。

本章最后讨论了作出推理的决定条件，一个重要概念是"沟通假设"（bridging assumption），如"a) Mary got some picnic supplies out of the car. b) The beer was warm"这两个句子似乎没有必然联系，但根据沟通假设，便可得出 c) The picnic supplies mentioned include some beer。所以，推理是作为潜隐联结（missing links）而出现的。当提到"a) I bought a bicycle yesterday；b) The frame is extra large"时，它们的潜隐连结是 c) The bicycle has a frame。如果我们说"dressing the baby — the clothes"这句话的推理具有自动联结（automatic connection）性，但在 picnic supplies 和 the beer 之间不存在必然的联系，这种联结是非自动的。在理解中充分利用推理来消除理解上的障碍十分重要，但对社会语言学来说，推理研究是十分棘手的工作，要真正理解人类推理的本质，还有大量的研究工作要做。

本书理论性较强，但涉及具体方法与实践不多，如某一理论在课堂教学或在话语轮换中的应用。作者在谈到会话含意时，探讨了 Grice 的合作原则，却忽略了会话含义的五个特征：可取消性、不可分离性、可推导性、非规约性和不确定性。介绍语境理论时，介绍了 co-context，但没有对 Halliday 的语境理论进行全面介绍。Halliday 把社会符号系统中的语境特征分为三种：场（field）、旨（tenor）和式（mode）。场指参与者正在从事的活动，语言被用来表示与此有关的内容；旨用来表示参与者之间的社会关系，可影响句型和语气的选择；式指语言所起的作用，影响到话语的衔接和风格。这一分析方法是比较全面和系统的，似乎可以介绍一些。当然，作者在撰写这本话语分析的著作时，话语分析这门学科尚处于起步阶段，作者必然受到种种局限，但可以肯定地说，它仍不失为一本话语分析入门的好书。

PREFACE

The term 'discourse analysis' has come to be used with a wide range of meanings which cover a wide range of activities. It is used to describe activities at the intersection of disciplines as diverse as sociolinguistics, psycholinguistics, philosophical linguistics and computational linguistics. Scholars working centrally in these different disciplines tend to concentrate on different aspects of discourse. Sociolinguists are particularly concerned with the structure of social interaction manifested in conversation, and their descriptions emphasise features of social context which are particularly amenable to sociological classification. They are concerned with generalising across 'real' instances of language in use, and typically work with transcribed spoken data. Psycholinguists are particularly concerned with issues related to language comprehension. They typically employ a tight methodology derived from experimental psychology, which investigates problems of comprehension in short constructed texts or sequences of written sentences. Philosophical linguists, and formal linguists, are particularly concerned with semantic relationships between constructed pairs of sentences and with their syntactic realisations. They are concerned, too, with relationships between sentences and the world in terms of whether or not sentences are used to make statements which can be assigned truth-values. They typically investigate such relationships between constructed sentences attributed to archetypal speakers addressing archetypal hearers in (minimally specified) archetypal contexts. Computational linguists working in this field are particularly concerned with producing models of discourse processing and are constrained, by their methodology, to working with short texts constructed in highly limited contexts. It must be obvious that, at this relatively early stage in the evolution of discourse analysis, there is often rather little in common between the various approaches except the discipline which they all, to varying degrees, call upon: *linguistics*.

In this book we take a primarily linguistic approach to the analysis of discourse. We examine how humans use language to communicate and, in particular, how addressers construct linguistic messages for addressees and how addressees work on linguistic messages in order to interpret them. We call on insights from all of the inter-disciplinary areas we have mentioned, and survey influential work done in all these fields, but our primary interest is the traditional concern of the descriptive linguist, to give an account of how forms of language are used in communication.

Since the study of discourse opens up uncircumscribed areas, interpenetrating with other disciplines, we have necessarily had to impose constraints on our discussion. We deal, for example, only with English discourse, in order to be able to make direct appeal to the reader's ability to interpret the texts we present, as well as to well-described and relatively well-understood features of English syntax and phonology. Many of the issues we raise are necessarily only briefly discussed here and we have to refer the reader to standard works for a full account. Even within English we have chosen only to deal with a few aspects of discourse processing and have ignored other tempting, and certainly profitable, approaches to the investigation (tense, aspect, modality etc.). We try to show that, within discourse analysis, there are contributions to be made by those who are primarily linguists, who bring to bear a methodology derived from descriptive linguistics. We have assumed a fairly basic, introductory knowledge of linguistics and, where possible, tried to avoid details of formal argumentation, preferring to outline the questions addressed by formalisms in generally accessible terms.

Throughout the book we have insisted on the view which puts the speaker / writer at the centre of the process of communication. We have insisted that it is people who communicate and people who interpret. It is speakers / writers who have topics, presuppositions, who assign information structure and who make reference. It is hearers / readers who interpret and who draw inferences. This view is opposed to the study of these issues in terms of sentences considered in isolation from communicative contexts. In appealing to this pragmatic approach, we have tried to avoid the dangerous extreme of advocating the individual (or idiosyncratic) approach to the interpretation of each discourse fragment which appears to characterise the hermeneutic view. We have adopted a compromise position which suggests that discourse analysis on the one hand includes the study of linguistic forms and the regularities of their distribution and, on the other hand, involves a consideration of the general principles of interpretation by which people normally make sense of what they hear and read. Samuel Butler, in a notebook entry, points out the necessity of such a compromise position, and its inherent dangers, in a warning which discourse analysts ought to take to heart:

Everything must be studied from the point of view of itself, as near as we can get to this, and from the point of view of its relations, as near as we can get to them. If we try to see it absolutely in itself, unalloyed with relations, we shall find, by and by, that we have, as it were, whittled it away. If we try to see it in its relations to the bitter end, we shall find that there is no corner of the universe into which it does not enter.

ACKNOWLEDGEMENTS

Many friends and colleagues have contributed to this book more or less directly. We are particularly grateful to Anne Anderson, Mahmoud Ayad, Keith Brown, Karen Currie de Carvalho, Jim Miller, Nigel Shadbolt, Richard Shillcock, Henry Thompson, Hugh Trappes-Lomax and Michele Trufant for helpful discussion, in some cases lasting over several years. Our Series editor, Peter Matthews, made many detailed and helpful comments on a draft version. We are grateful too, to many former students of the Department as well as to members of the School of Epistemics Seminar who have made us think. Finally we must thank Marion Law and Margaret Love for typing the manuscript.

We are grateful for permission to reproduce and to quote the following materials: extract on p. 97 from William Wharton, *Birdy* (1979), © Jonathan Cape Ltd and Alfred A. Knopf Inc.; diagrams on pp. 111 and 112 by W. Kintsch and J. Keenan (first appeared in *Cognitive Psychology* 5 (1973)); diagram on p. 118 from D. E. Rumelhart, 'Understanding and summarizing brief stories', in *Basic Processes in Reading* (1977), ed. D. Laberge and S. J. Samuels, © Laurence Erlbaum; diagram on p. 119 by P. W. Thorndyke (first appeared in *Cognitive Psychology* 9 (1977)); diagrams on pp. 122 and 123 from R. de Beaugrande, *Text, Discourse and Process* (1980), © Longman and Ablex Publishing Corp.

TRANSCRIPTION CONVENTIONS

The general issue of what a transcription represents is considered at length in 1.2. In the transcriptions we present in this book, a variable amount of detail is included from one to the next, for the straightforward reason that different extracts are studied for different purposes.

In the transcription of spoken data we always attempt to record as faithfully as possible what was said and we have avoided 'tidying up' the language used. Consequently some apparently ungrammatical forms, as well as occasional dialect forms, appear in several extracts. In addition, there are examples of repetition, hesitation, and incomplete sentences commonly found in transcripts of spoken data.

The occurrence of short pauses is marked by – , longer pauses by + , and extended pauses by ++ . A detailed discussion of pausing is presented in 5.1. In the intonational representations which accompany some extracts, a simple three-line stave is used. The lines of the stave represent the top, mid and low points of the speaker's pitch range (for a detailed discussion of intonational representation, see Brown, Currie & Kenworthy, 1980).

1

Introduction: linguistic forms and functions

1.1 The functions of language

The analysis of **discourse** is, necessarily, the analysis of language in use. As such, it cannot be restricted to the description of linguistic forms independent of the purposes or functions which those forms are designed to serve in human affairs. While some linguists may concentrate on determining the formal properties of a language, the discourse analyst is committed to an investigation of what that language is used for. While the formal approach has a long tradition, manifested in innumerable volumes of grammar, the functional approach is less well documented. Attempts to provide even a general set of labels for the principal functions of language have resulted in vague, and often confusing, terminology. We will adopt only two terms to describe the major functions of language and emphasise that this division is an analytic convenience. It would be unlikely that, on any occasion, a natural language utterance would be used to fulfil only one function, to the total exclusion of the other. That function which language serves in the expression of 'content' we will describe as **transactional**, and that function involved in expressing social relations and personal attitudes we will describe as **interactional**. Our distinction, 'transactional / interactional', stands in general correspondence to the functional dichotomies – 'representative / expressive', found in Bühler (1934), 'referential / emotive' (Jakobson, 1960), 'ideational / interpersonal' (Halliday, 1970b) and 'descriptive / social-expressive' (Lyons, 1977).

1.1.1 *The transactional view*

Linguists and linguistic philosophers tend to adopt a limited approach to the functions of language in society. While they frequently acknowledge that language may be used to perform many communicative functions, they nonetheless make the general assumption that the most important function is the communication of information. Thus Lyons (1977: 32) observes that the notion of communication is readily used 'of feelings, moods and attitudes' but suggests that he will be primarily interested in 'the intentional transmission of factual, or propositional, information'. Similarly Bennett (1976: 5) remarks 'it seems likely that communication is primarily a matter of a speaker's seeking either to inform a hearer of something or to enjoin some action upon him'.

The value of the use of language to transmit information is well embedded in our cultural mythology. We all believe that it is the faculty of language which has enabled the human race to develop diverse cultures, each with its distinctive social customs, religious observances, laws, oral traditions, patterns of trading, and so on. We all believe, moreover, that it is the acquisition of written language which has permitted the development within some of these cultures of philosophy, science and literature (see Goody, 1977). We all believe that this development is made possible by the ability to transfer information through the use of language, which enables man to utilise the knowledge of his forebears, and the knowledge of other men in other cultures.

We shall call the language which is used to convey 'factual or propositional information' *primarily transactional language*. In primarily transactional language we assume that what the speaker (or writer) has primarily in mind is the efficient transference of information. Language used in such a situation is primarily 'message oriented'. It is important that the recipient gets the informative detail correct. Thus if a policeman gives directions to a traveller, a doctor tells a nurse how to administer medicine to a patient, a householder puts in an insurance claim, a shop assistant explains the relative merits of two types of knitting wool, or a scientist describes an experiment, in each case it matters that the speaker should make what he says (or writes) clear. There will be unfortunate (even disastrous) consequences in the real world if the message is not properly understood by the recipient.

1.1.2 *The interactional view*
Whereas linguists, philosophers of language and psycho-

linguists have, in general, paid particular attention to the use of language for the transmission of 'factual or propositional information', sociologists and sociolinguists have been particularly concerned with the use of language to establish and maintain social relationships. In sociological and anthropological literature the *phatic* use of language has been frequently commented on – particularly the conventional use of language to open talk-exchanges and to close them. Conversational analysts have been particularly concerned with the use of language to negotiate role-relationships, peer-solidarity, the exchange of turns in a conversation, the saving of face of both speaker and hearer (cf. Labov, 1972a; Brown and Levinson, 1978; Sacks, Schegloff & Jefferson, 1974; Lakoff, 1973). It is clearly the case that a great deal of everyday human interaction is characterised by the primarily interpersonal rather than the primarily transactional use of language. When two strangers are standing shivering at a bus-stop in an icy wind and one turns to the other and says 'My goodness, it's cold', it is difficult to suppose that the primary intention of the speaker is to convey information. It seems much more reasonable to suggest that the speaker is indicating a readiness to be friendly and to talk. Indeed a great deal of ordinary everyday conversation appears to consist of one individual commenting on something which is present to both him and his listener. The weather is of course the most quoted example of this in British English. However a great deal of casual conversation contains phrases and echoes of phrases which appear more to be intended as contributions to a conversation than to be taken as instances of information-giving. Thus a woman on a bus describing the way a mutual friend has been behaving, getting out of bed too soon after an operation, concludes her turn in the conversation by saying:

> Aye, she's an awfy woman. (awfy = Sc awful)

This might be taken as an informative summary. Her neighbour then says reflectively (having been supportively uttering *aye, aye* throughout the first speaker's turn):

> Aye, she's an awfy woman.

Pirsig (1976: 313) remarks of such a conversation: 'the conversation's pace intrigues me. It isn't intended to go anywhere, just fill the time of day . . . on and on and on with no point or purpose other than to fill the time, like the rocking of a chair.'

What seems to be primarily at issue here is the sharing of a common point of view. Brown & Levinson point out the importance for social relationships of establishing common ground and agreeing on points of view, and illustrate the lengths to which speakers in different cultures will go to maintain an appearance of agreement, and they remark 'agreement may also be stressed by *repeating* part or all of what the preceding speaker has said' (1978: 117).

Whereas, as we shall note, written language is, in general, used for primarily transactional purposes, it is possible to find written genres whose purpose is not primarily to inform but to maintain social relationships – 'thank you' letters, love letters, games of consequences, etc.

1.2 Spoken and written language

1.2.1 *Manner of production*

From the point of view of production, it is clear that spoken and written language make somewhat different demands on language-producers. The speaker has available to him the full range of 'voice quality' effects (as well as facial expression, postural and gestural systems). Armed with these he can always override the effect of the words he speaks. Thus the speaker who says 'I'd really like to', leaning forward, smiling, with a 'warm, breathy' voice quality, is much more likely to be interpreted as meaning what he says, than another speaker uttering the same words, leaning away, brow puckered, with a 'sneering, nasal' voice quality. These paralinguistic cues are denied to the writer. We shall generally ignore paralinguistic features in spoken language in this book since the data we shall quote from is spoken by co-operative adults who are not exploiting paralinguistic resources against the verbal meanings of their utterances but are, rather, using them to reinforce the meaning.

Not only is the speaker controlling the production of communicative systems which are different from those controlled by the writer, he is also processing that production under circumstances which are considerably more demanding. The speaker must monitor what it is that he has just said, and determine whether it matches his intentions, while he is uttering his current phrase and monitoring that, and simultaneously planning his next utterance and fitting that into the overall pattern of what he wants to say and monitoring, moreover, not only his own performance but its reception by his hearer. He has no permanent record of what he has said earlier, and only under unusual circumstances does he have notes which remind him what he wants to say next.

The writer, on the contrary, may look over what he has already written, pause between each word with no fear of his interlocutor interrupting him, take his time in choosing a particular word, even looking it up in the dictionary if necessary, check his progress with his notes, reorder what he has written, and even change his mind about what he wants to say. Whereas the speaker is under considerable pressure to keep on talking during the period allotted to him, the writer is characteristically under no such pressure. Whereas the speaker knows that any words which pass his lips will be heard by his interlocutor and, if they are not what he intends, he will have to undertake active, public 'repair', the writer can cross out and rewrite in the privacy of his study.

There are, of course, advantages for the speaker. He can observe his interlocutor and, if he wishes to, modify what he is saying to make it more accessible or acceptable to his hearer. The writer has no access to immediate feedback and simply has to imagine the reader's reaction. It is interesting to observe the behaviour of individuals when given a choice of conducting a piece of business in person or in writing. Under some circumstances a face-to-face interaction is preferred but, in others, for a variety of different reasons, the individual may prefer to conduct his transaction in writing. Whereas in a spoken interaction the speaker has the advantage of being able to monitor his listener's minute-by-minute reaction to what he says, he also suffers from the disadvantage of exposing his own feelings ('leaking'; Ekman & Friesen, 1969) and of having to speak clearly and concisely and make immediate response to whichever way his interlocutor reacts.

1.2.2 *The representation of discourse: texts*

So far we have considered in very general terms some of the differences in the manner of production of writing and speech. Before we go on to discuss some of the ways in which the forms of speech and writing differ, we shall consider, in the next two sections, some of the problems of representing written and spoken language. We shall place this within a general discussion of what it means to represent 'a text'. We shall use **text** as a technical term, to refer to the verbal record of a communicative act. (For another approach to text cf. discussion in Chapter 6.)

1.2.3 *Written texts*

The notion of 'text' as a printed record is familiar in the study of literature. A 'text' may be differently presented in different editions, with different type-face, on different sizes of paper, in one or two columns, and we still assume, from one edition to the next, that the different presentations all represent the same 'text'. It is important to consider just what it is that is 'the same'. Minimally, the words should be the same words, presented in the same order. Where there are disputed readings of texts, editors usually feel obliged to comment on the crux; so of Hamlet's

O, that this too too sullied flesh would melt

(1.ii.129)

Dover Wilson makes it clear that this is an interpretation, since the second Quarto gives 'too too sallied' and the first Folio 'too too solid' (Dover Wilson, 1934). Even where there is no doubt about the identity of words and their correct sequence, replicating these alone does not guarantee an adequate representation of a text. Consider the following extract of dialogue from *Pride and Prejudice*:

'Mr. Bennet, how can you abuse your own children in such a way? You take delight in vexing me. You have no compassion on my poor nerves.'
'You mistake me, my dear. I have a high respect for your nerves. They are my old friends. I have heard you mention them with consideration these twenty years at least.'

It is clear that more than simply reproducing the words in their correct order is required. It is necessary to replicate punctuation conventions, as well as the lineation which indicates the change of speaker. The extract reads as gobbledygook if it is read as a speech by one individual. An adequate representation of a text must assign speeches to the correct characters, sentences to the correct paragraphs, and paragraphs to the correct chapters. The author's organisation and staging of his work must be preserved.

In a piece of expository prose, the author's indication of the development of the argument contributes to the reader's experience of the text. Thus titles, chapter headings, sub-divisions and sub-headings all indicate to the reader how the author intends his argument to be chunked. The detail of lineation rarely matters in expository or descriptive prose. However it clearly becomes crucial in the reproduction of poetry. The work of those seventeenth-century poets who created poems in the shape of diamonds or butterflies would be largely incomprehensible if the form were not preserved.

The notion of 'text' reaches beyond the reproduction of printed material in some further printed form. A letter, handwritten in purple ink with many curlicues, may have its text reproduced in printed form. Similarly, neutral printed versions may be produced of handwritten shopping lists, slogans spray-painted on to hoardings, and public notices embossed on metal plates. In each case the 'text' will be held to have been reproduced if the words, the punctuation and, where relevant, the lineation are reproduced accurately.

Where the original text exploits typographical variety, a text reproduced in one type-face may lack some of the quality of the original. An obvious example is a newspaper item which may exploit several different type-faces, different sizes of type and a particular shape of lay-out. It is interesting to observe that publishers regularly reproduce conscious manipulation of the written medium on the part of the writer. Thus Jane Austen's expression of contrast is reproduced by publishers in italics:

> 'Nay,' said Elizabeth, 'this is not fair. *You* wish to think all the world respectable, and are hurt if I speak ill of any body. *I* only want to think you *perfect* . . .'

Similarly Queen Victoria's use of underlining in her handwritten journal is represented by her publishers in the printed version with an italic type-face to represent the emphasis she wishes to indicate when writing of Lord Melbourne:

> he gave me *such* a kind, and I may say, *fatherly* look
> (Thursday, 28 June 1838)

Where the writer is deliberately exploiting the resources of the written medium, it seems reasonable to suggest that that manipulation constitutes part of the text.

A further illustration of this is to be found in the conventions governing spelling. In general we assume that words have a standardised spelling in British English. The fact of the standardisation enables authors to manipulate idiosyncratic spelling to achieve special effects. Thus in *Winnie-the-Pooh* the publishers reproduce the notice outside Owl's house in one inset line, using capitals, and with the author's own spelling:

PLEZ CNOKE IF AN RNSR IS NOT REQID

The point that the author makes with this particular spelling would be lost if the words were reproduced in their standard form. It might then be claimed that such a form of the text was incomplete or inadequate, because the point which the author wishes to make is no longer accessible from the written text. Indeed the importance of the correct citing of an author's spelling is regularly marked by the insertion of *sic* into a citation by a second author who wishes to disclaim responsibility for an aberrant spelling.

We have so far been making the simplifying assumption that it is clear, in all cases, what the original text consists of. Where handwritten texts are at issue, it is often the case that the individual reproducing the text in a printed version has to make a considerable effort of interpretation to assign a value to some of the less legible words. In literature, as we have remarked already, uncertainty may give rise to cruces, to disputed texts. In letters, prescriptions, shopping lists, school essays, the reader normally pushes through a once-for-all interpretation of a text which may never be read again. It must be clear however, that a printed version of a handwritten text is, in an important sense, an interpretation. This is particularly clear in the handwritten attempts of very young children where the adult is obliged to assign each large painstakingly formed letter token to a particular type of letter, which he may then re-interpret in the light of the larger message. Thus we have before us a page with a drawing of a large animal (reported to be a lion) and a table with a goldfish bowl on it. The five-year-old writes below what might be transliterated as:

1.　　　the lion wos the fish to ti it

2.　　　the cat wants to get dwon the steis

3.　　　with qwt to dsthhb thelion

A possible *interpretation* of the text thus represented might be:

The lion wants the fish, to eat it. The cat wants to get down the stairs without to disturb the lion.

The transliteration of the original with *qwt*, in line 3, reasonably accurately represents the first letter (which might also be represented as a figure nine if nine has a straight back stroke). A more charitable and *interpretive* transliteration would render it as *a* (i.e. 'unhatted' *a* with a long backstroke (ɑ). We shall return to the problem of the interpretive work of the reader / listener in identifying the words which constitute the text, in the next section.

1.2.4　*Spoken texts*

The problems encountered with the notion of 'text' as the verbal record of a communicative act become a good deal more complex when we consider what is meant by spoken 'text'. The simplest view to assume is that a tape-recording of a communicative act will preserve the 'text'. The tape-recording may also preserve a good deal that may be extraneous to the text – coughing, chairs creaking, buses going past, the scratch of a match lighting a cigarette. We shall insist that these events do not constitute part of the text (though they may form part of the relevant context, cf. Chapter 2).

In general the discourse analyst works with a tape-recording of an event, from which he then makes a written transcription, annotated according to his interests on a particular occasion – transcriptions of the sort which will appear in this book. He has to determine what constitutes the verbal event, and what form he will transcribe it in. Unless the analyst produces a fine-grained phonetic transcription (which very few people would be able to read fluently) details of accent and pronunciation are lost. In general, analysts represent speech using normal orthographic conventions. The analyst may hear an utterance which might be transcribed phonemically as / greɪpbrɪtn /. Is he to render this orthographically as *grape britain*? Hardly. He will interpret what he hears and normalise to the conventional orthographic form *Great Britain* inserting conventional word boundaries in the orthographic version which do not, of course, exist in the acoustic signal. If he hears a form / gənə /, is he to render this in the orthography as *gonna* (which for some readers may have a peculiarly American association) or *gointuh* or *going to*? The problem is a very real one, because most speakers constantly simplify words phonetically in the stream of speech (see Brown, 1977: ch. 4). If the analyst normalises to the conventional written form, the words take on a formality and specificity which necessarily misrepresent the spoken form.

Problems with representing the segmental record of the words spoken pale into insignificance compared with the problems of representing the suprasegmental record (details of intonation and rhythm). We have no standard conventions for representing the paralinguistic features of the utterance which are summarised as 'voice quality', yet the effect of an utterance being said kindly and sympathetically is clearly very different from the effect if it is said brutally and harshly. Similarly it is usually possible to determine from a speaker's voice his or her sex, approximate age and educational status, as well as some aspects of state of health and personality (see Abercrombie, 1968; Laver, 1980). It is not customary to find any detail relating to these indexical features of the speaker in transcriptions by discourse analysts. In general, too, rhythmic and temporal features of speech are ignored in transcriptions; the rhythmic structure which appears to bind some groups of words more closely together than others, and the speeding up and slowing down of the overall pace of speech relative to the speaker's normal pace in a given speech situation, are such complex variables that we have very little idea how they are exploited in speech and to what effect (but, cf. Butterworth, 1980). It seems reasonable to suggest, though, that these variables, together with pause and intonation, perform the functions in speech that punctuation, capitalisation, italicisation, paragraphing etc. perform in written language. If they constitute part of the textual record in written language, they should be included as part of the textual record in spoken language. If it is relevant to indicate Queen Victoria's underlining, then it is surely also relevant to indicate, for example, a speaker's use of high pitch and loudness to indicate emphasis.

The response of most analysts to this complex problem is to present their transcriptions of the spoken text using the conventions of the written language. Thus Cicourel (1973) reproduces three utterances recorded in a classroom in the following way:

1.   Ci: Like this?

2.   T: Okay, yeah, all right, now . . .

3.   Ri: *Now* what are we going to do?

In 1 and 3 we have to assume that the ? indicates that the utterance functions as a question – whether it is formally marked by, for instance, rising intonation in the case of 1, we are not told. Similarly the status of commas in the speech of the T(eacher) is not made explicit – presumably they are to indicate pauses in the stream of speech, but it may be that they simply indicate a complex of rhythmic and intonational cues which the analyst is responding to. What must be clear in a transcript of this kind is that a great deal of interpretation by the analyst has gone on before the reader encounters this 'data'. If the analyst chooses to italicise a word in his transcription to indicate, for example, the speaker's high pitch and increased loudness, he has performed an interpretation on the acoustic signal, an interpretation which, he has decided, is in effect equivalent to a writer's underlining of a word to indicate emphasis. There is a sense, then, in which the analyst is creating the text which others will read. In this creation of the written version of the spoken text he makes appeal to conventional modes of interpretation which, he believes, are shared by other speakers of the language.

It must be further emphasised that, however objective the notion of 'text' may appear as we have defined it ('the verbal record of a communicative act'), the perception and interpretation of each text is essentially subjective. Different individuals pay attention to different aspects of texts. The content of the text appeals to them or fits into their experience differently. In discussing texts we idealise away from this variability of the experiencing of the text and assume what Schutz has called 'the reciprocity of perspective', whereby we take it for granted that readers of a text or listeners to a text share the same experience (Schutz, 1953). Clearly for a great deal of ordinary everyday language this assumption of an amount of overlap of point of view sufficient to allow mutual comprehension is necessary. From time to time however we are brought to a halt by different interpretations of 'the same text'. This is particularly the case when critical attention is being focussed on details of spoken language which were only ever intended by the speaker as ephemeral parts, relatively unimportant, of the working-out of what he wanted to say. It seems fair to suggest that discourse analysis of spoken language is particularly prone to over-analysis. A text frequently has a much wider variety of interpretations imposed upon it by analysts studying it at their leisure, than would ever have been possible for the participants in the communicative interaction which gives rise to the 'text'. Once the analyst has 'created' a written transcription from a recorded spoken version, the written text is available to him in just the way a literary text is available to the literary critic. It is important to remember, when we discuss spoken 'texts', the transitoriness of the original.

It must be clear that our simple definition of 'text' as 'the verbal record of a communicative act' requires at least two hedges:

(i)   the representation of a text which is presented for discussion may in part, particularly where the written representation of a spoken text is involved, consist of a prior analysis (hence interpretation) of a fragment of discourse by the discourse analyst presenting the text for consideration

(ii)   features of the original production of the language, for example shaky handwriting or quavering speech, are somewhat arbitrarily considered as features of the text rather than features of the context in which the language is produced.

1.2.5   *The relationship between speech and writing*

The view that written language and spoken language serve, in general, quite different functions in society has been forcefully propounded, hardly surprisingly, by scholars whose main interest lies in anthropology and sociology. Thus Goody & Watt (1963) and Goody (1977) suggest that analytic thinking followed the acquisition of written language 'since it was the setting down of speech that enabled man clearly to separate words, to manipulate their order and to develop syllogistic forms of reasoning' (Goody, 1977: 11). Goody goes on to make even larger claims about the ways in which the acquisition of writing, which permits man to reflect upon what he has thought, has permitted the development of cognitive structures which are not available to the non-literate (cf. also the views of Vygotsky, 1962). He examines the use of 'figures of the written word' in various cultures, particularly the 'non-speech uses of language' which develop systems of classification like lists, formulae, tables and 'recipes for the organisation and development of human knowledge' (1977: 17).

Goody suggests that written language has two main functions: the first is the storage function which permits communication over time and space, and the second is that which 'shifts language from the oral to the visual domain' and permits words and sentences to be examined out of their original contexts, 'where they appear in a very different and highly "abstract" context' (1977: 78).

It seems reasonable to suggest that, whereas in daily life in a literate culture, we use speech largely for the establishment and maintenance of human relationships (primarily interactional use), we use written language largely for the working out of and transference of information (primarily transactional use). However, there are occasions when speech is used for the detailed transmission of factual information. It is noteworthy, then, that the recipient often writes down the details that he is told. So a doctor writes down his patient's symptoms, an architect writes down his client's requirements, Hansard records the proceedings of the British Parliament, we write down friends' addresses, telephone numbers, recipes, knitting patterns, and so on. When the recipient is not expected to write down the details, it is often the case that the speaker repeats them sometimes several times over. Consider the typical structure of a news broadcast which opens with the 'headlines' – a set of summary statements – which are followed by a news item that consists of an expansion and repetition of the first headline, in which is embedded a comment from 'our man on the spot' that recapitulates the main points again, then, at the end of the broadcast, there is a repetition of the set of headlines. There is a general expectation that people will not remember detailed facts correctly if they are only exposed to them in the spoken mode, especially if they are required to remember them over an extended period of time. This aspect of communication is obviously what written language is supremely good at, whether for the benefit of the individual in remembering the private paraphernalia of daily life, or for the benefit of nations in establishing constitutions, laws and treaties with other nations.

The major differences between speech and writing derive from the fact that one is essentially transitory and the other is designed to be permanent. It is exactly this point which D. J. Enright makes in the observation that 'Plato may once have thought more highly of speech than of writing, but I doubt he does now!' (Review in *The Sunday Times*, 24 January 1982).

1.2.6 *Differences in form between written and spoken language*

It is not our intention here to discuss the many different forms of spoken language which can be identified even within one geographical area like Britain. Clearly there are dialectal differences, accent differences, as well as 'register' differences depending on variables like the topic of discussion and the roles of the participants (see e.g. Trudgill, 1974 and Hudson, 1980 for discussion of these sorts of differences). There is however, one further distinction which is rarely noted, but which it is important to draw attention to here. That is the distinction between the speech of those whose language is highly influenced by long and constant immersion in written language forms, and the speech of those whose language is relatively uninfluenced by written forms of language. It is of course the case that it is the speech of the first set whose language tends to be described in descriptions of the language (grammars), since descriptions are typically written by middle-aged people who have spent long years reading written language. In particular situations the speech of, say, an academic, particularly if he is saying something he has said or thought about before, may have a great deal in common with written language forms. For the majority of the population, even of a 'literate' country, spoken language will have very much less in common with the written language. This, again, is a point appreciated by Goody: 'Some individuals spend more time with the written language than they do with the spoken. Apart from the effects on their own personalities . . . what are the effects on language? How do written languages differ from spoken ones?' (1977: 124). In the discussion which follows we shall draw a simplistic distinction between spoken and written language which takes highly literate written language as the norm of written language, and the speech of those who have not spent many years exposed to written language (a set which will include most young undergraduate students) as the norm for spoken language.

In 1.2.1 we discussed some of the differences in the manner of production of speech and writing, differences which often contribute significantly to characteristic forms in written language as against characteristic forms in speech. The overall effect is to produce speech which is less richly organised than written language, containing less densely packed information, but containing more interactive markers and planning 'fillers'. The standard descriptive grammars of English (e.g. Quirk, Greenbaum, Leech & Svartvik, 1972) typically describe features of the written language, or that form of the spoken language which is highly influenced by written language. From the descriptive work of a number of scholars studying spoken language (e.g. Labov, 1972a; Sinclair & Coulthard, 1975; Chafe, 1979; Ochs, 1979; Cicourel, 1981; Goffman, 1981) we can extract some (by no means all) features which characterise spoken language:

(a)   the syntax of spoken language is typically much less structured than that of written language
  - i. spoken language contains many incomplete sentences, often simply sequences of phrases
  - ii. spoken language typically contains rather little subordination
  - iii. in conversational speech, where sentential syntax can be observed, active declarative forms are normally found. In over 50 hours of recorded conversational speech, Brown, Currie and Kenworthy (1980) found very few examples of passives, it-clefts or wh-clefts. Crystal (1980) also presents some of the problems encountered in attempting to analyse spontaneous speech in terms of categories like *sentence* and *clause*.

As a brief example, notice how this speaker pauses and begins each new 'sentence' before formally completing the previous one:

> *it's quite nice the Grassmarket since + it's always had the antique shops but they're looking + they're sort of + em + become a bit nicer +*

(b)   in written language an extensive set of metalingual markers exists to mark relationships between clauses (*that* complementisers, *when / while* temporal markers, so-called 'logical connectors' like *besides, moreover, however, in spite of*, etc.), in spoken language the largely paratactically organised chunks are related by *and, but, then* and, more rarely, *if*. The speaker is typically less explicit than the writer: *I'm so tired* (because) *I had to walk all the way home*. In written language rhetorical organisers of larger stretches of discourse appear, like *firstly, more important than* and *in conclusion*. These are rare in spoken language.

(c)   In written language, rather heavily premodified noun phrases (like that one) are quite common – it is rare in spoken language to find more than two premodifying adjectives and there is a strong tendency to structure the short chunks of speech so that only one predicate is attached to a given referent at a time (simple case-frame or one-place predicate) as in: *it's a biggish cat + tabby + with torn ears*, or in: *old man McArthur + he was a wee chap + oh very small + and eh a beard + and he was pretty stooped*.

The packaging of information related to a particular referent can, in the written language, be very concentrated, as in the following news item:

> *A man who turned into a human torch ten days ago after snoozing in his locked car while smoking his pipe has died in hospital.*
>
> (*Evening News* (Edinburgh), 22 April 1982)

(d)   Whereas written language sentences are generally structured in subject–predicate form, in spoken language it is quite common to find what Givón (1979b) calls topic–comment structure, as in *the cats + did you let them out.*

(e)   in informal speech, the occurrence of passive constructions is relatively infrequent. That use of the passive in written language which allows non-attribution of agency is typically absent from conversational speech. Instead, active constructions with indeterminate group agents are noticeable, as in:

Oh everything they do in Edinburgh + they do it far too slowly

(f)   in chat about the immediate environment, the speaker may rely on (e.g.) gaze direction to supply a referent: (looking at the rain) *frightful isn't it.*

(g)   the speaker may replace or refine expressions as he goes along: *this man + this chap she was going out with*

(h)   the speaker typically uses a good deal of rather generalised vocabulary: *a lot of, got, do, thing, nice, stuff, place* and *things like that.*

(i)   the speaker frequently repeats the same syntactic form several times over, as this fairground inspector does: *I look at fire extinguishers + I look at fire exits + I look at what gangways are available + I look at electric cables what + are they properly earthed + are they properly covered*

(j)   the speaker may produce a large number of prefabricated 'fillers': *well, erm, I think, you know, if you see what I mean, of course, and so on.*

Some of the typical distinctions between discourse which has been written and that which has been spoken can be seen in the following two descriptions of a rainbow. (No direct comparison is intended, since the two pieces of discourse were produced in strictly non-comparable circumstances for very different purposes.)

Introduction: linguistic forms and functions

(1)   And then, in the blowing clouds, she saw a band of faint
iridescence colouring in faint shadows a portion of the hill.
And forgetting, startled, she looked for the hovering colour
and saw a rainbow forming itself. In one place it gleamed
fiercely, and, her heart anguished with hope, she sought the
shadow of iris where the bow should be. Steadily the colour
gathered, mysteriously, from nowhere, it took presence upon
itself, there was a faint, vast rainbow.

        (D. H. Lawrence, *The Rainbow*, chapter 16)

In the first extract (1), the rich lexis and well-organised structure
are indications that the writer has taken time in the construction,
and possibly reconstruction after several rewritings, of the final
product. There are complete sentences, containing subordinations,
frequent modifications via adjectives and adverbs, and more than
single predicates per referential expression. In extract (2), there are
frequent pauses, often interrupting major syntactic units, repetitions, incomplete sentences, generalised vocabulary, fillers and one
example of a tongue-slip.

(2)   normally after + very heavy rain + or something like that +
and + you're driving along the road + and + far away + you
see + well + er + a series + of + stripes + + formed like a
bow + an arch + + very very far away + ah + seven colours
but + + I guess you hardly ever see seven it's just a + a series
of + colours which + they seem to be separate but if you try to
look for the separate (kʌz) – colours they always seem + very
hard + to separate + if you see what I mean + +

        (Postgraduate student speaking informally)

The speaker planning in the here-and-now, possibly threatened
with his interlocutor wanting to take a turn, typically repeats
himself a good deal, using the same syntactic structure, the same
lexical items, using the first word that comes to mind rather than
hunting for the *mot juste*, filling in pauses with 'fillers'. The overall
effect is of information produced in a much less dense manner than
is characteristic of written language. We must assume that the
density of information packing in spoken language is appropriate
for the listener to process comfortably. Most people have experienced expository prose read aloud which they have found difficult
to follow in the spoken mode. Few people can extract a great deal
from a lecture which is read aloud with no visual support. Goody

points out that the written form of language releases us from the linear experiential mode: 'the fact that it takes a visual form means that one can escape from the problem of the succession of events in time, by backtracking, skipping, looking to see who-done-it before we know what it is they did. Who, except the most obsessive academic, reads a book as he hears speech? Who, except the most avant-garde of modern dramatists, attempts to write as they speak?' (1977: 124).

1.3　Sentence and utterance

It might seem reasonable to propose that the features of spoken language outlined in the preceding section should be considered as features of utterances, and those features typical of written language as characteristic of sentences. In this convenient distinction, we can say, in a fairly non-technical way, that utterances are spoken and sentences are written and that we will apply these terms to what Lyons describes as 'the products of ordinary language-behaviour'. In the case of the term **sentence**, it is important to be clear about the type of object one is referring to. Lyons makes a distinction between 'text-sentences' and 'system-sentences'. He describes the latter in the following way:

> system-sentences never occur as the products of ordinary language-behaviour. Representations of system-sentences may of course be used in metalinguistic discussion of the structure and functions of language: and it is such representations that are customarily cited in grammatical descriptions of particular languages.
>
> (Lyons, 1977: 31)

Since the linguistic exemplification presented in support of our discussion throughout this book is overwhelmingly drawn from 'ordinary language behaviour', we shall generally employ the term 'sentence' in the 'text-sentence', and not the 'system-sentence' sense.

Although the linguist who undertakes the analysis of discourse has ultimately the same aims as a linguist who uses 'system-sentences' in his grammatical description of a language, there are important methodological differences involved in the two approaches. Both linguists wish to produce accurate descriptions of the particular language studied. In pursuit of this goal, the grammarian will concentrate on a particular body of data and attempt to produce an exhaustive but economical set of rules which will account for all and only the acceptable sentences in his data. He will not normally seek to account for the mental processes involved in any language-user's production of those sentences, nor to describe the physical or social contexts in which those sentences occur. On each of these issues, concerning 'data', 'rules', 'processes' and 'contexts', the discourse analyst will take a different view.

1.3.1 *On 'data'*

The grammarian's 'data' is inevitably the single sentence, or a set of single sentences illustrating a particular feature of the language being studied. It is also typically the case that the grammarian will have constructed the sentence or sentences he uses as examples. This procedure is not often made explicit, but an overt commitment to the constructed-data approach has recently been expressed in the following terms:

I shall assume . . . that invented strings and certain intuitive judgements about them constitute legitimate data for linguistic research.

(Gazdar, 1979: 11)

In contrast, the analysis of discourse, as undertaken and exemplified in this book, is typically based on the linguistic output of someone other than the analyst. On the few occasions where constructed data is used as illustration (of a paradigm, for example, in Chapter 4), it is inevitably directed towards accounting for the range of formal options available to a speaker or writer. More typically, the discourse analyst's 'data' is taken from written texts or tape-recordings. It is rarely in the form of a single sentence. This type of linguistic material is sometimes described as 'performance-data' and may contain features such as hesitations, slips, and non-standard forms which a linguist like Chomsky (1965) believed should not have to be accounted for in the grammar of a language.

Although these two views of 'data' differ substantially, they are not incompatible, unless they are taken in an extreme form. A discourse analyst may regularly work with extended extracts of conversational speech, for example, but he does not consider his data in isolation from the descriptions and insights provided by sentence-grammarians. It should be the case that a linguist who is primarily interested in the analysis of discourse is, in some sense, also a sentence-grammarian. Similarly, the sentence-grammarian cannot remain immured from the discourse he encounters in his daily life. The sentence he constructs to illustrate a particular linguistic feature must, in some sense, derive from the 'ordinary language' of his daily life and also be acceptable in it.

A dangerously extreme view of 'relevant data' for a discourse analyst would involve denying the admissibility of a constructed sentence as linguistic data. Another would be an analytic approach to data which did not require that there should be linguistic evidence in the data to support analytic claims. We shall return to the issue of 'relevant data' for discourse analysis in Chapter 2. An over-extreme view of what counts as data for the sentence-grammarian was, according to Sampson (1980), noticeable in some of the early work of generative grammarians. Chomsky gave an indication of the narrowness of view which could be taken, when, immediately before his conclusion that 'grammar is autonomous', he stated:

Despite the undeniable interest and importance of semantic and statistical studies of language, they appear to have no direct relevance to the problem of determining or characterising the set of grammatical utterances.

(Chomsky, 1957: 17)

The essential problem in an extreme version of the constructed-sentence approach occurs when the resulting sentences are tested only against the linguist's introspection. This can (and occasionally did) lead to a situation in which a linguist claims that the 'data' he is using illustrates acceptable linguistic strings because he says it does, as a result of personal introspection, and regardless of how many voices arise in disagreement. The source of this problem, as Sampson (1980: 153) points out, is that the narrow restriction of 'data' to constructed sentences and personal introspection leads to a 'non-testability', in principle, of any claims made. One outcome of this narrow view of data is that there is a concentration on 'artificially contrived sentences isolated from their communicative context' (see Preface to Givón (ed.), 1979). Although we shall appeal frequently, in the course of this book, to the insights of sentence-grammarians, including those working within a generative framework, we shall avoid as far as possible the methodology which depends on what Lyons (1968) described as regularised, standardised and decontextualised data.

1.3.2 *Rules versus regularities*

A corollary to the restricted data approach found in much of Chomskyan linguistics is the importance placed on writing **rules** of grammar which are fixed and true 100% of the time. Just as the grammarian's 'data' cannot contain any variable phenomena, so the grammar must have categorial rules, and not 'rules' which are true only some of the time. It is typical of arguments concerning the 'correct rules' of the language in the Chomskyan approach, and that of most other sentence-grammarians, that they are based on the presentation of 'example' and 'counterexample'. After all, a single (accepted) sentence, which is presented as a counterexample, can be enough to invalidate a rule of the categorial type. In this sense, the 'rules' of grammar appear to be treated in the same way as 'laws' in the physical sciences. This restricts the applicability of such rules since it renders them unavailable to any linguist interested in diachronic change or synchronic variation in a language. It should be emphasised that this is an extreme version of the sentence-grammarian's view and one which is found less frequently, in contemporary linguistics, than it was fifteen years ago.

The discourse analyst, with his 'ordinary language' data, is committed to quite a different view of the rule-governed aspects of a language. Indeed, he may wish to discuss, not 'rules' but **regularities**, simply because his data constantly exemplifies non-categorial phenomena. The regularities which the analyst describes are based on the frequency with which a particular linguistic feature occurs under certain conditions in his discourse data. If the frequency of occurrence is very high, then the phenomenon described may appear to be categorial. As Givón says:

> what is the communicative difference between a rule of 90% fidelity and one of 100% fidelity? In psychological terms, next to nothing. In communication, a system with 90% categorial fidelity is a highly efficient system.
>
> (Givón, 1979a: 28)

Yet the frequency of occurrence need not be as high as 90% to qualify as a regularity. The discourse analyst, like the experimental psychologist, is mainly interested in the level of frequency which reaches significance in perceptual terms. Thus, a regularity in discourse is a linguistic feature which occurs in a definable environment with a significant frequency. In trying to determine such regularities, the discourse analyst will typically adopt the traditional methodology of descriptive linguistics. He will attempt to describe the linguistic forms which occur in his data, relative to the environments in which they occur. In this sense, discourse analysis is, like descriptive linguistics, a way of studying language. It may be regarded as a set of techniques, rather than a theoretically predetermined system for the writing of linguistic 'rules'. The discourse analyst attempts to *discover* regularities in his data and to *describe* them.

1.3.3 *Product versus process*

The regularities which the discourse analyst describes will normally be expressed in dynamic, not static, terms. Since the data investigated is the result of 'ordinary language behaviour', it is likely to contain evidence of the 'behaviour' element. That is, unless we believe that language-users present each other with prefabricated chunks of linguistic strings (sentences), after the fashion of Swift's professors at the grand academy of Lagado (*Gulliver's Travels*, part 3, chapter 5), then we must assume that the data we investigate is the result of active processes.

The sentence-grammarian does not in general take account of this, since his data is not connected to behaviour. His data consists of a set of objects called 'the well-formed sentences of a language', which can exist independently of any individual speaker of that language.

We shall characterise such a view as the **sentence-as-object** view, and note that such sentence-objects have no producers and no receivers. Moreover, they need not be considered in terms of function, as evidenced in this statement by Chomsky (1968: 62):

If we hope to understand human language and the psychological capacities on which it rests, we must first ask what it is, not how or for what purposes it is used.

A less extreme, but certainly related, view of natural language sentences can also be found elsewhere in the literature which relates to discourse analysis. In this view, there are producers and receivers of sentences, or extended texts, but the analysis concentrates solely on the product, that is, the words-on-the-page. Much of the analytic work undertaken in 'Textlinguistics' is of this type.

Typical of such an approach is the 'cohesion' view of the relationships between sentences in a printed text (e.g. the approach in Halliday & Hasan, 1976). In this view, cohesive ties exist between elements in connected sentences of a text in such a way that one word or phrase is linked to other words or phrases. Thus, an anaphoric element such as a pronoun is treated as a word which substitutes for, or refers back to, another word or words. Although there are claims that cohesive links in texts are used by text-producers to facilitate reading or comprehension by text-receivers (cf. Rochester & Martin 1977, 1979; Källgren, 1979), the analysis of the 'product', i.e. the printed text itself, does not involve any consideration of how the product is produced or how it is received. We shall describe such an approach as deriving from a **text-as-product** view. This view does not take account of those principles which constrain the production and those which constrain the interpretation of texts.

In contrast to these two broadly defined approaches, the view taken in this book is best characterised as a **discourse-as-process** view. The distinction between treating discourse as 'product' or 'process' has already been made by Widdowson (1979b: 71). We shall consider words, phrases and sentences which appear in the textual record of a discourse to be evidence of an attempt by a producer (speaker / writer) to communicate his message to a recipient (hearer / reader). We shall be particularly interested in discussing how a recipient might come to comprehend the producer's intended message on a particular occasion, and how the requirements of the particular recipient(s), in definable circumstances, influence the organisation of the producer's discourse. This is clearly an approach which takes the communicative function of language as its primary area of investigation and consequently seeks to describe linguistic form, not as a static object, but as a dynamic means of expressing intended meaning.

There are several arguments against the static concept of language to be found in both the 'sentence-as-object' and 'text-as-product' approaches. For example, Wittgenstein (1953: 132) warns that 'the confusions that occupy us arise when language is like an engine idling, not when it is doing work'. In the course of describing how a sentence-as-object approach, based exclusively on syntactic descriptions, fails to account for a variety of sentential structures, Kuno (1976) concludes that 'it is time to re-examine every major syntactic constraint from a functional point of view'. Similar conclusions are expressed by Creider (1979), Givón (1976, 1979b), Rommetveit (1974) and Tyler (1978). In criticising the text-as-product view of cohesion in text, Morgan (1979) argues that we see a link between a particular pronoun and a full noun phrase in a text because we assume the text is coherent and not because the pronoun 'refers back' to the noun phrase. We seek to identify the writer's intended referent for a pronoun, since a pronoun can, in effect, be used to refer to almost anything. That is, what the textual record means is determined by our interpretation of what the producer intended it to mean.

The discourse analyst, then, is interested in the function or purpose of a piece of linguistic data and also in how that data is processed, both by the producer and by the receiver. It is a natural consequence that the discourse analyst will be interested in the results of psycholinguistic processing experiments in a way which is not typical of the sentence-grammarian. It also follows that the work of those sociolinguists and ethnographers who attempt to discuss language in terms of user's purposes will also be of interest. In the course of this book, we shall appeal to evidence in the psycholinguistic and sociolinguistic literature which offers insights into the way in which discourse, produced in describable contexts for recognisable purposes, is processed and comprehended.

1.3.4 On 'context'

We have constantly referred to the 'environment', 'circumstances' or **context** in which language is used. In Chapter 2 we shall explore the problem of specifying the relevant context. Here we simply remark that in recent years the idea that a linguistic string (a sentence) can be fully analysed without taking 'context' into account has been seriously questioned. If the sentence-grammarian wishes to make claims about the 'acceptability' of a sentence in determining whether the strings produced by his grammar are correct sentences of the language, he is implicitly appealing to contextual considerations. After all, what do we do when we are asked whether a particular string is 'acceptable'? Do we not immediately, and quite naturally, set about constructing some circumstances (i.e. a 'context') in which the sentence could be acceptably used?

Any analytic approach in linguistics which involves contextual considerations, necessarily belongs to that area of language study called **pragmatics**. 'Doing discourse analysis' certainly involves 'doing syntax and semantics', but it primarily consists of 'doing pragmatics'. When the principles which we have expounded in 1.3 are placed alongside Morris's definition of pragmatics as 'the relations of signs to interpreters' (1938: 6), the connection becomes quite clear. In discourse analysis, as in pragmatics, we are concerned with what people using language are doing, and accounting for the linguistic features in the discourse as the means employed in what they are doing.

In summary, the discourse analyst treats his data as the record (text) of a dynamic process in which language was used as an instrument of communication in a context by a speaker / writer to express meanings and achieve intentions (discourse). Working from this data, the analyst seeks to describe regularities in the linguistic realisations used by people to communicate those meanings and intentions.

2

The role of context in interpretation

2.1 Pragmatics and discourse context

In Chapter 1, we emphasised that the discourse analyst necessarily takes a pragmatic approach to the study of language in use. Such an approach brings into consideration a number of issues which do not generally receive much attention in the formal linguist's description of sentential syntax and semantics. We noted, for example, that the discourse analyst has to take account of the context in which a piece of discourse occurs. Some of the most obvious linguistic elements which require contextual information for their interpretation are the deictic forms such as *here*, *now*, *I*, *you*, *this* and *that*. In order to interpret these elements in a piece of discourse, it is necessary to know (at least) who the speaker and hearer are, and the time and place of the production of the discourse. In this chapter we shall discuss these and other aspects of contextual description which are required in the analysis of discourse.

There are, however, other ways in which the discourse analyst's approach to linguistic data differs from that of the formal linguist and leads to a specialised use of certain terms. Because the analyst is investigating the use of language in context by a speaker / writer, he is more concerned with the relationship between the speaker and the utterance, on the particular occasion of use, than with the potential relationship of one sentence to another, regardless of their use. That is, in using terms such as **reference, presupposition, implicature** and **inference**, the discourse analyst is describing what speakers and hearers are doing, and not the relationship which exists between one sentence or proposition and another.

2.1.1 *Reference*

In presenting the traditional semantic view of reference, Lyons (1968: 404) says that 'the relationship which holds between words and things is the relationship of *reference*: words *refer to* things'. This traditional view continues to be expressed in those linguistic studies (e.g. lexical semantics) which describe the relationship between a language and the world, in the absence of language-users. Yet, Lyons, in a more recent statement on the nature of reference, makes the following point: 'it is the speaker who refers (by using some appropriate expression): he invests the expression with reference by the act of referring' (1977: 177). It is exactly this latter view of the nature of reference which the discourse analyst has to appeal to. There is support for such a pragmatic concept of reference in Strawson's (1950) claim that '"referring" is not something an expression does; it is something that someone can use an expression to do'; and in Searle's view that 'in the sense in which speakers refer, expressions do not refer any more than they make promises or give orders' (1979: 155). Thus, in discourse analysis, reference is treated as an action on the part of the speaker / writer. In the following conversational fragment, we shall say, for example, that speaker A uses the expressions *my uncle* and *he* to refer to one individual and *my mother's sister* and *she* to refer to another. We will not, for example, say that *he* 'refers to' *my uncle*.

(1)   A: my uncle's coming home from Canada on Sunday + he's due in +
        B: how long has he been away for or has he just been away?
        A: Oh no they lived in Canada eh he was married to my mother's sister + + well she's been dead for a number of years now +

The complex nature of discourse reference will be investigated in greater detail in Chapters 5 and 6.

2.1.2 *Presupposition*

In the preceding conversational fragment (1), we shall also say that speaker A treats the information that she has an uncle as presupposed and speaker B, in her question, indicates that she has accepted this presupposition. We shall take the view that the notion of presupposition required in discourse analysis is pragmatic presupposition, that is, 'defined in terms of assumptions the speaker makes about what the hearer is likely to accept without challenge' (Givón, 1979a: 50). The notion of assumed 'common ground' is also involved in such a characterisation of presupposition and can be found in this definition by Stalnaker (1978: 321):

presuppositions are what is taken by the speaker to be the common ground of the participants in the conversation.

Notice that, in both these quotations, the indicated source of presuppositions is the speaker.

Consequently, we shall, as with reference, avoid attributing presuppositions to sentences or propositions. Thus, we can see little practical use, in the analysis of discourse, for the notion of logical presupposition which Keenan (1971: 45) describes in the following way:

A sentence S logically presupposes a sentence S′ just in case S logically implies S′ and the negation of S, ~ S, also logically implies S′.

If we take the first sentence of extract (1) as S, and present it below as (2a), we can also present the negation of S, as (2b), and the logical presupposition, S′, as (2c).

(2) a. My uncle is coming home from Canada.
    b. My uncle isn't coming home from Canada.
    c. I have an uncle.

Following Keenan's definition, we can say that (2a) logically presupposes (2c) because of constancy under negation.

However, it seems rather unnecessary to introduce the negative sentence (2b) into a consideration of the relationship between (2a) and (2c) which arises in the conversation presented earlier in (1). Though it may not be common knowledge that the speaker has an uncle, it is what Grice (1981: 190) terms 'noncontroversial' information. Moreover, since the speaker chose to say *my uncle* rather than *I have an uncle and he . . .*, we must assume she didn't feel the need to assert the information. What she appears to be asserting is that this person *is coming home from Canada*. Given this assertion, the idea that we should consider the *denial* of this assertion in order to find out whether there is a presupposition in what the speaker has not asserted seems particularly counterintuitive.

The introduction of the negative sentence (2b) into a consideration of (2a) creates an additional problem. For example, it has been suggested (cf. Kempson, 1975) that a sentence such as (2d) is a perfectly reasonable sentence of English and undermines the argument for logical presupposition, as it is defined above.

(2d)   My uncle isn't coming home from Canada because I don't have an uncle.

Sentences like (2d) always seem typical of utterances made by a speaker to deny another speaker's presupposition in a rather aggressive way. Yet the circumstances in which (2d) might be uttered are likely to be quite different from those in which the first sentence of extract (1) was uttered. *The speakers*, we may suggest, would have different presuppositions, in the two situations. If we rely on a notion of speaker, or pragmatic, presupposition, we can simply treat (2c) as a presupposition of the speaker in uttering (2a). Sentences (2b) and (2d) do not come into consideration at all.

In support of a view that hearers behave as if speakers' presuppositions are to be accepted, there is the rather disturbing evidence from Loftus' study (1975) of answers to leading questions. After watching a film of a car accident some subjects were asked the two questions in (3).

(3)   a. How fast was car A going when it turned right?
        b. Did you see a stop sign?

We can note that one of the speaker-presuppositions in asking (3a) is that *car A turned right*. A number (35%) answered yes to question (3b). Another group of subjects were asked the questions in (4).

(4)   a. How fast was car A going when it ran the stop sign?
        b. Did you see a stop sign?

One of the speaker-presuppositions in asking (4a) is that *car A ran the stop sign*. In this situation, a significantly larger group (53%) answered yes to question (4b).

It is worth noting that a number of subjects did not answer the *b* question in terms of truth or falsehood of fact, but according to what the speaker, in asking the preceding question, had appeared to presuppose. (For a more detailed discussion of this issue, see Loftus, 1975 and Loftus & Zanni, 1975.)

We shall reconsider the notion of presupposition in section 3.3.2, but generally avoid the complex arguments which revolve around the presuppositions of sentences and propositions. (See the contributions and bibliography in Oh & Dineen (eds.) 1979.)

2.1.3 *Implicatures*

The term 'implicature' is used by Grice (1975) to account for what a speaker can imply, suggest, or mean, as distinct from what the speaker literally says. There are **conventional implicatures** which are, according to Grice, determined by 'the conventional meaning of the words used' (1975: 44). In the following example (5), the speaker does not directly assert that one property (being brave) follows from another property (being an Englishman), but the form of expression used conventionally implicates that such a relation does hold.

(5)   He is an Englishman, he is, therefore, brave.

If it should turn out that the individual in question is an Englishman, and not brave, then the implicature is mistaken, but the utterance, Grice suggests, need not be false. For a fuller discussion of conventional implicature, see Karttunen & Peters (1979).

Of much greater interest to the discourse analyst is the notion of **conversational implicature** which is derived from a general principle of conversation plus a number of maxims which speakers will normally obey. The general principle is called the *Cooperative Principle* which Grice (1975: 45) presents in the following terms:

Make your conversational contribution such as is required, at the stage at which it occurs, by the accepted purpose or direction of the talk exchange in which you are engaged.

The conversational conventions, or maxims, which support this principle are as follows:

> *Quantity:* Make your contribution as informative as is required (for the current purposes of the exchange). Do not make your contribution more informative than is required.
>
> *Quality:* Do not say what you believe to be false. Do not say that for which you lack adequate evidence.
>
> *Relation:* Be relevant.
>
> *Manner:* Be perspicuous.
> Avoid obscurity of expression.
> Avoid ambiguity.
> Be brief (avoid unnecessary prolixity).
> Be orderly.

Grice does not suggest that this is an exhaustive list – he notes that a maxim such as *Be polite* is also normally observed – nor that equal weight should be attached to each of the stated maxims. (The maxim of manner, for example, does not obviously apply to primarily interactional conversation.) We might observe that the instruction *Be relevant* seems to cover all the other instructions. However, by providing a description of the norms speakers operate with in conversation, Grice makes it possible to describe what types of meaning a speaker can convey by 'flouting' one of these maxims. This flouting of a maxim results in the speaker conveying, in addition to the literal meaning of his utterance, an additional meaning, which is a conversational implicature. As a brief example, we can consider the following exchange:

(6)   A: I am out of petrol.
          B: There is a garage round the corner.

In this exchange, Grice (1975: 51) suggests that B would be infringing the instruction *Be relevant* if he was gratuitously stating a fact about the world via the literal meaning of his utterance. The implicature, derived from the assumption that speaker B is adhering to the Cooperative Principle, is that the garage is not only round the corner, but also will be open and selling petrol. We might also note that, in order to arrive at the implicature, we have to know certain facts about the world, that garages sell petrol, and that *round the corner* is not a great distance away. We also have to interpret A's remark not only as a description of a particular state of affairs, but as a request for help, for instance. Once the analysis of intended meaning goes beyond the literal meaning of the 'sentences-on-the-page', a vast number of related issues have to be considered. We shall investigate some of these issues in the course of this book, particularly in Chapters 6 and 7.

As a brief account of how the term 'implicature' is used in discourse analysis, we have summarised the important points in Grice's proposal. We would like to emphasise the fact that implicatures are pragmatic aspects of meaning and have certain identifiable characteristics. They are partially derived from the conventional or literal meaning of an utterance, produced in a specific context which is shared by the speaker and the hearer, and depend on a recognition by the speaker and the hearer of the Cooperative Principle and its maxims. For the analyst, as well as the hearer, conversational implicatures must be treated as inherently indeterminate since they derive from a supposition that the speaker has the intention of conveying meaning and of obeying the Cooperative Principle. Since the analyst has only limited access to what a speaker intended, or how sincerely he was behaving, in the production of a discourse fragment, any claims regarding the implicatures identified will have the status of interpretations. In this respect, the discourse analyst is not in the apparently secure position of the formal linguist who has 'rules' of the language which are or are not satisfied, but rather, is in the position of the hearer who has interpretations of the discourse which do, or do not, make sense. (For a more detailed treatment of conversational implicature, see Levinson, forthcoming.)

2.1.4 *Inference*

Since the discourse analyst, like the hearer, has no direct access to a speaker's intended meaning in producing an utterance, he often has to rely on a process of inference to arrive at an interpretation for utterances or for the connections between utterances. Such inferences appear to be of different kinds. It may be the case that we are capable of deriving a specific conclusion (7c) from specific premises (7a) and (7b), via deductive inference, but we are rarely asked to do so in the everyday discourse we encounter.

(7)   a. If it's sunny, it's warm.
           b. It's sunny.
           c. So, it's warm.

We are more likely to operate with a rather loose form of inferencing which leads us to believe that *the hats and coats* mentioned in (8) belong to visitors to the house which has *the dresser* in its kitchen.

(8)   in the kitchen there was a huge dresser and when anyone went in you see + the hats and coats were all dumped on this dresser

It may be, of course, that such an inference is wrong, but, as discourse processors, we seem to prefer to make inferences which have some likelihood of being justified and, if some subsequent information does not fit in with this inference, we abandon it and form another. As an illustration of this, consider the following example (9), taken from Sanford & Garrod (1981: 10):

(9)   John was on his way to school.

If we were to take a formal view of the entailments of such a declarative sentence (like that, for example, expressed in Smith & Wilson, 1979: 150f.), we would be obliged to accept as entailments a set of sentences which would include the following:

(10)   a. Someone was on his way to school.
          b. John was on his way to somewhere.
          c. Someone was on his way to somewhere.

This view of what we infer from reading (9) will only provide us with a limited insight into how readers interpret what they read. Most readers report that they infer from (9) that John is a schoolboy, among other things. When sentence (9) is followed later in the same text by sentence (11), readers readily abandon their original inference and form another, for example that John is a schoolteacher.

(11)   Last week he had been unable to control the class.

In order to capture this type of inference, which is extremely common in our interpretation of discourse, we need a relatively loose notion of inference based on socio-cultural knowledge. Gumperz (1977) presents an extended discussion of the types of factors involved in this type of pragmatic, as opposed to logical, inference. We shall discuss the influence of inference in more detail in Chapter 7.

For the moment, we simply present a view which claims that the terms *reference, presupposition, implicature* and *inference* must be treated as pragmatic concepts in the analysis of discourse. These terms will be used to indicate relationships between discourse participants and elements in the discourse. Since the pragmatic use of these terms is closely tied to the context in which a discourse occurs, we shall now investigate what aspects of context have to be considered in undertaking the analysis of discourse.

2.2 **The context of situation**

Since the beginning of the 1970s, linguists have become increasingly aware of the importance of context in the interpretation of sentences. The implications of taking context into account are well expressed by Sadock (1978: 281):

There is, then, a serious methodological problem that confronts the advocate of linguistic pragmatics. Given some aspects of what a sentence conveys in a particular context, is that aspect part of what the sentence conveys in virtue of its meaning . . . or should it be 'worked out' on the basis of Gricean principles from the rest of the meaning of the sentence and relevant facts of the context of utterance?

If we are to begin to consider the second part of this question seriously we need to be able to specify what are the 'relevant facts of the context of utterance'. The same problem is raised by Fillmore (1977: 119) when he advocates a methodology to which a discourse analyst may often wish to appeal:

The task is to determine what we can know about the meaning and context of an utterance given only the knowledge that the utterance has occurred . . . I find that whenever I notice some sentence in context, I immediately find myself asking what the effect would have been if the context had been slightly different.

In order to make appeal to this methodology, which is very commonly used in linguistic and philosophical discussion, we need to know what it would mean for the context to be 'slightly different'.

2.2.1 Features of context

Consider two invented scenarios in which an identical utterance is produced by two distinct speakers.

(a)   *speaker:* a young mother, *hearer:* her mother-in-law, *place:* park, by a duckpond, *time:* sunny afternoon in September 1962. They are watching the young mother's two-year-old son chasing ducks and the mother-in-law has just remarked that her son, the child's father, was rather *backward* at this age. The young mother says:

I do think *Adam's* quick

(b)   *speaker:* a student, *hearers:* a set of students, *place:* sitting round a coffee table in the refectory, *time:* evening in March 1980. John, one of the group, has just told a joke. Everyone laughs except Adam. Then Adam laughs. One of the students says:

I do think *Adam's* quick

(In each case phonological prominence is placed on *Adam*.)

Clearly we can do a formal analysis on these tokens and, in both cases, the speaker says of Adam that he is quick. It is clear, however, that the utterances in the contexts of situation in which they are cited, would be taken to convey very different messages. In (a) we shall simplistically assume that the referents of *I* and *Adam* are fixed by spatio-temporal co-ordinates. This 'Adam' is being compared (or contrasted), favourably, with his father. *Quick*, may be interpreted, in the context of *backward*, as meaning something like 'quick in developing'.

In (b) different referents for *I* and *Adam* are fixed spatio-temporally. This 'Adam' is being compared (or contrasted) not with his father and favourably, but with the set of other students unfavourably. In this case *quick* must be interpreted as meaning something like 'quick to understand / react / see the joke'. Moreover, since it is said in a context where Adam has just manifestly failed to react to the punch-line as quickly as the set of other students, the speaker (given this type of speaker to this type of hearer in this type of surroundings) will be assumed not to be intending to tell an untruth, but to be implicating the opposite of what she has said.

Is it possible to determine in any principled way what aspects of context of situation are relevant to these different interpretations of the same 'utterance' on two occasions?

J. R. Firth (regarded by many as the founder of modern British linguistics) remarked:

Logicians are apt to think of words and propositions as having 'meaning' somehow in themselves, apart from participants in contexts of situation. Speakers and listeners do not seem to be necessary. I suggest that voices should not be entirely dissociated from the social context in which they function and that therefore all texts in modern spoken languages should be regarded as having 'the implication of utterance', and be referred to typical participants in some generalised context of situation.

(1957: 226)

Firth, then, was concerned to embed the utterance in the 'social context' and to generalise across meanings in specified social contexts. He proposed an approach to the principled description of such contexts which bears a close resemblance to more recent descriptions which we shall go on to examine:

My view was, and still is, that 'context of situation' is best used as a suitable schematic construct to apply to language events . . . A context of situation for linguistic work brings into relation the following categories:
    A. The relevant features of participants: persons, personalities.
      (i) The verbal action of the participants.
      (ii) The non-verbal action of the participants.
    B. The relevant objects.
    C. The effect of the verbal action.
. . . A very rough parallel to this sort of context can be found in language manuals providing the learner with a picture of the railway station and the operative words for travelling by train. It is very rough. But it is parallel with the grammatical rules, and is based on the repetitive routines of initiated persons in the society under description.
(1957: 182; for a practical application of Firth's approach, see Mitchell, 1957.)

An approach similarly emphasising the importance of an ethnographic view of communicative events within communities has been developed by Hymes in a series of articles. Hymes views the role of context in interpretation as, on the one hand, limiting the range of possible interpretations and, on the other, as supporting the intended interpretation:

The use of a linguistic form identifies a range of meanings. A context can support a range of meanings. When a form is used in a context it

37

eliminates the meanings possible to that context other than those the form can signal: the context eliminates from consideration the meanings possible to the form other than those the context can support.

(Hymes, 1962, quoted in Wootton, 1975: 44)

Hymes (1964) sets about specifying the features of context which may be relevant to the identification of a type of speech event in a way reminiscent of Firth's. Like Firth, he seizes first on the 'persons' participating in the speech event. Generalising over speech events, he abstracts the roles **addressor** and **addressee**. The addressor is the speaker or writer who produces the utterance. The addressee is the hearer or reader who is the recipient of the utterance. (Later Hymes also distinguishes **audience**, since the presence of overhearers may contribute to the specification of the speech event.) Knowledge of the addressor in a given communicative event makes it possible for the analyst to imagine what that particular person is likely to say. Knowledge of his addressee constrains the analyst's expectations even further. Thus, if you know the speaker is the prime minister or the departmental secretary or your family doctor or your mother, and you know that the speaker is speaking to a colleague or his bank manager or a small child, you will have different expectations of the sort of language which will be produced, both with respect to form and to content. If you know, further, what is being talked about, Hymes' category of **topic**, your expectations will be further constrained. If then you have information about the **setting**, both in terms of where the event is situated in place and time, and in terms of the physical relations of the interactants with respect to posture and gesture and facial expression, your expectations will be still further limited.

The remaining features of context which Hymes discusses (in 1964) include large-scale features like **channel** (how is contact between the participants in the event being maintained – by speech, writing, signing, smoke signals), **code** (what language, or dialect, or style of language is being used), **message-form** (what form is intended – chat, debate, sermon, fairy-tale, sonnet, love-letter, etc.) and **event** (the nature of the communicative event within which a genre may be embedded – thus a sermon or prayer may be part of the larger event, a church service). In later recensions Hymes adds other features, for example **key** (which involves evaluation – was it a good sermon, a pathetic explanation, etc.), and

purpose (what did the participants intend should come about as a result of the communicative event).

Hymes intends that these contextual features should be regarded rather as general phonetic features are regarded. Just as a phonetician may select, from the general phonetic features available, the features *voiced*, *bilabial* and *stop*, but not *lateral*, to characterise a [b], so, he suggests, the analyst may choose from the contextual features, those necessary to characterise a particular communicative event. Just as the phonetician may wish to make a more detailed, more specific description of the [b] under consideration, for example mentioning delayed onset of voicing and some protrusion of the lips during the period of closure, so may the ethnographer wish to specify some of the contextual features in great detail. We shall return to this point. Hymes' features constitute essentially a checklist which would enable a visiting ethnographer to arrive by helicopter in a location where a communicative event is in process and to check off the detail of the nature of the communicative event.

Let us consider such an ethnographer as an invisible witness to a particular speech event. He would begin, presumably, by noting the larger-scale features of context: what *channel* is being used (we shall say *speech*), what language *code* is being used (we shall specify it is *English*), what *message-form* is being performed (we shall specify it is *conversation*), what *event* is it embedded in (we shall specify it is part of an *interview*). He can identify the participants: the *addressor* is a young scientist who is being interviewed by the *addressee* who is doing research on language. The setting is physically located in the addressee's territory in Edinburgh University and a prominent physical feature is a tape-recorder which is switched on. The time is during the later 1970s (so it is reasonable to expect that they will speak modern English, with Scottish accents). It has just been agreed that they will talk about the young scientist's work, the tape-recorder is switched on and he says:

(12)   I must admit I'm very nervous.

His *topic* at this point, we shall simplistically assume (see further discussion in Chapter 3), is his nervousness.

Given the knowledge of context the analyst has, he should find this a fairly unsurprising utterance. It is very rarely the case in real life that we can predict in detail the form and content of the language which we will encounter, but, given all of the ethnographic information we have specified, the actual occurring utterance is much more likely (hence, we assume, much more readily processed by the addressee) than any of the following 'utterances' which did not occur:

(13)   a. Please pass the marmalade.
       b. My cat has just been sick again.
       c. Get into the box.
       d. I am about to make the first incision.

The more the analyst knows about the features of context, the more likely he is to be able to predict what is likely to be said (see 2.4).

It is further the case that the ethnographic features will give us a value for the deictic forms occurring in the utterance which was actually produced. Thus *I*, *must*, and *am* must be interpreted with respect to the speaker, the young scientist, at the time of making the utterance. (The context here makes the other possible reading, that the speaker is characteristically nervous all of the time, so unlikely as not to be considered apparently by the addressee, or indeed by the analyst until the process of analysis was brought to conscious attention.) In 2.1 we pointed out that deictic elements of the utterances can only be interpreted with respect to the context in which they are uttered. Hymes' checklist of ethnographic features offers one characterisation of context to which we can relate such deictic elements. A more elaborate checklist is provided by the philosopher Lewis (1972), specifically to provide an index of those co-ordinates which a hearer would need to have specified in order that he could determine the truth of a sentence. Like most formal linguists, Lewis assumes that the *channel* is speech, the *code*, English, the *message-form* conversation and the *event* one where one individual is informing another. His interests lie, not with these general features of the communicative event, but with those particular co-ordinates which constitute 'a package of relevant factors, an index' (1972: 173) and which characterise the context against which the truth of a sentence is to be judged. The co-ordinates of the index are specified as follows:

(a)   **possible-world** co-ordinate: this is to account for states of affairs which *might be*, or *could be supposed to be* or *are*

(b)   **time** co-ordinate: to account for tensed sentences and adverbials like *today* or *next week*

(c)   **place** co-ordinate: to account for sentences like *here it is*

(d)   **speaker** co-ordinate: to account for sentences which include first person reference (*I, me, we, our,* etc.)

(e)   **audience** co-ordinate: to account for sentences including *you, yours, yourself,* etc.

(f)   **indicated object** co-ordinate: to account for sentences containing demonstrative phrases like *this, those,* etc.

(g)   **previous discourse** co-ordinate: to account for sentences including phrases like *the latter, the aforementioned,* etc.

(h)   **assignment** co-ordinate: an infinite series of things (sets of things, sequences of things . . .)

Rather similar lists are proposed by scholars who are concerned with the construction of formal discourse domains (see discussion in Chapter 3). For our present purposes we should note that Lewis' list, like Hymes', makes reference to the *speaker* and *hearer* in order to assign values to the deictic categories of speaker and audience (addressor / addressee) realised in first and second person pronouns. Hymes' category *setting* is expanded to take explicit and distinct account of *time* and *place*. Hymes' generalised feature of *topic* is now distributed between the deictic co-ordinate *indicated object*, the *assignment* co-ordinate and the *previous discourse* co-ordinate. This last co-ordinate specifically enables the hearer to interpret what is said in the light of what has already been said. It builds in a cumulative temporal structure to the index, in that the hearer must continually update the information in his *previous discourse* component, to take account of what has most recently been added.

It is, obviously, not possible for us in a textbook to permit you to have the experience of everyday discourse in what Stenning (1978) calls a 'normal context', where the hearer is part of the context and then experiences the text. We have to have recourse to what Stenning calls 'abnormal' contexts, where the analyst reads the text and then has to try to provide the characteristics of the context in which the text might have occurred. We are going to provide you with three written fragments, abstracted from the contexts in which they appeared. The first two are printed, the third spraygunned on a wall. We ask you to consider what, if any, difficulty you have in understanding them, in terms of the co-ordinates of Lewis' index.

(14)   a. Place two fingers in the two holes directly to the left of the finger stop. Remove finger nearest stop.
          b. He seemed to resent them on that occasion and will not wear them today.
          c. SQUASHED INSECTS DONT BITE MAD MENTAL RULE

We have not, as yet, introduced any satisfactory way of handling your experience of previous similar texts (see discussion in 2.4). For the moment we shall suppose that you probably recognise the type of writer in (a) as some impersonal / institutionalised writer addressing a general reader rather than a particular individual (paying attention to *Place* and *Remove* and the ellipsis in the second sentence (the) *finger* nearest (to the) *stop*). If you have difficulty in interpreting this fragment it is probably partly because you are not sure of the referents of the expression *the two holes* and *the finger stop*. You may work out that the two holes have to be of a suitable size for an individual (?) to put two fingers in, possibly near enough to each other to put two fingers of the same hand in, and, having established this scale, it seems likely that the object referred to as *the finger stop* is only centimetres removed, rather than kilometres removed. It would certainly help you to have the following information:

The *addressor* is the Post Office.

The *addressee* is you as a telephone user.

You can probably work out the rest if you did not know it already. However we shall spell out some more:

The *time* of utterance in clock or calendar time does not seem relevant, but what certainly is relevant is that you should know whether this instruction still applies. (It does.)

The *place* of the original utterance is hardly relevant but where you would encounter the text is. (Look in your telephone directory.)

The *possible world* that is relevant is specified in the *previous discourse*: 'It is worth remembering how to dial 999 in darkness or smoke.'

(We should point out that you are not here being asked to use the co-ordinates for the purpose Lewis intended them for, to determine the truth of a sentence. It is a matter of debate whether truth can be assigned to sentences in the imperative form.)

In text *b* the problem of interpretation arises because of not knowing the referents for the expressions *He*, *them*, *on that occasion* and *them* and not having a value to fix the time expression *today*. You may be able to work out that *He* refers to an animate masculine entity, the subject of both clauses. You may wonder why it is reported that *He seemed to resent them*, which may suggest that he was unable to express his own resentment, which may limit your range of potential interpretations of the expression *He*. You note that he *resented them*, where *them* is plural, and you may consider what plural entity may be both *resented* and *worn* (or not worn). This example has all the characteristics of a sentence occurring within a larger piece of text, and illustrates quite clearly the need for a 'previous discourse' co-ordinate, as well as the more obvious 'time' and 'place' co-ordinates. This text appeared in *The Sporting Chronicle* on 4 June 1980. In the preceding part of the text, the writer has been describing a particular racehorse (*He*) which had been fitted with blinkers (*them*) for its previous race (*on that occasion*).

The third text, *c*, offers more thorny problems. Whereas the language of *a* and *b* is quite straightforward and all you require to arrive at an interpretation are values for expressions being used to refer, you may feel that the language here is obscure, perhaps not even meaningful. It is relevant that the time at which this text appeared was in the late 1970s. Your experience of previous similar texts in the 1970s may have familiarised you with the form *X rule OK* which may permit you to divide this unpunctuated sequence into two parts:

SQUASHED INSECTS DONT BITE
MAD MENTAL RULE

The place at which it appeared is relevant. It was spraygunned on a wall in Glasgow. The form of the text, together with the information about place, may suggest to you, if you have previous experience of such texts, that this text derives from an interaction between street gangs. Encyclopaedic knowledge of the world might inform you that the writer is a member of 'Mad Mental' (a street gang) and that the intended addressees are members of 'The Insects' (another street gang). You then need to make appeal to previous discourse in which the Insects had proclaimed INSECTS BITE. (You might then appeal to your knowledge of what Hymes calls 'message-form' which informs you that street gang interactions on walls consists of taunts and counter-taunts. Thus you might arrive at an attribution of intention in the warning SQUASHED INSECTS DONT BITE and the straight assertion MAD MENTAL RULE – without the *OK* tag, which might be taken to invite assent on the part of the addressee.)

Texts *a* and *b*, addressed to the general reader, are relatively accessible fragments of language which require only specification of the intended referents to make them readily interpretable. Text *c* is intended for specific addressees, not for the general public, and it is hard for the general public to interpret without access to shared presuppositions and previous experience which cannot comfortably be forced into the framework proposed by Lewis. In order to take account of this, we are going to need some way of making appeals to notions like 'shared presuppositions', 'encyclopaedic knowledge', 'intention / purpose in uttering' and 'experience of previous similar text' which we have simply appealed to in an *ad hoc* way in our discussion so far. We return to these questions in 2.3.

What we have shown in this section is that the contextual features suggested by Hymes, supplemented with the index of co-ordinates proposed by Lewis (put forward, remember, with quite different purposes in mind) do enable us to give a partial account of what the undifferentiated term 'context' may mean. From this it follows that we could give some account of what it might mean to 'change the context' in the sense in which Fillmore (1977: 119) envisages this when he says 'I . . . find myself asking what the effect would have been if the context had been slightly different.' We could reply that if you alter the condition specified by any of the co-ordinates, you alter the context.

At this point we shall consider only the alteration of one co-ordinate, the speaker co-ordinate. Obviously, if Jane says *I'm skipping* and Mary says *I'm skipping* we observe that on one occasion it is Jane who announces that she is skipping and on another it is Mary. In each case the sentence is true if the person who spoke was skipping at the time of the utterance. However, if we are further told that speaker Jane is only three years old, we may, in addition to paying attention to the announcement, consider that it is a remarkable feat for a three-year-old. Whereas if Mary is eight years old and known to be an intrepid skipper, the announcement may be one of a depressingly predictable series. We pay different amounts of attention to the announcements and react to them differently, because one aspect of the context, the speaker, is significantly different.

Consider the following fragment of conversation:

(15) A: are you often here
      B: quite often + about once a month + actually ++ I come
         up to see my children

You have to suppose of B that B is of an age to have children. What we are interested in is the different sorts of inferences which we make as addressees, depending on variables like the age and sex of the speaker, as a result of hearing what B says. Suppose B is a man of seventy. We assume that B's children will be grown-up. Nothing particular follows from the fact that he visits them once a month, except perhaps we infer that he has a close relationship with them. Suppose the speaker is a young man in his thirties. We assume that children he has will be young children, children of an age who usually live with their parents. We may then wonder why B's children are not living with their father, wonder whether the exigences of his professional life, or of his relationship with the children's mother, constrains him to live apart from them. Suppose the speaker is a young woman in her thirties. Again we assume that she would have young children, children who would normally be expected to be living with her. Since, in the case of the parents being separated, young children usually live with their mother in our society, we might infer that the woman's children are in some form of institutional or educational care. (In the conversation we quote from, the speaker was a man in his early thirties and the children were living with his estranged wife, all inferences which had been drawn by A before B went on to explain that this was the case.)

Observe that the sorts of inferences we have been discussing are not sanctioned by the form of language used. The different inferences arise because of the alteration of the context, in the simple manipulation of age and sex of the addressor. It is the interpretation of the utterance in context which permits the hearer to draw such inferences (see Chapter 7 for further discussion of inferences).

2.2.2 Co-text

In our discussion so far we have concentrated particularly on the physical context in which single utterances are embedded and we have paid rather little attention to the *previous discourse* co-ordinate. Lewis introduced this co-ordinate to take account of sentences which include specific reference to what has been mentioned before as in phrases like *the aforementioned*. It is, however, the case that any sentence other than the first in a fragment of discourse, will have the whole of its interpretation forcibly constrained by the preceding text, not just those phrases which obviously and specifically refer to the preceding text, like *the aforementioned*. Just as the interpretation of the token α in the child's representation of 'without to disturb the lion' and the token [p] in [greɪpbrɪtn] are determined by the context in which they appear, so the words which occur in discourse are constrained by what, following Halliday, we shall call their **co-text**. Consider the following lexical items in a number of verbal contexts cited almost at random from Darwin's *Journal during the Voyage of HMS Beagle round the World*:

(16)   a. The children of the Indians are saved, to be sold or given away as servants, or rather slaves for as long a time as the

> owners can make them believe themselves slaves. But I
> believe in their *treatment* there is little to complain of.
> (114)
> b. The same evening I went on shore. The first *landing* in any
> new country is very interesting. (169)
> c. When we came within hail, one of the four natives who
> were present advanced to receive us and began to shout
> most vehemently, wishing to direct us where to land. When
> we were on shore the *party* looked rather alarmed. (206)
> d. After crossing many low hills, we descended into the small
> land-locked plain of Guitron. In the *basins*, such as this
> one, which are elevated from one thousand to two thousand
> feet above the sea, two species of acacia . . . grow in large
> numbers. (257)
>
> (1892 edition)

The point we wish to make here should be an obvious one and
can of course be made with respect to many of the other items
which we have not italicised in the cited texts. However, consider
the sort of lexical content you would expect to find associated with
the forms *treatment*, *landing*, *party* and *basin* in a dictionary entry,
and note how finding the forms embedded within a co-text
constrains their interpretation.

Just as the interpretation of individual lexical items is constrained
by co-text, so is the interpretation of utterances within a discourse.
Consider this text of the beginning of a sixteen-year-old Scottish
pupil's account of a Sempé cartoon:

(17)   a. a man and woman sitting in the living room + the woman
         sitting reading quite happily – the man's bored goes to the
         window looks out the window + and gets himself ready and
         goes out +

The reader must interpret *the woman sitting reading quite happily*
as the 'woman' already mentioned, hence must construct an
interpretation which has her 'sitting reading quite happily *in the
living room*'. Similarly the *window* which the man approaches must
be interpreted as 'the window of the living room'. The speaker
continues with a change of location and we have to assume that
what follows is within the newly introduced location:

         b. goes to his goes to a club + has a drink talks to the barman
         + then he starts dancing with a beautiful girl long black
         hair + has a good time +

We interpret everything that happens here as happening to the man we met in the living room who is now at *a club*. So he *has a drink, talks to the barman, starts dancing* and *has a good time* all at the 'club'. The speaker announces another change of location

> c. then he goes home and he calls her + and his wife overhears him +

Again we assume that we are still talking about the same man, that he has returned *home* to the location where the 'living room' we first met was located. Now the analyst may be in some doubt how to interpret *and he calls her*, since the man might reasonably go into the house and call (shout for) his wife. However this interpretation is ruled out by the following co-text *and his wife overhears him*. So we are obliged to interpret *calls* as meaning 'phones' and *her* as referring to 'the beautiful girl with long black hair with whom he danced and had a good time'.

Within the co-text, as we have seen in (17) above, a further context may be constructed which has its own index of co-ordinates. Indeed within that constructed context, further contexts may be nested. Consider the following passages:

(18)   About four months before the time I am writing of, my Lady had been in London, and had gone over a Reformatory . . . The matron, seeing my Lady took an interest in the place, pointed out a girl to her, named Rosanna Spearman, and told her a most miserable story: which I haven't the heart to repeat here; for I don't like to be made wretched without any use, and no more do you. The upshot of it was, that Rosanna Spearman had been a thief . . .

                                    (Wilkie Collins, *The Moonstone*)

The actual place and time of writing of the manuscript by the author, Wilkie Collins, or indeed the identity of the author, is not a necessary piece of information for the reader to interpret the text. We may assume, however, that he will have a better understanding of the purpose of the author in constructing the text in the way it is constructed if he knows that it is written in the late nineteenth century (which will account for some differences in *code*, in Hymes' terms) in Victorian England (which will account for the reference to a *Reformatory*) and that the author is constructing the first English detective story, narrating the events from the point of view of four different participants, whose characters are in part revealed by the narrative style which the author assigns to them. We have then, an author and an actual time and place of writing the novel (or a series of times and places). Then to each narrator is assigned a time and place of the writing of his contribution. It is presumably that time which is relevant to the comment *which I haven't the heart to repeat here* where *I* refers to the current narrator. Immediately preceding this extracted fragment, the narrator has been describing an incident relevant to the main story. This is referred to in the expression *the time I am writing of*. The narrator then proceeds to give some background information, which he situates in a previous time *About four months before*. He introduces *Rosanna Spearman*, who, at the time four months before was a resident of the *Reformatory*, but at some previous time to that, *Rosanna Spearman had been a thief*. Within the time domain of 'four months before' a new speaker and hearer are introduced:

(19)   My Lady . . . said to the matron upon that, 'Rosanna Spear-
         man shall have her chance, in my service'. In a week after-
         wards, Rosanna Spearman entered this establishment as our
         second housemaid.

At the time of utterance, *four months before the time I am writing of*, the beneficent lady speaks of the future, *shall have her chance*. In the following sentence the narrator comments on what happened a week later than the time of the lady's speech, from the point of view of his context at the time of writing his contribution to the novel, *In a week afterwards . . .*

This brief introduction does scant justice to the interest of the temporal structure of this passage. It does, however, indicate the complexity of nested contexts established by co-text which, as hearers / readers, we are capable of interpreting.

In Chapter 6 we shall discuss the issue of anaphoric reference which is generally held to depend crucially on co-text for interpreta-tion.

For the moment the main point we are concerned to make is to stress the power of co-text in constraining interpretation. Even in the absence of information about place and time of original utterance, even in the absence of information about the speaker / writer and his intended recipient, it is often possible to reconstruct at least some part of the physical context and to arrive at some interpretation of the text. The more co-text there is, in general, the more secure the interpretation is. Text creates its own context. As Isard (1975: 377) remarks: 'communications do not merely depend on the context for their interpretation, they change that context'.

2.3 The expanding context

In our discussion so far, we have been concerned to impose some sort of analytic structure on the lumpen mass of context. We have abstracted away from particular contexts, across communicative contexts in general, to arrive at a set of features, some of which seem relevant to the identification of a speech event as being of a particular kind, to the ability of the hearer to predict what sort of thing the speaker is likely to say in a given type of context, and to the constraining of interpretation in context. The observant reader will have noticed that we have helped ourselves to the content of the features proposed by Hymes and the co-ordinates proposed by Lewis in a fairly arbitrary way. So we have given variable amounts of information about the *speaker* or the *hearer* or the *time* or the *place* as we have discussed different fragments of discourse. This behaviour is consistent with Hymes' own expectations about how his framework would be used. You will remember that he thought that contextual features might be considered in the way that general phonetic features are considered: sometimes, but not always relevant, and specifiable to variable degrees of delicacy for different purposes (2.2.1).

A problem for the discourse analyst must be, then, to decide when a particular feature is relevant to the specification of a particular context and what degree of specification is required. Are there general principles which will determine the relevance or nature of the specification, or does the analyst have to make *ad hoc* judgements on these questions each time he attempts to work on a fragment of discourse? For the moment, we shall limit our discussion of this question to those features which relate directly to the **deictic context**, those features which will permit interpretation for deictic expressions like the temporal expression *now*, the spatial expression *here*, and the first person expression *I*. Are there standard procedures for determining what information is relevant to the interpretation of these expressions?

Lyons (1977: 570) suggests that there might, in principle, be such standard procedures:

> Every actual utterance is spatiotemporally unique, being spoken or written at a particular place and at a particular time; and provided that there is some standard system for identifying points in space and time, we can, in principle, specify the actual spatiotemporal situation of any utterance act.

There clearly are standard systems for locating points in time and space. It would be possible to specify the time of an utterance as stretching between say 9.33 a.m. and 9.34 a.m. on 5 June 1961, specifying the utterance in terms of clock and calendar time, good standard systems. We could, then, presumably, if we had the relevant instrumentation, specify the place of the utterance in terms of a fine interaction of latitude and longitude. It is not at all clear, however, that these particular standard systems produce the relevant information on all occasions. Presumably some patrol ship on the high seas might log messages in this way, but it is clear that, as humans, our experience of utterances is not that we have recorded in memory a list of utterances to which are attached standard tags specifying time and place in these terms. A friend can attempt to recall to your mind some utterance which you both experienced by a variety of place and time tags:

(20)   a. But you just said he wasn't. (Place: maintained; time: only minutes ago)
        b. You said in the staff meeting yesterday that he wasn't.
        c. You said last week at the staff meeting that he wasn't.
        d. You said last year when we met in Toronto that he wasn't.

The further away in time the message was situated, the less likely the speaker is to remember precisely the date and time at which it occurred, and the larger the time-span he is likely to make available for it to have occurred in. It seems unlikely then, that 'standard procedures' of recording space and time are going to be relevant to the unique identification of utterance acts.

Perhaps the standard procedures will enable us to fix the relevant space spans for the interpretation of deictic expressions like *here*. Suppose X is talking to Y, standing on the blue border of the carpet in X's office, in a given street, in Manchester, in England, in

Britain, in Western Europe ... Y might produce any of the following utterances:

(21)   a. There's another worn section which needs repair here.
        b. You've got a very nice room here.
        c. It's a really nasty day here.
        d. You have a comparatively mild climate here.

It must be clear that the spatial location identified by *here* in each of these expressions could be interpreted as a series of concentric rings spreading out from the speaker and encompassing different amounts of physical space, but the interpretation of the spatial range of the expression *here* on any particular occasion of use will have to be sought in the context of what the speaker is talking about. What appears to be stable in interpretations of *here* (apart from curious usages deriving from long-distance telephonic communication and long-distance travel, discussed in Lyons, 1977) is that the deictic centre is located where the speaker is.

Very similar problems arise with the interpretation of the temporal deictic expression *now*. Consider the following possible utterances:

(22)   a. Clap altogether NOW. (gym mistress to class)
        b. I think you should begin the next chapter now. (supervisor to student)
        c. Now I'm getting older I really do find policemen look younger.
        d. From the iron age till now, man has been making increasingly complex artefacts.

In *c* and *d* the utterances appear to be located within different temporal spans, one relating to the speaker's advancing age (involving a span of 20–30 years) as opposed to the advancement of man (involving a span at least of decades and possibly centuries). Utterances *a* and *b* are different in that the action specified is to follow the utterance, immediately in the case of *a*, but after some expanse of time in *b*. Once again we suggest that the deictic centre is located within the context of utterance by the speaker, but that the interpretation of the expression *now* as relating duratively or subsequently to the utterance, and the time-span involved, must be determined with respect to the content of the utterance.

We should note that this fixing of the deictic centre is particularly appropriate to what Lyons (1977: 637) calls

the canonical situation of utterance: this involves one-one, or one-many, signalling in the phonic medium along the vocal-auditory channel, with all the participants present in the same actual situation able to see one another and to perceive the associated non-vocal paralinguistic features of their utterances, and each assuming the role of sender and receiver in turn.

It is, of course, possible to use the expressions *here* and *now* in what might be described as 'displaced contexts'. Consider how you would interpret the utterance *We'll land here* said by one astronaut to another, on earth, as they study a map of the moon. Or, how you interpret the message on each sheet of one brand of government-issue toilet roll, which reads *NOW WASH YOUR HANDS, PLEASE*. Speakers, or writers, do have the option of transferring the deictic centre to the hearer's, or reader's, spatio-temporal situation in which the text will be encountered.

From our discussion of the spatio-temporal co-ordinates which seem, in principle, peculiarly accessible to standard specification, it must be obvious first, that deictic expressions may retain a standard deictic centre but must be interpreted with respect to the content of the utterance in which they occur and, second, that the relevant standard temporal description of an utterance, for instance *9.22 a.m. on Tuesday 28 June 1873*, as opposed to *in the late nineteenth century*, will vary depending on the knowledge and intention of the analyst (or speaker) in referring to the utterance as located in time. That is to say, even if there were an agreed, standard system for tagging utterances with spatio-temporal features, there is no guarantee that that tagging system provides the relevant information. Thus in 2.2.1. we discussed a fragment of discourse:

> He seemed to resent them on that occasion and will not wear them today

where we specified the time of utterance as 4 June 1980. The newspaper article from which this fragment was extracted did indeed appear on that date. However, for anyone who knows what the expression *the Derby* means, it would almost certainly have been more informative to tag the time of utterance as *Derby Day, 1980*.

The space–time co-ordinates cannot be regarded as simple

unstructured cues to interpretation in context. Similarly, the other co-ordinates relevant to the deictic context, *speaker*, *hearer* and *indicated object*, cannot be regarded as simple unstructured cues which demand standard specification. What does it mean to specify, for instance, the indicated object co-ordinate? We could identify a person by name. We could report *Ellen Blair said she'd like to come*. This might be adequate to identify the speaker, indeed the expression *Ellen* might be sufficient. If, however, you do not know who this person is, or might be, it would be more helpful if we were to give some indication of why we have introduced her into the conversation. So we might say *my friend Ellen Blair*, or *the former chairman Ellen Blair*, or *a nurse in the ward called Ellen Blair*, giving, in some sense, 'credentials' for her existence and for her relationship to the speaker who is responsible for introducing her into the conversation. Morgan (1975: 442) asks 'What can we infer about the speaker's intentions from the fact that he has chosen this particular description, rather than any of the others which would call to mind the same referent?' For any individual there will be an immense number of possible descriptions which will be more or less appropriate in different contexts. We may identify the person from external physical cues: *the woman in the corner*, *the man with a beard*, *the student who has had his hair dyed*, *the child in the pink dress* or, more or less flatteringly, *the tall distinguished-looking man / the man with a big nose and stringy hair*. We may identify people from a description of what they are doing: *the woman who is chatting up the Admiral*, *the man who's fixing the car*, etc.

The variable which interests us most is that which is concerned with the various roles played by the individual. Lyons (1977: 574ff.) distinguishes between the **deictic role** of an individual (which assigns, for instance, first, second and third person pronouns) and his **social role** or 'status'. Lyons points out that, for example, the terms of address used by a social inferior to a social superior may be different from those used between peers, as in vocative terms like 'Sir' or 'Doctor' or 'My Lord' (in the courtroom). In different social contexts, then, different terms of address will be found. (Consider for instance, the distribution of the *tu / vous* pronouns in French.) In general we may assume that, in a particular social context, only one role is taken by an individual at one particular time. A glance at any newspaper will yield a rich crop of identifications of individuals in terms of the social role relevant to the news item. Here are just a few:

(23)   a. *Daily Telegraph cartoonist Nicholas Garland* showing how he sees *the Prime Minister.*
                    (*Stop Press*, 27 February 1982)
     b. *Frank Silbey, chief investigator for the Senate Labor and Human Resources Committee*, picked up his telephone.
                    (*Time*, 31 May 1982)
     c. *Sophia Loren, the film actress*, awoke in a prison cell in Caserta, near Naples, today.
                    (*The Times*, 21 May 1982)
     d. *Mr. Robert Mugabe, the Prime Minister of Zimbabwe* yesterday sought to reassure prospective investors in his country.
                    (*The Times*, 21 May 1982)
     e. *Senor Jorge Blanco of the ruling Revolutionary Party* was officially declared winner.
                    (*The Times*, 21 May 1982)

In each case the individual is identified either by the role which is relevant to the content of the article, or by the role by which he is known to the public. Each individual may play many other roles – parent, child, niece, brother, chess player, gardener, diarist, but these roles are not relevant in this context, so not mentioned on this occasion.

It is possible for more than one social role to be relevant at one time. Rommetveit (1974: 45) discusses a sentence introduced in Chomsky (1972: 67):

I am not against MY FATHER, only against THE LABOR MINISTER

Rommetveit argues that the sentence is not necessarily self-contradictory even if the individual referred to by the two nominal expressions is the same individual. It merely expresses the ambivalence which is a common human experience where some aspect of an entity pleases you and some other aspect fails to please. Rommetveit argues against 'the notion of identifying reference as an unequivocally defined point in a monistic and epistemological transparent space, constructed on axiomatic prerequisites for specific operations within formal logic' . . . where 'the severe laws of truth values prescribe that the speaker must know him (the indicated entity) fully or not at all' (1974: 48).

It is possible for speakers, hearers or indicated entities to be regarded from the perspective of more than one role. Consider:

(24)   a. As his neighbour I see quite a lot of him, as his colleague I hardly ever see him.

          b. As a colleague you're deficient but as a neighbour you're marvellous.

          c. I quite like her as a colleague and she's very pleasant as a casual friend but she's impossible to live with.

It is clear that we can hold partially or severely differing opinions about the same individual in different roles.

In the following extract from a report in *The Times* (15 May 1982) the same individual is referred to by a number of different expressions which relate to the multiple roles that the reporter considers relevant to the incident:

(25)   *Priest is charged with Pope attack* (Lisbon, May 14)

          A *dissident Spanish priest* was charged here today with attempting to murder the Pope.

          Juan Fernandez Krohn, aged 32, was arrested after *a man armed with a bayonet* approached the Pope while he was saying prayers at Fatima on Wednesday night.

          According to the police, *Fernandez* told the investigating magistrates today *he* had trained for the past six months for the assault. *He* was alleged to have claimed the Pope 'looked furious' on hearing *the priest's* criticism of his handling of the church's affairs.

          If found guilty, *the Spaniard* faces a prison sentence of 15–20 years.

We have italicised the expressions relating to the man identified in the headline as *Priest*. The relevance of his role as priest (referred to by the expressions *Priest, a dissident . . . priest, the priest's*) is presumably as a priest of the Roman Catholic Church of which the Pope is Head. Since the incident reported takes place in Portugal (*Lisbon*) and any subsequent prison sentence will be served in Portugal, it is relevant that the priest is not Portuguese (*a . . . Spanish priest, the Spaniard*). A potentially confusing indefinite referring expression, *a man armed with a bayonet*, apparently relates back to the period before he was identified as 'a dissident Spanish priest'. He is identified by his name, as an individual, in the set constituted by the intersection of the various relevant roles (*Juan Fernandez Krohn, Fernandez*). As Levy (1979: 193) remarks, 'the speaker by *making reference* may not simply identify but may *construct* the object by selecting from a field of relations those properties that *are* relevant at the *moment of utterance*'.

Consider the response of a five-and-a-half-year-old girl in a Yorkshire infant school where she is asked to say how two pictures are different from each other. She replies:

(26)   a. That one's over there in *that* but it in't *there*.

The teacher then holds the little girl's hands, so she can't point, shuts her own eyes and says to the child:

     b. Now I can't see the picture. Tell me the difference again.

This time the child says:

     c. In this picture the teddy's on the chair but there ain't no teddy in that one.

The pictures are identical except in three respects: the presence or absence of a teddy bear sitting on the chair, a difference in the pattern on the counterpane, a difference in the position of a mirror. For the child the teddy bear is clearly the salient object. She relies in her first response on the teacher's access to the shared visual context to interpret what she says. She points to the teddy bear (*that one*) in the first picture and then points to the empty chair in the second picture (*there*) and assumes that the teacher is paying attention to what she is pointing to in their shared context of situation. When the teacher inhibits the child from pointing and pretends not to be able to see the picture, the child understands that the communicative situation has changed, that she can no longer rely on the shared visual context and she makes her reference explicit (*the teddy*), locates him verbally rather than by pointing to him (*on the chair*) and makes explicit how the second picture differs from the first (*there ain't no teddy*). A salient aspect of the addressee, her ability to see what the child can see, has been changed by the utterance of *b* and the acts accompanying the utterance.

Speakers, hearers and indicated objects are not featureless, colourless spheres. Nor do they come simply tagged with proper names appropriate to all occasions together with one identifying description appropriate to all occasions. They are, characteristically, endowed with immense numbers of physical and social properties, any one of which may be the property which is relevant to a particular communicative act. The philosopher's crisp index, which permits the identification of speaker and hearer as X and Y, is only relevant in a restricted model world. The discourse analyst working in the real world has to be able to extract, see as relevant, just those properties of the features of context which are relevant to the particular communicative act which he is describing, and which contribute to the interpretation (or intended meaning) of the utterance. As Enkvist (1980: 79) remarks, 'The context analyst's first embarrassment is richness.' How is he to determine which properties of which features of context are relevant on a particular occasion? Are there general principles to appeal to? Is it reasonable to assume, as we tend to do, that those features of context which are salient to the speaker are equally salient to the hearer? Ought we not rather to think in terms of partially intersecting views of context? Bar-Hillel (1970: 79) states that 'the depth of the pragmatic context which is necessary for the full understanding of various sentence-tokens, is different, of course, from case to case'. As yet we have only a very limited understanding of how we might set about determining 'the depth of the pragmatic context which is necessary' for interpretation. We outline a possible approach to the problem in the next section and in Chapter 3.

2.4 The principles of 'local interpretation' and of 'analogy'

In 2.3 we have discussed the problems for the discourse analyst in specifying what aspects of the apparently illimitable features of context are to be taken into account in the interpretation of discourse. How is he to determine the relevant span of time in the interpretation of a particular utterance of 'now' or the relevant aspects of a character referred to by the expression 'John'? We must assume that the problem for the discourse analyst is, in this case, identical to the problem for the hearer. There must be principles of interpretation available to the hearer which enable him to determine, for instance, a relevant and reasonable interpretation of an expression 'John' on a particular occasion of utterance. One principle which we can identify we shall call the **principle of local interpretation**. This principle instructs the hearer not to construct a context any larger than he needs to arrive at an interpretation. Thus if he hears someone say 'Shut the door' he will look towards the nearest door available for being shut. (If that door is shut, he may well say 'It's shut', rather than consider what other doors are potentially available for being shut.) Similarly if his host says 'Come early', having just invited him for eight o'clock, he will interpret 'early' with respect to the last-mentioned time, rather than to some previously mentioned time.

Consider again extract (17) presented here as (27).

(27) a man and woman sitting in the living room . . . the man's bored goes to the window looks out the window . . . and goes out + goes to his goes to a club + has a drink talks to the barman

In our discussion in 2.2.2, we pointed out the effect of 'co-text' in limiting the interpretation of what follows. The initial setting of the co-text determines the extent of the context within which the hearer will understand what is said next. He assumes that entities referred to will remain constant, that the temporal setting will remain constant, that the locational setting will remain constant, unless the speaker indicates some change in any of these, in which case the hearer will minimally expand the context. Not only does the hearer assume it is the same 'man' who is being talked about throughout, he also assumes that the man will stay in the same place unless the speaker announces that he moves. When the hearer hears *goes to the window*, he assumes it is 'the window' in that same 'living room' which has already been mentioned, and he assumes that the man 'goes to the window' on the same occasion, within minutes of the original setting 'sitting in the living room'. When the man *goes to a club*, the hearer assumes that the 'club' is in the same town, that the man has not caught an aeroplane and flown to Las Vegas. Again the minimal expansion of the spatio-temporal setting will suggest that the man *has a drink* and *talks to the barman* within that same club and on that same occasion, within a restricted time-span, say an hour rather than a year.

It is this principle, which instructs the hearer not to construct a context any larger than necessary to secure an interpretation, which accounts for how we understand Sacks' (1972) much-quoted sequence:

(28)   The baby cried.
            The mommy picked it up.

It is possible, of course, to imagine that the first of these sentences describes one event and the second describes another, quite unrelated, event (so the person identified as 'a mother' may be picking up a chair in the course of cleaning a room). The principle of local interpretation however, will guide us to construct a limited context in which 'the mother' is the mentioned baby's mother and the expression *it* is used to refer to the previously mentioned baby. Moreover the sequence of events will be understood as happening adjacently in time and situated adjacently in place. It does not even occur to the reader that the baby might have cried one year in Singapore and be picked up by its mother a year later in Aden. It would, of course, be possible to establish a setting in which such a sequence of events would be plausible, but, if no such setting is established, the reader will assume a local interpretation in respect of time, place and participants.

It must be obvious that 'local interpretation' may only be vaguely conceptualised. It seems unlikely that in interpreting (28) the reader postulates any exact physical distance between the mother and the baby at the point before the mother picks the child up, or that he bothers to wonder whether the mother picks the child up after it has finished crying (and if so how long after, in terms of minutes or seconds) or whether the child was still crying when the mother picked it up. Similarly it seems unlikely that the reader will bother to construct a three-dimensional, photographic representation of 'the baby' which cries in the first sentence and which is picked up in the second sentence. 'Local interpretation' probably relates to another strategy which instructs the hearer / reader to do as little processing as possible, only to construct a representation which is sufficiently specific to permit an interpretation which is adequate for what the hearer judges the purpose of the utterance to be.

Everything that we have said so far in this section leans heavily on the hearer's / reader's ability to utilise his knowledge of the world and his past experience of similar events in interpreting the language which he encounters. It is the experience of similar events which enables him to judge what the purpose of an utterance might be. It is his knowledge of the world which constrains his local interpretation. Consider again (27) presented here as (29).

(29)   a man and woman sitting in the living room . . . the man's bored goes to the window . . . goes out . . . goes to a club

We suggested that *goes to the window* will be interpreted as meaning that 'he goes to the window in the living room', whereas *goes to a club* will be interpreted as meaning 'goes to a club in the same town', i.e. not 'in the living room', nor even 'in the same house'. Knowledge of the world tells us that houses which contain living rooms do not usually contain bars. *Goes out* cannot be simply interpreted as meaning 'goes out of the room', it has to be interpreted as meaning 'goes out of the house'. (In Chapter 7 we return to a discussion of 'knowledge of the world'.)

We must suppose that an individual's experience of past events of a similar kind will equip him with expectations, hypotheses, about what are likely to be relevant aspects of context. Bartlett, one of the founders of modern psychology, comments on the importance of relating a particular experience to other similar experiences:

it is legitimate to say that all the cognitive processes which have been considered, from perceiving to thinking, are ways in which some fundamental 'effort after meaning' seeks expression. Speaking very broadly, such effort is simply the attempt *to connect something that is given with something other than itself.*

(1932: 227, our emphasis)

The individual, he suggests, generalises over particular experiences and extracts from these a number of *types* of experience. This notion is, of course, implicit in the construction of the sets of features of context which we have been considering in this chapter. In order to construct a notion of 'speaker in a context' it is necessary to generalise over contexts and to determine what characteristics speakers in different contexts share. Similarly, in order to construct a notion of 'genre', it is necessary to generalise across experience and determine what it is that is common to fairy stories, chats, news broadcasts, epic poems, debates or salesmen's routines which enables us to recognise one as being a token of the generalised type.

On the basis of experience then, we recognise types of communicative events which take place against the background of a mass of below-conscious expectations also based on past experience which we might summarise, following van Dijk (1977: 99), as 'the ASSUMED NORMALITY of the world'. We assume that our muscles will continue to move normally, that doors which normally open will continue to open, that hair grows on heads, that dogs bark, that towns retain their geographical locations, that the sun will shine, and so on. It is interesting to observe the powerful constraints on creators of surrealist or science fiction in this respect. Alice may enter a looking-glass world where unexpected things happen, but she is still constituted like a human being: walking may take her in an unexpected direction, but the nature of the physical act of walking is taken for granted. If too many expectations are flouted, the writer may be suspected of being mentally unbalanced, of being incapable of seeing the world in a normal way.

Thus, on the one hand, expectations make interpretation possible and, on the other, they constitute an extension or further affirmation of their own validity. Popper makes the point cogently: 'we are born with expectations: with "knowledge" which, although not *valid a priori, is psychologically or genetically a priori*, i.e. prior to all observational experience. One of the most important of these expectations is the expectation of finding a regularity. It is connected with an inborn propensity to look out for regularities, or with a *need* to *find* regularities' (1963: 47, original emphasis). Furthermore, as Lewis (1969: 38) points out, 'fortunately we have learned that all of us will mostly notice the same analogies'. Not only are we all primed to look for regularities, we tend to perceive the same regularities. Clearly the smaller the community, the more notions of regularity will be shared, since the contexts which the members of the community share will be very similar.

Once the individual begins to establish regularities, to generalise over experience, it becomes possible for him not only to recognise a particular experience as being one of a type, say a scolding or an interview, it also becomes possible to predict what is likely to happen, what are likely to be the relevant features of context, within a particular type of communicative event. It follows that the hearer in a speech situation is not in the position of trying to pay attention to every feature of the context (in principle an impossible task). He only pays attention to those features which have been necessary and relevant in similar situations in the past. Bartlett suggests that the individual has 'an overmastering tendency simply to get a general impression of the whole; and on the basis of this he constructs the probable detail' (1932: 206). We pay attention to those salient features which are constitutive of the type of genre, and expect that the peripheral features will be as they have been in the past. Obviously there will be types of occasions which have not occurred within our past experience. We have cultural stereotypes which suggest that such occasions are difficult for us, potentially embarrassing, because we do not know the appropriate responses. Thus, if it is the first time someone tells you a particular genre of joke, you may not know the appropriate type of response. The second time around, however, you feel more confident of what to expect. (Tolstoy, in *War and Peace*, gives a brilliant account of the insecurity engendered by the first occasion of a new type of experience in his description of Pierre's induction into membership of a masonic brotherhood.)

Our experience of particular communicative situations teaches us what to expect of that situation, both in a general predictive sense (e.g. the sort of attitudes which are likely to be expressed, the sort of topics which are likely to be raised) which gives rise to notions of 'appropriacy', and in a limited predictive sense which enables us to interpret linguistic tokens (e.g. deictic forms like *here* and *now*) in the way we have interpreted them before in similar contexts. We must assume that the young child's acquisition of language comes about in the context of expanding experience, of expanding possible interpretations of forms like *here* and *now* in different contexts of situation, contexts which come to be recognised, and stored as types.

Against the background of this mass of expectations which derives from and constitutes our experience, it must become possible to identify the relevant properties of features of the context of situation in terms of norms of expectation within a particular genre. The more highly constrained and ritualised the genre, the more likely we are to be able to identify norms. Thus it seems likely

that examination questions in chemical engineering at degree level
will bear certain similarities of form and content, and share certain
presuppositions, in institutions throughout the world. The less
constrained the genre, primarily interactional 'chat', for example,
the less likely it is that we can confidently state norms of expectation which will generalise even over the experience of the English-
speaking population. For the individual participant in a chatting
relationship, this does not constitute a difficulty, because he has
plenty of previous personal and local experience to call upon. For
the discourse analyst, on the other hand, the more personal and
particular the occasion for the participants, the more limited and
circumspect he must be in his interpretation. Confronted with data
of the following sort, an extract from a private diary only intended
to remind the elderly writer of how she passed a day in January
1982, the discourse analyst may not be able to proceed very far in
his analysis.

(30)   Did more to Ivy's letter. A.A. rang me at 4 o/c she returned on
        2nd and had had grand time with Gwenda and families. As was
        nice p.m. I went to Evensong (rev. Carlil) and walked back
        with Mrs. Nicholls (85!!) and daughter. Cos' Doris rang 8.15
        and will come tomorrow! Bed. 11.15.

Of course, if the discourse analyst experiences a great deal of data
like this, he will feel more confident in his description and
interpretation. He, too, is constrained in his interpretation by past
similar experience, by interpreting in the light of what we might
call the **principle of analogy**.

   The principle of analogy will provide a reasonably secure
framework for interpretation for the hearer and for the analyst most
of the time. Most of the time, things will indeed conform to our
expectations. However, conventions can be flouted and expectations upset, either deliberately for a stylistic effect, or by accident
or oversight. Note that where the speaker / writer is deliberately
flouting a convention, upsetting an expectation for a stylistic effect,
he can only bring off that effect because the convention / expectation exists. The 'non-limerick' which follows only makes an effect
in the light of the conventional structure for limericks which have a
characteristic rhythm and an *aabba* rhyme scheme:

(31)   There was a young girl of St Bees,
         Who was stung on the nose by a wasp,
         When asked 'Does it hurt?'
         She replied 'Yes it does,
         But I'm glad it wasn't a hornet.'

The principle of analogy is one of the fundamental heuristics which hearers and analysts adopt in determining interpretations in context. They assume that everything will remain as it was before unless they are given specific notice that some aspect has changed. Dahl (1976: 46) formulates a principle for speakers: 'Indicate only things which have changed and omit those which are as they were before.' To repeat what is known to be shared knowledge, 'things as they were before', flouts Grice's maxim of quantity. (Speakers do, of course, remind each other of knowledge which they share, in order to make that knowledge part of the activated context of discourse, as McCawley (1979) points out.)

Discourse is interpreted in the light of past experience of similar discourse, by analogy with previous similar texts (remember the relevance of experience of previous similar texts in the interpretation of (14c) in Chapter 2, SQUASHED INSECTS DONT BITE MAD MENTAL RULE). Relevant previous experience, together with the principle of local interpretation, will impel hearers / readers to try to interpret sequential utterances as relating to the same topic. When two sentences are placed together in sequence by a writer who does not want us to consider them as a continuous text, their separateness or disconnectedness must be positively indicated. In a linguistics textbook, the following two sentences were presented as separate citation examples to illustrate structural ambiguity.

(32)   1. The bride and groom left early last night.
         2. He greeted the girl with a smile.
                                    (Brown & Miller, 1980: 84)

In the context of a linguistics textbook, expecially one on syntax, we would not expect to have to interpret two continuous cited sentences as describing an event sequence. In most contexts, however, the natural 'effort after meaning' will impel the hearer / reader to try to co-interpret chunks of language which he finds close

65

to each other on a page, or a stone or a wall and, where possible, to interpret the language as relevant to the physical context.

This last point leads us to an important, but frequently misunderstood, concept in the analysis of discourse. The imperative *'need* to *find* regularities' which Popper speaks of, coupled with Bartlett's 'effort after meaning', constitute a powerful expectation in human beings that what is said or written will make sense in the context in which it appears. Even in the most unpropitious circumstances, the natural reaction of man appears to be to make sense of any sign resembling language, resembling an effort to communicate. The reaction of the man who finds what are apparently signs etched in a stone in the middle of a desert is to try to decipher their meaning. The reaction of parents to infants, and of friends to the speech of those who are gravely ill, is to attribute meaning to any murmur which can be interpreted as relevant to the context of situation, and, if at all possible, to interpret what appears to be being said as constituting a coherent message, permitting the hearer to construct a coherent interpretation. The natural effort of hearers and readers alike is to attribute relevance and coherence to the text they encounter until they are forced not to.

The normal expectation in the construction and interpretation of discourse is, as Grice suggests, that relevance holds, that the speaker is still speaking of the same place and time, participants and topic, unless he marks a change and shows explicitly whether the changed context is, or is not, relevant to what he has been saying previously. Similarly the normal expectation is that the discourse will be coherent. The reaction of some scholars to the question of 'coherence' is to search for cues to coherence within the text and this may indeed yield a descriptive account of the characteristics of some types of text. It ignores, however, the fact that human beings do not require formal textual markers before they are prepared to interpret a text. They naturally assume coherence, and interpret the text in the light of that assumption. They assume, that is, that the principles of analogy and local interpretation constrain their experience.

There are as many linguistic 'cues to coherence' (a concept to be discussed in detail in Chapter 6) holding between the pairs of sentences:

(33)   1. The bride and groom left early last night.
        2. He greeted the girl with a smile.

as there are between:

(34)   The baby cried.
        The mommy picked it up.

It is not the sequence of sentences which represents 'coherent discourse'. Rather it is the reader, driven by the principles of analogy and local interpretation, who assumes that the second sequence describes a series of connected events and interprets linguistic cues (like *baby – it*) under that assumption. Encountering the first pair of sentences in the context in which they occur, the reader does not assume that they describe a connected sequence of events and consequently does not interpret the potential linguistic cues (like *groom – he*) as referring to the same entity. The principles of analogy (things will tend to be as they were before) and local interpretation (if there is a change, assume it is minimal) form the basis of the assumption of coherence in our experience of life in general, hence in our experience of discourse as well.

3
Topic and the representation of discourse content

In the course of this chapter, we shall examine some of the uses of the term *topic* in the study of discourse. In the process, we shall explore some recent attempts to construct a theoretical notion of 'topic', a notion which seems to be essential to concepts such as 'relevance' and 'coherence', but which itself is very difficult to pin down. We shall suggest that formal attempts to identify topics are doomed to failure, but that the discourse analyst may usefully make appeal to notions like 'speaking topically' and 'the speaker's topic' within a 'topic framework'. We shall also consider briefly how markers of 'topic-shift' may be identified in written and spoken discourse. In particular, we shall insist on the principle that it is speakers and writers who have topics, not texts.

We shall then go on to consider how the notion of 'topic' relates to representations of discourse content. Since many of the representations proposed are based on a hierarchical organisation of discourse content, we shall consider critically the possibility of characterising 'topic' in terms of the top-most elements in the hierarchical representation.

3.1 Discourse fragments and the notion 'topic'

We have already argued that the data used in discourse analysis will inevitably reflect the analyst's particular interests. Moreover, the piece of data chosen for study can only be partially analysed. If the investigation is undertaken by someone primarily interested in intonation, for example, the data selected has to meet certain requirements. It must be spoken, audible, and, depending on the level of investigation involved, clear enough to allow instrumental analysis, and accompanied by additional information on the age, sex and linguistic background of the speaker. In practice, any single investigation will have much stricter data requirements than this rather general list. Having selected the data, the investigators will study features such as the pitch, rhythm and loudness of syllables in the data, and spend relatively little or no time studying the lexis or the morphology. In its most extreme form, this narrowing of the investigation in terms of the data selected and the analysis undertaken can lead to a constructed text being carefully read aloud in a phonetics laboratory by a speaker of standard Southern British English. The results of the investigation may then be used to make 'empirical' claims about the intonation of English. Although this is an extreme example, it serves to illustrate the selectiveness which characterises linguistic investigation generally, and which is also present to a certain degree in most analysis of discourse.

The data studied in discourse analysis is always a fragment of discourse and the discourse analyst always has to decide where the fragment begins and ends. How does the analyst decide what constitutes a satisfactory unit for analysis?

There do exist ways of identifying the boundaries of stretches of discourse which set one chunk of discourse off from the rest. Formulaic expressions such as 'Once upon a time . . . and they lived happily ever after' can be used explicitly to mark the boundaries of a fragment. Other familiar markers are 'Have you heard the one about . . . ?', 'Did I tell you what happened to me last week . . . ?' and various other forms which can be used to mark the beginning of a joke or anecdote. These markers can help the analyst decide where the beginning of a coherent fragment of discourse occurs. However, speakers often do not provide such explicit guidelines to help the analyst select chunks of discourse for study.

In order to divide up a lengthy recording of conversational data into chunks which can be investigated in detail, the analyst is often forced to depend on intuitive notions about where one part of a conversation ends and another begins. There are, of course, points where one speaker stops and another starts speaking, but every speaker-change does not necessarily terminate a particular coherent fragment of conversation. Which point of speaker-change, among the many, could be treated as the end of one chunk of the conversation? This type of decision is typically made by appealing to an intuitive notion of **topic**. The conversationalists stop talking about 'money' and move on to 'sex'. A chunk of conversational discourse, then, can be treated as a unit of some kind because it is on a particular 'topic'. The notion of 'topic' is clearly an intuitively satisfactory way of describing the unifying principle which makes one stretch of discourse 'about' something and the next stretch 'about' something else, for it is appealed to very frequently in the discourse analysis literature.

Yet the basis for the identification of 'topic' is rarely made explicit. In fact, 'topic' could be described as the most frequently used, unexplained, term in the analysis of discourse.

3.2 Sentential topic

One use of the term 'topic' is associated with descriptions of sentence structure. According to Hockett, a distinction can be made between the **topic** and the **comment** in a sentence, in that 'the speaker announces a topic and then says something about it . . . In English and the familiar languages of Europe, topics are usually also subjects and comments are predicates' (1958: 201). It is clear from Hockett's examples, reproduced here as (1) and (2), that this 'sentential topic' may coincide with the grammatical subject, as in (1), but need not, as in (2).

(1)   John / ran away

(2)   That new book by Thomas Guernsey / I haven't read yet

The treatment of 'topic' as a grammatical term, identifying a constituent in the structure of a sentence (or the deep structure analysis, at least) is also noticeable in the work of grammarians such as Dahl (1969) and Sgall et al. (1973). Transformational generative grammars would also account for the structure of example (2) in terms of a movement transformation called 'topicalisation'. The term 'topic', then, as found in descriptions of sentence structure, is essentially a term which identifies a particular sentential constituent. As such, it has been used in the study of discourse, by Grimes (1975: 337) for example, to describe the different methods used in various languages to mark the 'topic constituent' of sentences. It has also been used by Givón (1979a) in his argument that, in the development of a language, sentential subjects are derived from 'grammaticalised topics'.

However, we are not, for the moment, concerned with the structure of linguistic units comparable to the simple sentence (see Chapter 5). Nor are we considering 'topic' as a grammatical constituent of any kind. We are primarily interested in the general pretheoretical notion of 'topic' as 'what is being talked about' in a conversation. This type of 'topic' is unlikely to be identifiable as one part of a sentence. Accordingly, we agree with Morgan that 'it is not sentences that have topics, but speakers' (Morgan, 1975: 434).

3.3 Discourse topic

In an attempt to distinguish their notion of topic from the grammarians' sentential topic, Keenan & Schieffelin (1976) used the term **discourse topic**. They were particularly anxious to avoid having 'topic', in discourse study, treated as if it were somehow expressible by a simple noun phrase, as often happens in the treatment of sentential topics. (Some ontological reasons for this type of treatment are suggested by Lyons, 1977: 502.) What Keenan & Schieffelin (1976: 380) emphasise is that 'discourse topic is not a simple NP, but a proposition (about which some claim is made or elicited)'. It may be because their investigation is primarily concerned with children's speech, but, in describing the discourse topic as the 'question of immediate concern', Keenan & Schieffelin appear to replace the idea of a single correct noun phrase as expressing the topic with the idea of a single correct phrase or sentence. The implication in their study is that there must be, for any fragment of conversational discourse, a single proposition (expressed as a phrase or sentence) which represents the discourse topic of the whole of the fragment. Such a view is certainly too simplistic, as we hope to show by considering some experimental work in which 'the topic' was treated as the equivalent of a title. (We shall consider the possibility of representing 'the discourse topic' as a proposition when we investigate the proposition-based analysis of discourse in section 3.7.)

In a series of experiments reported by Bransford & Johnson (1973) subjects were presented with constructed texts to read, comprehend, and, later, recall. The aim of the experiments was to demonstrate that the comprehension of English texts depends not only on knowledge of the language, but also on extra-linguistic knowledge, particularly related to the contexts in which the texts occur. There are examples of texts which appear to depend on accompanying visual material for comprehension and others, such as example (3) reproduced below, for which 'the topic' must be provided.

(3)   The procedure is actually quite simple. First you arrange things into different groups. Of course, one pile may be sufficient depending on how much there is to do. If you have to go somewhere else due to lack of facilities that is the next step, otherwise you are pretty well set. It is important not to overdo things. That is, it is better to do too few things at once than too many. In the short run this may not seem important but complications can easily arise. A mistake can be expensive as well. At first the whole procedure will seem complicated. Soon, however, it will become just another facet of life. It is difficult to foresee any end to the necessity for this task in the immediate future, but then one never can tell. After the procedure is completed one arranges the materials into different groups again. Then they can be put into their appropriate places. Eventually they will be used once more and the whole cycle will then have to be repeated. However, that is part of life.

(from Bransford & Johnson, 1973: 400)

Because it was constructed for a specific purpose, this text is fairly unusual in that there are few lexical clues to what the text might be 'about'. Predictably, the experiments showed that comprehension and recall of this passage were significantly better when subjects were provided, before reading, with what Bransford & Johnson called 'the topic of the passage'. The topic of this passage was 'Washing clothes'. The reader can judge for himself whether his comprehension would have been fuller if he had known this topic.

The use of the word 'topic' in this type of experiment suggests that the topic of a text is equivalent to the title and that, for any text, there is a single correct expression which is 'the topic'. This would be the case if texts could only be understood completely as long as they were accompanied by the single, correct title. However, it should not be too difficult to imagine several different titles for passage (3), each of which could equally facilitate comprehension. One could indicate that the text contains a set of instructions by producing a title such as 'How to Do the Laundry' or 'A Guide to Getting your Clothes Cleaner'. One could incorporate the text's philosophical final statement in a title such as 'Doing the Laundry as a Philosophy of Life' or 'An Orderly Life through Good Laundry Procedure'. These latter titles contain as much information for the reader as the title 'Washing Clothes', which Bransford & Johnson describe as 'the topic'. The implication, surely, is that, for any text, there are a number of possible titles. Correspondingly, we will suggest, there is, for any text, a number of different ways of expressing 'the topic'. Each different way of expressing 'the topic' will effectively represent a different judgement of what is being written (or talked) about in a text. As an illustration of this point, consider the text in (3) as a dusty fragment, recovered during an archaeological dig in the ruins of Minneapolis in the year 2500 A.D. When asked what the text is 'about', the discourse analyst in the expedition might report that it is about 'procedures used in mid-twentieth-century American middle-class culture for maintaining cleanliness in their garments'. (Note the temporal and locational elements included here – elements which we shall consider more fully later.) Another discourse analyst, providing a second opinion, might report that it is about something else entirely, and a debate would ensue in the discourse analysis literature. The same 'text' is considered by both analysts. Their disagreement would be over ways of expressing 'the topic'. (Literary critics are still exercised about the topic of *Hamlet*.)

The difficulty of determining a single phrase or sentence as 'the topic' of a piece of printed text is increased when fragments of conversational discourse are considered. In any conversation, 'what is being talked about' will be judged differently at different points and the participants themselves may not have identical views of what each is talking about. People do, however, regularly report on what a conversation was 'about'. There are informal ways of expressing the topic, even in conversational discourse.

3.3.1 *Topic framework*

The discourse analyst, then, is faced with several problems when he wishes to use the very attractive pretheoretical notion of 'topic' as 'what is being talked/written about'. The notion is attractive because it seems to be the central organising principle for a lot of discourse. It may enable the analyst to explain why several

73

sentences or utterances should be considered together as a set of some kind, separate from another set. It might also provide a means of distinguishing fragments of discourse which are felt to be good, coherent, examples of English from those that are, intuitively, incoherent concatenations of sentences.

Consider, for example, the following discourse fragment, taken from Rochester & Martin (1979: 95).

(4)   Interviewer: A stitch in time saves nine. What does that mean?

Thought-disordered
Speaker: Oh! that's because all women have a little bit of magic to them – I found that out – and it's called – it's sort of good magic – and nine is sort of a magic number + like I've got nine colors here you will notice – I've got yellow, green, blue, grey, orange, blue, and navy – and I've got black – and I've got a sort of clear white – the nine colors to me they are the whole universe – and they symbolize every man, woman and child in the world +

Rochester & Martin attempt to describe the connections existing between sentences in discourse of this type, produced by thought-disordered and schizophrenic speakers, in terms of conceptual associations and lexical ties. They point out, however, that such connections are 'unrelated to the conversational topic'. The notion of 'topic', though undefined, seems to provide Rochester & Martin with a natural criterion for distinguishing between the connected, yet incoherent, discourse of thought-disordered speakers and the coherent discourse of normal speakers.

If there are, as we have already argued, a potentially large number of different ways of expressing 'the topic' of even a short written text, how does the analyst determine which is the one correct expression of the topic for the text? One answer, of course, is to say that, for any practical purposes, there is no such thing as the one correct expression of the topic for any fragment of discourse. There will always be a set of possible expressions of the topic. In the terms used by Tyler (1978: 452), the 'topic' can only be 'one possible paraphrase' of a sequence of utterances. What is required is a characterisation of 'topic' which would allow each of the possible expressions, including titles, to be considered (partially) correct, thus incorporating all reasonable judgements of 'what is being talked about'. We suggest that such a characterisation can be developed in terms of a **topic framework**.

In Chapter 2, we discussed the problem for the discourse analyst of deciding just what features of context were relevant in the interpretation of a particular fragment of discourse. We suggested there that the strategy available to him would be, on the one hand, to work predictively in terms of his previous experience (similar speakers, similar genres, etc.) and on the other hand to examine the content of the text. From the content of the text the analyst can, in principle, determine what aspects of the context are explicitly reflected in the text as the formal record of the utterance. Those aspects of the context which are directly reflected in the text, and which need to be called upon to interpret the text, we shall refer to as *activated features of context* and suggest that they constitute the contextual framework within which the topic is constituted, that is, *the topic framework*.

As a way of characterising the type of feature which will be required in a topic framework, we shall examine a fragment of conversational discourse and try to determine what is 'being talked about'. The fragment, presented as (5), is not a constructed piece of text, it is taken from a recorded conversation. As an example of discourse analysis data, it has been selected for a particular purpose. It is not a difficult fragment to work with, it has a definable beginning and end, and, for most of the fragment, there is one participant talking, in response to another's request for information. This request for information provides a direction for the conversational fragment, so that we are considering speech with some purpose and not just social chat used to pass the time. One might also say that the content of the request for information could provide some basis for the content of the response, especially when the request is for the meaning of an expression to be given. That is, it would seem, at first glance, to be a simple matter to produce 'the topic' for this discourse fragment, for it is contained in the question asked. Immediately prior to the following extract, the speaker has been asked the meaning of the expression, 'smoke the houses'.

(5)   R: in those days + when we were young + there was no local
fire engine here + it was just a two-wheeled trolley which
was kept in the borough + in the borough eh store down on
James Street + and whenever a fire broke out + it was just
a question of whoever saw the fire first yelling 'Fire' + and
the nearest people ran for the trolley and how they got
on with it goodness knows + nobody was trained in
its use + anyway everybody knew to go for the
trolley + well + when we were children + we used to use
this taw [tɔː] + it smouldered furiously + black thick
smoke came from it and we used to get it burning + and
then go to a letter box and just keep blowing + open the
letter box + and just keep blowing the smoke in + you
see + till you'd fill up the lower part of the house with
nothing but smoke + there was no fire + but just fill it up
with smoke + just to put the breeze up + just as a
joke + and then of course + when somebody would open a
window or a door the smoke would come pouring
out + and then + everybody was away then for the
trolley + we just stood and watched all of them + +

       S: so that's what 'smoke the houses' is?

       R: probably + probably + we called it 'the taw' +

If we were to say that the topic of this discourse fragment is 'the
meaning of the expression "smoke the houses"', we could not claim
to have said very much of analytic interest. It may be that, for
participant S, the above expression represents the best way of
summarising what speaker R was talking about, as evidenced by her
response. However, even if we take that summarising phrase as one
possible expression of the topic of speaker R's lengthy contribution,
we have surely not adequately characterised what this speaker was
talking about. We might suggest that the speaker is talking about *a
joke* or a prank. In doing so, he talks about an object called 'the taw'
which produces a lot of *smoke*. He talks about the process of *putting
the smoke into houses* through the letter box and how *smoke would
come out* of the window or door. He also talks about an object
known as *the trolley*, a type of fire engine, and *the events* associated
with its use. He talks about *people going for the trolley* when the
smoke comes out of a house. Thus one account of what this speaker
is talking about would contain the following elements: a joke – the
taw – smoke – into houses – out of houses – people get trolley – the
use of the trolley.

    This set of objects and events could be taken as a set of elements which would have to be included in a representation of this speaker's topic, i.e. what he was talking about. It is not a complete set. In this fragment, the speaker is also talking 'about' a particular time and place, and 'about' a specific person. He is talking about his own childhood (*when we were children*) in Stornoway (*here*). This last element presents a problem, because there is nothing in the text of the conversational fragment to indicate this location. Yet it is a piece of knowledge relevant to what the speaker is talking about and, importantly, knowledge which the speaker assumes is available, to his hearer. Presumably, the speaker can also assume that, because his hearer knows, approximately, the speaker's age, the hearer can judge the time (i.e. forty years before and not ten years before) of the events described.

Aspects of the speaker's assumptions about his hearer's knowledge must also be considered in relation to the elements which the speaker does make explicit in his contribution. Do the first lines of this fragment contribute to answering the question asked? Strictly speaking they do not. Yet one would hesitate to describe these lines as irrelevant. They are relevant to what the speaker wishes to provide as an answer to the question, *given the particular hearer* he has. This young American hearer, visiting Stornoway, may have a quite inappropriate idea of the type of object, and the associated behaviour, involved in dealing with a fire in Stornoway forty years before. Without knowing about the trolley, the hearer may not (in the speaker's assessment perhaps) appreciate the full flavour of the joke or prank being described.

It may be argued that this last point has more to do with why the speaker talked about something than with what he talked about. Any consideration of topic involves asking why the speaker said what he said in a particular discourse situation. As Coulthard (1977: 76), following Sacks (1971), points out, there is a constant analysis in conversation of what is said in terms of 'why that now and to me'. In the present discussion we have already partially answered the reader's primary 'why' question about the discourse fragment being studied by providing the previous speaker's question. That is, attempting to provide an account of what a person is talking about is always built on an assumption that we know why that person says what he says. The point may be clearer if we consider a possible reaction to the expression, 'Roses are red, violets are blue' being included in (5) after the speaker has said *nobody was trained in its use*. Would the expression simply be included in the list of what was talked about, or would it prompt the question 'Why does he say that here?' The acceptance of extract (5) as a reasonable piece of English conversational discourse involves implicitly assessing each expression in terms of the 'why?' question above and finding a suitable answer. Part of the process of analysing discourse in terms of 'topic' is an attempt to make explicit the basis for our intuitive ability to recognise why what is said is appropriate in a particular discourse fragment.

Certain elements which constrain the topic can be determined before this discourse begins. These elements are part of what, in the previous chapter, were described as the context of a speech event. In relating contextual features to a particular speech event, however, we are particularly interested in only those activated features of context pertaining to the fragment of discourse being studied. For example, aspects of the time and place of the discourse in (5) are important because they have a bearing on what the speaker says in the fragment (forty years after the described event took place, but still in Stornoway). Similarly, certain facts about the speaker and hearer, as we pointed out earlier, have to be included. As a first approximation, then, we could produce a partial representation of a 'framework' for extract (5) in terms of the following set of activated contextual features.

> Conversation between Participant R (50+ years, Scottish, male, . . .) and Participant S (20+ years, American, female, . . .) in location p (Stornoway, . . .) at time t (late 1970s, . . .)

This simple set of features which we have claimed are necessary for a discussion of topic are required, quite independently of topic considerations, in any form of discourse analysis. For ethnographers and sociolinguists considering linguistic interaction, these elements and others have to be made explicit in the analysis of features such as code-switching and role-relationships. For the formal semanticist, these elements are required in the assignment of values to indexicals such as *I, you, here* and *now*. That is, in building a framework for the analysis of topic, we are not adding any machinery to the apparatus of the discourse analyst which he does not have to employ already.

Those contextual features we have described above are, of course, derived from the physical context. They are external to the text. There is, for most conversational fragments, a set of discourse-internal elements which are derived from the conversation prior to the particular fragment being studied. These elements are introduced in the preceding co-text and form part of what has been described as 'the domain of discourse' (cf. Karttunen, 1974). Within the domain of a particular discourse fragment are the people, places, entities, events, facts, etc. already activated for both participants because they have been mentioned in the preceding conversation. If the fragment of discourse one wished to study was only the part of (5) beginning, *when we were children we used to use this taw*, then accounting for the speaker's mention of *the trolley* near the end of this fragment would have to be done in terms of the preceding discourse (i.e. all the first section before *the taw* is mentioned) in which *the trolley* is introduced and characterised.

We have introduced some basic components which would be required in a characterisation of the topic framework for any discourse fragment. The topic framework consists of elements derivable from the physical context and from the discourse domain of any discourse fragment. Notice that we have concentrated on only those elements which are *activated*, that is, relevant to the interpretation of what is said. If we say that characterising the topic framework is a means of making explicit some of the assumptions a speaker can make about his hearer's knowledge, we are not talking about the *total* knowledge which the speaker believes he shares with his hearer. We are describing only that activated part which is required in the analysis of the discourse fragment under consideration. This approach is crucially different from some other proposals we shall examine.

3.3.2 *Presupposition pools*

What we have described as a *topic framework* has much in common with Venneman's proposal that, for a discourse, there is a **presupposition pool** which contains information 'constituted from general knowledge, from the situative context of the discourse, and from the completed part of the discourse itself'

(Venneman, 1975: 314). In this approach, each participant in a discourse has a presupposition pool and his pool is added to as the discourse proceeds. Each participant also behaves as if there exists only one presupposition pool shared by all participants in the discourse. Venneman emphasises that this is true in 'a normal, honest discourse'.

Within the presupposition pool for any discourse, there is a set of *discourse subjects* and each discourse is, in a sense, about its discourse subjects. Because it is part of the shared assumptions of the discourse participants that these discourse subjects exist, they do not need to have their existence asserted in the discourse. Examples of expressions used for discourse subjects might be *the Queen, John, John's wife* (in the presupposition pool by virtue of general knowledge), *your hat, today* (from the situative context) and *a concert of the Berlin Philharmonic's last year, several essays* (from the preceding part of the text of the discourse).

The number of discourse subjects in a presupposition pool shared by participants in a discourse, particularly participants who know each other quite well, is potentially very large. How does the discourse analyst decide which discourse subjects to include in the presupposition pool for a particular piece of conversational discourse? Remembering that any discourse data to which the analyst has access will only be a fragment, it would be extremely difficult for the analyst to predetermine the complete set of discourse subjects which participants share prior to a particular discourse fragment. The most he could hope to provide would be a partial set. The problem to be faced is that of limiting the choice of the contents of even a partial set, in some non-arbitrary way.

The most important principle involved in this selection of Venneman's discourse subjects must have to do with their relevance to the particular discourse fragment under consideration. If, in a stretch of conversational discourse, the participants involved can be independently known to have potential discourse subjects such as 'the Queen', 'the Pope', or even 'the King of Siam', within their shared presupposition pool, but do not mention the individuals, so identified, in their conversation, it is surely unnecessary to refer to those individuals in the analysis of that particular discourse fragment. They are, in our terms, not 'activated'. This would lead to the conclusion that the relevant 'discourse subjects' for a particular discourse fragment must be those to which reference is made in the text of the discourse. If 'mentioned-in-the-text' is taken as the basis for selection of discourse subjects, it should be noted that the analyst is, in fact, attempting to reconstitute the presupposition pool which the participants must have had prior to the discourse fragment being analysed. Such a process may be comparable to the experience one has when switching on the radio in the middle of a discussion programme and trying to understand the discussion through a partial reconstruction of what must have been said already, who the participants must be, and so on. It does suggest that the only information the discourse analyst has access to is that contained in the text of a discourse fragment.

3.3.3 *Sentential topic and the presupposition pool*

Of course, the data for discourse analysis is not limited to anonymous, decontextualised texts, as we have argued already in Chapter 2. Concentrating solely on the text, however, remains a common approach in many accounts of discourse. It is also characteristic of this approach that the text to be analysed is constructed by the analyst to illustrate the points he wishes to make. This, unfortunately, is the method used by Venneman who, despite the promising breadth of analysis suggested by the concept of a presupposition pool shared by participants, restricts his investigation to describing the relationship between pairs of sentences. The notion of 'topic' considered by Venneman reflects the limitations of his investigation. He considers

the expression 'topic' or 'topic of a discourse' as referring to a discourse subject on which the attention of the participants of the discourse is concentrated. Such concentration of attention is usually, though not always, brought about by an immediately preceding textual mentioning of the discourse subject.

(Venneman, 1975: 317)

This definition of topic has a certain intuitive appeal, in the sense that what two participants are concentrating on, in their conversational talk for example, is a reasonable candidate for 'the topic'. There are, however, two basic problems here. First, this definition of topic seems to be based on the same 'topic = single term title' notion which we challenged earlier. As we pointed out then, although a stretch of discourse can appear to be largely concerned with a single individual, or one discourse subject, so that the discourse may be loosely reported as being 'about' that individual, this should not lead us to claim that all discourses are about single individuals or can be given convenient one-word titles.

A second objection is that it is far from clear how we would decide, in any principled way, what the participants in a discourse fragment are, in fact, 'concentrating' on. An attempt is made by Venneman to provide a formal means of identifying the topic in a discourse fragment. He suggests that like 'all phenomena whose unique existence is presupposed, topics can be referred to by means of individual names, deictic expressions, and definite descriptions' (Venneman, 1975: 317). Using this guide, the analyst must find that the following two discourse fragments, one each from stretches of spoken and written discourse, have several such 'topics'.

(6)   what was interesting was that little Richard came home from his Toronto school with his Newfie jokes the content of which the substantive content was identical to Irish jokes which my son comes home with from Edinburgh schools

(7)   so can he, but the main point about this system is the strain it puts on the other players

What is 'the topic' of (6) – *little Richard* or *his Toronto school* or *his Newfie jokes*, etc.; and is *he*, *this system* or *the other players* the topic of (7)? It is possible to make a guess at what the speaker of (6) and the writer of (7) were concentrating on, but the guess is probably based on an elaborate reconstruction of what the most probable context was, both verbal and non-verbal, for these two discourse fragments. That is, the reader will be forced to use these 'texts' to reconstruct, not just some relevant discourse subjects in the presupposition pool, following Venneman, but rather some of the elements of the topic framework existing when these discourse fragments were produced. It is also likely that the reader, if asked to give the topic for each fragment, would not simply produce a single-term 'title'.

If the same reader were faced with the type of 'discourse' fragment created by Venneman, reproduced as (8) below, he might quite readily provide support for Venneman's analysis by saying that 'the topic' is *Mary*.

(8)   Mary is singing strangely.

The reader presumably can just as easily reconstruct an alternative context (e.g. a description of the effects of marijuana on a Nativity play performance) in which *Mary* would not be proposed as 'the topic of the discourse'. Thus, while there may be preferences discernible in the choice of elements most-likely-to-be-concentrated-on within a sentence if that sentence is presented in isolation, such preferences may reflect the rather trivial fact that names are more salient than anything else, in isolation. That these preferences do have significance for an analysis of the syntactic structure of sentences has been argued by Kuno & Kaburaki (1977). However, it is, in principle, impossible for a discourse to consist of a single decontextualised sentence and, in practice, rare for discourse participants to have to work out 'the topic of discourse' one sentence at a time. The most a discourse analyst could say about a discourse fragment such as the sentence in (8) above is that *Mary* is potentially part of the topic of the discourse in which (8) occurred, but more information is required, as indeed is also the case for both extracts (6) and (7). It should be apparent that the use of single constructed sentences as the basis for making claims about notions such as 'the topic of a discourse' is extremely misleading.

3.4 Relevance and speaking topically

The topic framework, as we have described it, represents the area of overlap in the knowledge which has been activated and is shared by the participants at a particular point in a discourse. Once the elements in the topic framework and the interrelationships between them have been identified, the analyst has some basis for making judgements of **relevance** with regard to conversational contributions.

The technical use of the term 'relevance' in the analysis of conversation is derived from the conversational maxims proposed by Grice (1975). If, as Grice suggests, there is a general agreement of co-operation between participants in conversation, then each participant can expect the other to conform to certain conventions in speaking. These conventions or maxims have to do with the *quantity* (or informativeness), the *quality* (truthfulness), the *manner* (clearness) and *relevance* of conversational contributions.

Although he discusses and exemplifies the other maxims, Grice does not elaborate on the simple instruction 'Be relevant.' The discourse analyst wishing to make use of this notion is immediately confronted with the problem of deciding 'relevant to what?' One way of solving this problem is to translate the maxim 'Be relevant' into a more practically useful form as 'Make your contribution relevant in terms of the existing topic framework.'

What we have characterised as a convention of conversational discourse – 'making your contribution relevant in terms of the existing topic framework' – could be captured more succinctly in the expression **speaking topically**. We could say that a discourse participant is 'speaking topically' when he makes his contribution fit closely to the most recent elements incorporated in the topic framework. This is most noticeable in conversations where each participant 'picks up' elements from the contribution of the preceding speaker and incorporates them in his contribution, as in the following fragment:

(9)   E: I went to Yosemite National Park
         F: did you
         E: yeah – it's beautiful there right throughout the year +
         F: I have relations in California and that's their favourite Park
            because they + enjoy camping a lot
         E: oh yeah
         F: they go round camping +
         E: I must admit I hate camping +

This type of 'speaking topically' is an obvious feature of casual conversation in which each participant contributes equally and there is no fixed direction for the conversation to go. In contrast, there is the type of conversational situation in which the participants are concentrating their talk on one particular entity, individual or issue. In such a situation, the participants may, in fact, 'speak topically', but they might also be said to be **speaking on a topic**. An extreme example of 'speaking on a topic' would be in a debate where one participant ignored the previous speaker's contribution on 'capital punishment', for example, and presented his talk quite independently of any connection with what went before. In practice, we should find that any conversational fragment will exhibit patterns of talk in which both 'speaking topically' and 'speaking on a topic' are present.

Both forms are based on the existing topic framework, but the distinction derives from what each individual speaker treats as the salient elements in the existing topic framework. It is quite often the case that a speaker will treat what he was talking about in his last contribution as the most salient elements and what the other speaker talked about, though more recent, as less salient. This facet of conversational discourse quite naturally leads to a consideration of the individual speaker's topics within what we have been discussing as the conversational topic. Before we explore the influence of 'speaker's topic', we shall try to illustrate in some detail the way in which conversational participants 'speak topically', by making their contributions relevant to the existing topic framework.

In the representation of the topic framework, we shall present the elements involved as a list. It is difficult to imagine an appropriate 'diagram' which could incorporate both the sequential pattern of elements introduced and the interrelatedness of those elements with each other and with the contextual features. For the moment, we shall identify some of the elements and links which are pertinent to an analysis of one fragment.

(10)   Partial topic framework existing in a conversation
        between K   (20+, female, Edinburgh-resident, university stu-
                     dent, . . .)
        and J   (60+, male, Edinburgh-resident, retired, . . .)
        in P   Working Men's Club, Edinburgh, . . .)
        at T   (early evening, spring, 1976, . . .)
        mentioning (J's three children – J's brothers – the schools they
                     attended – the schools J attended – that J did badly
                     at school – J left school at fourteen)
        when   K asks J what he did after he left school

        J   oh I done odd jobs like + paper boy + chemist's
                     shop worked in a chemist shop + and done two or
                     three others + and I finally started in the
                     bricklaying + so I served my time as a bricklayer +
        K: that's good money
        J: nowadays it is but in that + when my time was out
                     it wasn't + it was only three pounds nine a
                     week + so + +
        K: my father was a stonemason and he started at
                     home + and they were paid a halfpenny an hour
                     extra for being left-handed + +

Given a fragment of conversation and a topic framework as in (10), it is possible for the analyst to point out some ways in which each participant 'speaks topically'. Such an undertaking can appear to be a matter of stating the obvious – that speaker J, in his first contribution, for example, is answering the 'what' question in terms of an understood-to-be-known location and a time which is known from an interaction between knowledge of J's age (context) and knowledge that J was at least fourteen (domain). We might highlight the 'topicality' or 'relevance' of J's first contribution by asking how K might have reacted if J had talked about one of his brothers, or about the type of work to be had in Australia, or training to be a brain surgeon. Given this topic framework, J is constrained from talking about these things *unless* he introduces into the topic framework some additional information which he could then treat as shared by his hearer – that one of his brothers had gone to Australia to train as a brain surgeon and he considered doing the same, but settled for bricklaying instead. Thus, J's first contribution here can be judged to be relevant in terms of the existing topic framework and also to add some information to the topic framework. In this first contribution, he doesn't talk about 'being fourteen or older' or 'Edinburgh', but he does talk about 'starting work as a bricklayer' (when I was fourteen or older, in Edinburgh) and, as a co-operative conversationalist, he would have to state *explicitly* if the information 'being fourteen or older, in Edinburgh' was not applicable.

More interesting is speaker K's first contribution in (10). First, its connection to the preceding discourse depends on a general inference that if one works (e.g. as a bricklayer) one receives money. (We shall discuss the role of inference in discourse in Chapter 7.) Second, this contribution has the potential to produce some conflict within the conversation, since 'what is being talked about' up to this point is not present time. The speaker appears to be generalising to a time which includes her own experience. Within the existing topic framework, speaker K's saying *that's good money* is an example of speaking topically, *for her*, but, for speaker J, the time co-ordinate within the topic framework has been narrowed down by his preceding remarks. There is, then, a discrepancy between what each participant is talking about, within the topic framework. We shall examine this effect of individual speaker's topics in the next section.

Speaker J relates his subsequent remarks to the two salient time co-ordinates within the topic framework and adds some specific information on the 'money' element introduced by speaker K.

Speaker K's next contribution exhibits a series of complex ties with the existing topic framework. Speaker J, in his preceding contribution, has talked about the money received for his work at a particular point in the past. Speaker K's contribution 'picks up' the past time element, moving closer to speaker J's time while maintaining the personal reference in *my father*, who also did work (*stonemason*) comparable to J's (*bricklayer*) and received money for this work. Putting her contribution even closer to J's preceding remarks, K makes her comments about her father relate to his 'starting' work and so comparable to J's *started* and *when my time was out*. With these complex connections made, speaker K adds some new elements to the conversation (extra pay for being left-handed).

We have tried to list the connections existing across contributions in this discourse fragment to emphasise the ways speakers make what *they're* talking about fit into a framework which represents what *we* (as discourse participants) are talking about in conversational discourse. For the discourse analyst, as an overhearer, those connections can signal the coherence relations which make each contribution relevant to the discourse as a whole. Identifying the elements in the topic framework at any point in the discourse allows the analyst to make claims about what is involved in 'speaking topically'. It also enables him to produce a version of 'what is being talked about', i.e. the topic of conversation, which is much more comprehensive, and certainly of greater analytic interest, than the single word-or-phrase-type title which is often used in a fairly trivial way to characterise 'topic' in the study of conversation.

3.5 Speaker's topic

So far we have considered the notion of 'topic' in discourse in terms of what the participants share. The 'topic framework', as an analytic device, is essentially a means of characterising the area of overlap in contributions to a discourse. By concentrating on the way conversational contributions overlap, however, we may neglect aspects of conversational discourse associated with different speakers having different personal 'topics'. So far, we have been concentrating on describing the 'conversational topic', but neglecting the notion of **speaker's topic**. As we have already pointed out, the analyst typically treats conversational data as something complete, as a static product of some recorded interaction. In doing so, he may lose sight of the fact that conversational discourse is dynamic, and that his data represents a process. If we can treat any piece of conversational data as a process in which two or more participants speak within the topic framework, we should also find in their contributions elements which characterise their own personal 'speaker's topics'. We shall look at a fragment of spoken discourse, not in terms of how we would characterise the participants' shared information, but in terms of a process in which each participant expresses a personal topic within the general topic framework of the conversation as a whole. Prior to extract (11), the participants, L (female, 20+, unmarried, Edinburgh-resident, and M (female, 30+, married with young children, Edinburgh-resident), have been talking about recent improvements to old buildings in different areas in Edinburgh.

(11)   L: I quite like the way they've done the Mile though + I think it's quite –
         M: yes[∧h∧] yes
         L: the bottom of it anyway
         M: it is – it is quite good they've certainly kept within the + em + + preserved it reasonably well or conserved it but we were up in Aberdeen this year for a holiday and we were staying right within the University complex there in Old Aberdeen + and + oh some of the buildings there are beautiful really they really are nice + but er I was quite impressed with it – it's the first holiday we've had up there +
         L: I was noticing – I was down by Queen Street or + the bottom of Hanover Street or somewhere + and they've just cleaned up some of the buildings down there + and what a difference it makes +
         M: yes I know because there are some beautiful buildings
         L: oh it was really nice

Extract (11) is representative of a common conversational situation in which each of the participants give examples from their personal experience to illustrate some general point. The general point in this case is something like 'the effect of restoring old buildings' which is already part of the topic framework established by the preceding discourse. Notice that speaker M's second contribution in this extract is not just 'about' that general point. She is also talking about her recent holiday in Aberdeen, for example. We could describe this 'holiday in Aberdeen' element as, at this point, a part of speaker M's personal topic which could become, in the developing conversation, a shared topic area for both speakers. Speaker L could have followed on, with a question, for example, about the holiday, Aberdeen, or even with some personal observations on the buildings in Old Aberdeen or the University. Speaker L, however, does not 'pick up' any elements from speaker M's personal topic, but continues on her own personal topic area (i.e. Edinburgh's old buildings after restoration). When participant M speaks again near the end, she does not return to her 'holiday' or 'Old Aberdeen', but makes her contribution relate closely to L's immediately preceding remarks.

There are two points worth noting about this fragment of conversational discourse. First, it is a feature of a lot of conversation that 'topics' are not fixed beforehand, but are negotiated in the process of conversing. Throughout a conversation, the next 'topic' of conversation is developing. Each speaker contributes to the conversation in terms of both the existing topic framework and his or her personal topic. It is clear from extract (11) that some elements in a speaker's personal topic do not become salient elements in the conversation if neither the other participant nor the speaker herself mention them again. To use the 'negotiation' metaphor, we can say that speaker M offers elements in her personal topic (in her second contribution) as possible elements to be included in the conversational business, but speaker L does not take up the offer.

A second point to be noted in this, and in a large number of other conversational fragments, is that personal topics are frequently introduced through first person reference in one form or another. Although the points made in extract (11) could have been expressed objectively as statements that certain buildings in certain locations are more beautiful since restoration, both speakers relate such statements to personal experience. It is as if speakers feel obliged to offer some personal warrant for the statements they will make about the world. A statement that the buildings in Old Aberdeen are beautiful is embedded within an assertion that the speaker was recently in Old Aberdeen, and stayed there for a period, and so she has a warrant for making the statement.

If we reconsider the earlier extract (5) as one participant wanting to know the meaning of an expression and the other offering a possible explanation, we can see that the explanation is offered in personal terms (*when we were young* and *we called it 'the taw'*) based on the speaker's personal experience. It may be that this explanation is not an acceptable answer to the question, but it is presented by the speaker in a form which conveys 'what I think we're talking about' in this part of the conversation. Characterising the individual speaker's topic as 'what I think we're talking about' incorporates both that element which the conversational analyst tends to abstract as the 'topic of conversation' for the participants ('What we're talking about') and the individual speaker's version ('I think'), as he/she makes a conversational contribution. That speakers do introduce what they want to say via some form of personal reference has a noticeable effect on the structure of contributions in conversational discourse. We shall return to this point in the discussion of further details of discourse structure in Chapter 4.

From what we have proposed as speakers' topics in conversational discourse, it must occasionally happen that there are at least two versions of 'What I think we're talking about' which are potentially incompatible. It is a noticeable feature of co-operative conversational discourse, however, that this potential incompatibility rarely leads to conflict over the topic of conversation. What typically happens is that, in the negotiation process, one speaker realises that his version is incompatible with what the other appears to be talking about and makes his contributions compatible with 'what I think *you* (not we) are talking about'. We can illustrate this process in two conversational fragments and note two different strategies used to avoid conflict in the 'negotiations'.

In the first extract, (12), one piece of continuous conversational discourse has been divided up into chunks. Immediately before this extract, speaker B (female, 50+, aunt of speaker A) has been describing to speaker A (female, 20+) the first type of radio she had, forty years before.

(12)   A: but you'd have telephones around +
             B: mm oh yes oh aye oh aye I've had the telephone since nineteen thirty eight +
             A: hmm
             B: oh they were on a long while I think before that +

Speaker B had been talking about the radio she had in the 1930s and speaker A's first line here seems to continue within the temporal, locational and personal indices of the existing topic framework while introducing *telephones*. Speaker B treats this contribution as requiring an answer, following a pattern described by Labov in the rule: 'If (speaker) A makes a statement about a (speaker) B-event, it is heard as a request for confirmation' (1972b: 254). Speaker B expands on her answer, in personal terms, regarding *the telephone*. Speaker A offers no contribution and speaker B adds some additional information about *telephones*. We might characterise speaker B's view of 'what I think we're talking about now' as something involving herself, the 1930s, and the existence of telephones (as well as radios) at that time. The conversation continues:

             A: 'cause there was a man in – my father's in the Scouts +
             B: oh yes he was – is he still
             A: he's a county commissioner now
             B: oh is he + ah ha +

Speaker A appears to be offering some new elements as part of the conversational topic, again deriving from some personal reference (as in *my father*) which speaker B appears to accept. That is, speaker B does not insist on mentioning *telephones*, but moves on to this new area. Speaker B's view of 'what I think we're talking about now' must now involve speaker A, A's father, the Scouts and *a man* (who may have something to do with telephones). We might expect speaker B to be a little confused about how these elements relate to the preceding conversation. Speaker A continues, as follows:

             A: and eh one of his oldest + scoutmasters wa- ha- was reaching his hundredth birthday +
             B: is that so +

We suspect that, by this point, although speaker B can identify 'what's being talked about', she can play no part in negotiating the topic, because she may not be able to see *why* this individual entity is being talked about. The contributions of speaker B cease to be attempts to add anything to the conversational topic. Speaker B's view of the conversation has consequently become one in which she is no longer expressing a personal topic, but is waiting to discover 'what I think *you* (not we) are talking about'. Throughout the rest of this fragment, speaker B simply makes 'interested' noises as speaker A gradually gets to the point.

> A: so father was making up a big + sort of remembrance book –
> B: aha
> A: to give him and he was writing just at the beginning he was – writing the whole – for each year of his life he wrote something in that had – had been invented or +
> B: oh yes
> A: ah a book that had been written or a piece of music that had been written or a painting or a –
> B: very interesting yes
> A: or whatever you know and + within his lifetime the telephone had been invented +
> B: had it + really + fancy +

In this extract as a whole, we can trace speaker B's attempt to contribute to what she thinks they're about, by first offering some remarks on *telephones* and then on the *father*, but gradually reducing her comments to the type of contentless noises described by Duncan (1973) as *back channels*. *Back channel behaviour*, which can also include nods and sentence completions is used when a participant wants to indicate to the person speaking that he should continue. Speaker B stops trying to take turns in the negotiation of topic and waits for speaker A to make it clear how what she is saying has some connection to the existing topic framework. Eventually, as we can see in A's final remarks, a connection is made. There is evidence in speaker A's contributions that what she is trying to say is not very well organised before she starts to speak. There are false starts, hesitations and repetitions. Everyday conversational discourse is, not infrequently, characterised by this lack of pre-planning. The resulting structure of speaker A's contributions is, in fact, quite common in discourse and will be discussed in some detail later in terms of 'staging' (see Chapter 4).

Speaker B's strategy, then, in a situation where she finds that she is unsure about what she thinks they're talking about, is to stop talking. In the following extract (13), there is another example of a mismatch between speakers' topics, brought about by a misunderstanding of the intended meaning of a particular word. In the immediately preceding conversation, speaker C (female, 20+, American, visiting Edinburgh) has been finding out from speaker D (male, 40+, Edinburgh-resident) where there are good places to go for bicycle rides in and around Edinburgh.

(13)   C: what about going down by the – the Firth of Forth
                D: that should be fun shouldn't it yes you could –
                C: is it
                D: yes you can cycle all – you can ride right along the edge you know + without falling in you can ride right along the edge eh without em + going – keeping on the main road + that should be great actually + you could do that +
                C: is it very rough down there though
                D: well there are no cobbles as far as I remember – have you tried riding on the cobbles
                C: yes yes
                D: you must have done
                C: I went down to Muirhouse
                D: which is almost all cobbles isn't it
                C: it was rather rough
                D: hmm
                C: no but I was – I was thinking rather more rough in terms of the em + people +
                D: oh I see + you well I don't think so + I don't know + I – I – eh – parts of it are quite poor + particularly the Pilton area +

Looking back to speaker C's third question, we can propose two versions of 'what I think we're talking about'. For speaker C, it involves 'are the people rough?' and, for speaker D, 'are the roads rough?' Unlike the hearer (B) in extract (12), however, speaker C appears to be able to recognise speaker D's alternative topic and accepts what she thinks speaker D is talking about as 'what we're talking about', for a few turns. When speaker D stops talking about *cobbles* (i.e. rough for cycling on), speaker C can attempt to return to her topic (*rough in terms of the em + people*). Speaker D's response at the end of this fragment is, in effect, an answer to the question which speaker C originally intended him to answer.

We might think that by the end of this fragment there is once again a single version for both speakers of 'what I think we're talking about'. Indeed, most conversational analysis is undertaken with this single 'topic' concept as a working assumption. Yet, in extract (13) we can only reconstruct the intended meaning of C's third question because she actually explains her intended meaning later. If speaker D had gone on at some length about 'cobbles' or rough roads in general, or if the analysis only had part of this fragment, up to C's *it was rather rough*, then we might have had no evidence of a divergence in speakers' topics within the conversation. Our argument for the importance of considering individual speaker's topics in conversational discourse would consequently be weaker. We do not suggest that discourse analysts should spend their time looking for potential alternative meanings in what speakers say in a conversation, but we do suggest that the analyst should not simply assume that there is a single, static 'topic of conversation' in any conversational fragment. If there is an entity identifiable as 'the topic of conversation', the analyst should consider what evidence from each individual speaker's contributions he is using to make that identification. He should also remain aware of the fact that conversation is a process and that each contribution should be treated as part of the negotiation of 'what is being talked about'. Above all, he should remember that it is speakers, and not conversations or discourses, that have 'topics'.

3.6 Topic boundary markers

In our discussion of 'topic', we have concentrated mainly on considerations of 'content' and neglected the influence of 'form'. Yet our interpretation of *what* a speaker is talking about is inevitably based on *how* he structures what he is saying. We shall now investigate some formal aspects of topic-structure in discourse. In this section we shall look at the formal devices used to mark the boundaries of chunks of both written and spoken discourse which form large units of some kind, such as paragraphs. Aspects of the internal structuring of these chunks will be discussed in Chapter 4.

It has been suggested (e.g. by Schank, 1977: 424; Maynard, 1980) that instead of undertaking the difficult task of attempting to define 'what a topic is', we should concentrate on describing what we recognise as **topic-shift**. That is, between two contiguous pieces of discourse which are intuitively considered to have two different 'topics', there should be a point at which the shift from one topic to the next is marked. If we can characterise this marking of topic-shift, then we shall have found a structural basis for dividing up stretches of discourse into a series of smaller units, each on a separate topic. This type of approach to the analysis of discourse is based on the principle that, if we can identify the boundaries of units – where one unit ends and another begins – then we need not have a priori specifications for the content of such units. The burden of analysis is consequently transferred to identifying the formal markers of topic-shift in discourse.

3.6.1 *Paragraphs*

It might seem that identifying the formal demarcation of chunks of written or printed discourse is a relatively simple task. After all, written discourse is divided into paragraphs whose boundaries are marked by indentations. Topic-shifts in written discourse then could be identified with the beginning of each new paragraph. Unfortunately, it doesn't seem to be as simple as that. Those who use the term 'paragraph' to describe a unit in the structural analysis of written discourse go to some trouble to point out that they are not describing the orthographic paragraph. According to Longacre (1979: 116), the orthographic paragraph can result from a writer's stylistic concerns, 'partially dictated by eye appeal', or from printing conventions such as an indentation for each change of speaker. Hinds (1977: 83) also notes that the journalistic paragraph is often determined on the basis of appearance. He has a worked example in which a single structural paragraph derives from a newspaper article containing five orthographic paragraphs. Thus, it may be that the beginning of an orthographic paragraph indicates a point of topic-shift, but it need not do so.

Both Longacre (1979) and Hinds (1977) appeal to languages other than English for evidence that there are formal linguistic markers of the beginning and end of paragraphs. What is immediately noticeable in the discussion of these markers is that they are genre-specific. There are ways of indicating the beginning of a new paragraph in a piece of narrative, for example, which are not used in explanatory discourse. This general point is also made by

Grimes (1975: 109), who describes the marking of paragraph boundaries as one form of 'partitioning' in discourse. The principles on which partitioning depends are related to change of 'setting' (time or place) and 'theme' (the person or thing talked about), in narrative discourse, at least. Interesting though it may be to learn that there is a narrative-discourse-paragraph-introductory-particle in Huichol or Shipibo, it becomes decidedly less interesting when one discovers that the identification of the significance of these particles depends on a prior identification of the paragraph as a unit in which 'the speaker continues talking about the same thing' (Grimes, 1975: 103). Hinds (1977) bases his paragraph divisions on a similar principle, quoting Grimes as support, and emphasising the significance of 'participant orientation' – that is, the unity of a paragraph derives from its being mainly about a single participant. Longacre (1979) claims that 'in narrative discourse, a narrative paragraph is built around a thematic participant, occasionally a small set of thematic participants' (Longacre, 1979: 118).

In other words, only the paragraph structure of stretches of discourse about individual, primarily human, characters is being discussed. In effect, this limits the discussion to narrative discourse, or, as in Hinds (1977), a description or an obituary of a particular individual. It should be obvious why a single structural or 'semantic' paragraph in Hinds' (1977) analysis can extend over five orthographic paragraphs in a newspaper. Each of these orthographic paragraphs is 'about' the same individual. Yet, some obituaries extend to twenty or more orthographic paragraphs 'about' the one person, and whole chapters of novels, containing over a hundred lengthy orthographic paragraphs, may be 'about' the same individual. Surely such extended stretches of written discourse are not single 'paragraphs'?

We shall consider a stretch of written discourse, not from a source such as a Paez (Colombia) folk tale or a specially constructed text, but from a recent English novel. In the extract reproduced below (14), the orthographic paragraph boundaries as they appeared on the printed page have been ignored. The whole extract has two principal participants, but is quite clearly 'about' only one of them. If there are points of 'topic-shift' in English written discourse which lead writers, or their editors, to begin new orthographic paragraphs, then we should be able to identify likely points where the writer or the editor marked the division of this 'text' into separate chunks.

(14)   [1]After the first few days, when I come into the room, Birdie is down on the floor of the cage, running back and forth, looking out over the barrier that holds in the gravel. [2]I think she's glad to see me, not just because I give her treat food, but because she's lonely. [3]I'm her one friend now, the only living being she gets to see. [4]By the end of the week, I rubberband the treat food dish onto the end of an extra perch and put it into the cage through the door. [5]I lock the door open with a paper clip. [6] At first, Birdie's shy, but then she jumps onto the perch I'm holding and side-hops over to the treat dish. [7]It's terrific to see her without the bars between us. [8]She sits eating the treat food at the opening to the door and looking at me. [9]How does she know to look into my eyes and not at the huge finger next to her. [10]After she's finished eating, she retreats to the middle of the perch. [11]I lift it gently to give her a ride and a feeling the perch is part of me and not the cage. [12]She shifts her body and flips her wings to keep balance, then looks at me and makes a new sound, like peeEEP; very sharp. [13]She jumps off the perch to the bottom of the cage. [14]I take out the perch and try to talk to her but she ignores me. [15]She drinks water. [16]She doesn't look at me again till she's wiped off her beak and stretched both wings, one at a time. [17]She uses her feet to help stretch the wings. [18]Then, she gives a small queeEEP?. [19]Generally, Birdie looks at me more with her right eye than her left. [20]It doesn't matter which side of the cage I stand. [21]She turns so she can see me with her right eye. [22]Also, when she reaches with her foot to hold the treat dish, or even her regular food dish, she does it with her right foot. [23]She'd be right-handed if she had hands; she's right-footed or right-sided. [24]She approaches and does most things from the right side.

(William Wharton, *Birdy*, Jonathan Cape, 1979, p. 47)

If there are orthographic paragraph divisions in the original version of this text which were made for the sake of appearance on the page, then we have little hope of identifying such divisions in any formal way. What kind of formal marks, if any, would we expect to find at the beginning of a new paragraph? The markers Longacre (1979) identifies in narrative discourse are inevitably adverbial expressions indicating temporal sequence. It may be that the general class of adverbials which can appear initially in a sentence could be taken as possible markers of 'topic-shift'. Quirk et al. (1972: ch. 8) provide lists of such adverbials in terms of adjuncts, conjuncts and disjuncts. In fact, extract (14) begins with an adverbial clause in initial position. There are two other points in this extract, sentences 4 and 10, where adverbial clauses occur in sentence-initial position. There are four other points where adverbial expressions occur sentence-initially, sentences 6 (*At first*), 18 (*Then*), 19 (*Generally*), and 22 (*Also*). This would give us six possible breaks, formally marked, in the structure of the piece of text.

The next question is – do all these adverbial expressions function in the same way? After all, we would like to distinguish between adverbials which indicate a connection between one sentence and the next and those adverbials used to link a set of sentences to another set. The use of *then* in 18 seems to introduce a final action in a temporal sequence of actions. We can conceive of this one sentence being separated from the previous set as a form of distinct climax. We might expect, however, that it would more typically occur as the final sentence of a paragraph, not as a climax, but as describing an action which culminates a series of actions. It is followed by a sentence which does not continue the series of actions and which begins with what Quirk et al. (1972: 509) would characterise as a 'style disjunct'. This use of *generally*, in 19, effectively separates the previous set of sentences from the next set describing a particular habit of the individual involved. Within this latter set, one sentence begins with the additive adjunct, *also*, in 22, which could be indicating that there are two parts to this set. It is more likely that the sentence beginning with *also* is adding more detail to support the general conclusion that the individual concerned is *right-sided* and is part of the internal structure of a paragraph beginning with *Generally*.

The other adverbial, *at first*, in 6, seems to be part of a sentence-internal construction, especially when we see the *then* which follows. The events described in this sentence fall within the set of events described as happening *by the end of the week* (in 4).

Thus, we have reduced the number of possible breaks in this text to three, so that we can suggest that there are four paragraphs, beginning at sentences 1, 4, 10 and 19. The reader may suggest other possible breaks, as, for example, in 9, where there is a sentence structure (an interrogative) quite different from the structure of the rest of the text sentences. An argument for a break here would seem quite reasonable since this sentence is structurally marked as separate. No doubt the reader could also think of an argument, mainly in stylistic terms, for treating this sentence as part of the preceding set. It may be the case that, taking stylistic considerations more generally, the reader would wish to divide this text into separate paragraphs at points where there are no formal markers at all. We would assume that the discussion, in such a case, would cease to be a discussion which appealed to primarily linguistic evidence in this piece of discourse.

On the basis of some formal linguistic markers, we have suggested that there are four paragraphs in extract (14). We may have been led to finding those four paragraphs because they are, in fact, the divisions which actually appear in the original and we merely sought additional evidence to support the way the author had divided up his discourse. Yet this point highlights the fact that the exercise we have performed on extract (14) was an extremely artificial treatment of written discourse. We began by removing one of the primary indicators of 'topic-shift' available to a writer, that of indenting a line in his text. Rather than treat the indenting of the first line of a paragraph as simply some cosmetic device, as Longacre (1979) does, we might look upon it as an indication by a writer of what he intends us to treat as the beginning of a new part of his text. If the writer also uses adverbial expressions initially in the first sentence of this new part of his text, then we might say we have overwhelming evidence that the writer is marking a 'topic-shift' in his discourse. We are, after all, performing a descriptive and not a prescriptive exercise when we undertake discourse analysis. We do not wish to say how a writer should organise his written discourse into paragraphs before we have managed to characterise, in any comprehensive way, how writers typically do so.

The investigation of what writers typically do when marking the structure of their texts would seem to be a more appropriate goal of discourse analysis. For example, rather than dismiss the orthographic paragraph format to be found in newspaper articles as, in some way, a deviation from the 'true' paragraph structure of what is being written, it would be more appropriate for discourse analysts to describe the journalistic format as one form of written discourse organisation. The paragraph structure of different genres, such as scientific textbook writing, repair manuals, nineteenth-century novels, etc. could then be characterised, and statements could be made about, for example, the 'norms' or regular features of topic-shift in such genres.

On the basis of such genre-specific descriptions of 'topic-shift' markers, it should be possible to make linguistic, as opposed to literary, statements about the structure of English written discourse which reflect the writer's purpose. Thus, in producing a narrative, the writer must provide some indications of change of time and place, as Grimes (1975: 102) has pointed out. In presenting a philosophical argument, however, the writer can range over different times and places within a single paragraph, but must mark out changes in the direction of his argument. Taking a random page from the writings of Karl Popper, one can see the structure of the discourse in skeleton form by taking the first phrase or sentence of each paragraph.

(15)   para 1 : Other questions have sometimes been asked . . .
          para 2 : Another question sometimes asked is this . . .
          para 3 : The only correct answer is the straightforward
                   one . . .
          para 4 : It has also been said that the problem of induction
                   is . . .

                                        (Popper, 1963: 56)

Eventually, it should also be possible to specify those markers of 'topic-shift' which occur in all forms of written discourse. We might find that it is indeed the case that the use of 'But' at the beginning of a paragraph as described by van Dijk (1977: 139), is a very general marker of topic change. Other examples of what van Dijk (1977: 150) terms macro-structure connectives are 'furthermore', 'however', and 'so'. We shall discuss the concept of macro-structures in discourse in section 3.7 on the proposition-based analysis of discourse.

3.6.2 *Paratones*

So far we have concentrated on structural markers in written discourse. In spoken discourse, there is not the visual prompt of paragraph-initial line indentation to indicate a division in the discourse structure. How do speakers mark 'topic-shifts'? One suggestion is that there are, in fact, structural units of spoken discourse which take the form of 'speech paragraphs' and have been called **paratones** (see Brown, 1977: 86). Some support for the notion that there are ways of marking the boundaries of 'speech paragraphs' can be found in a common practice of people who are asked to read pieces of written text aloud. They use intonational cues to signal the start of a new paragraph. The 'speech paragraph', or paratone, like the orthographic paragraph, is identified by its boundary markers. The marking of the start of a paratone, then, is clearly one device which speakers can use to indicate a topic-shift. Since the paratone is a much less familiar concept than the orthographic paragraph, it may be useful to have its identifying features described.

At the beginning of a paratone, the speaker typically uses an introductory expression to announce what he specifically intends to talk about. This introductory expression is made phonologically prominent and the whole of the first clause or sentence in a paratone may be uttered with raised pitch. The end of a paratone is marked in a way similar to the 'turn signal' discussed by those who investigate conversational discourse as a process of social inter-action (cf. Duncan, 1974; Sacks et al., 1974). It can be marked by very low pitch, even on lexical items, loss of amplitude and a lengthy pause. Alternatively, the speaker can use a summarising phrase, often repeating the introductory expression, not necessarily low in pitch, but also followed by a lengthy pause. The most consistent paratone-final marker is the long pause, normally ex-ceeding one second.

We shall examine an extract from conversational discourse containing a longish paratone which illustrates the features just described. It is relevant that the topic framework for this extract (16) should contain information about the speaker (female, 20+, Edinburgh-resident) and the preceding discourse (the types of drinks the participants had encountered in different types of bars during their respective recent holidays in the United States). It is also worth noting that in Edinburgh Scottish English, phono-logically prominent syllables are typically uttered with raised or high pitch and need not have the type of pitch movement associated with phonological prominence in descriptions of standard southern English (cf. Brown et al., 1980). (For an explanation of the stave representation of intonation used, see the 'transcription conven-tions' on p. xii.)

(16)   I found my drink was a great problem with them because

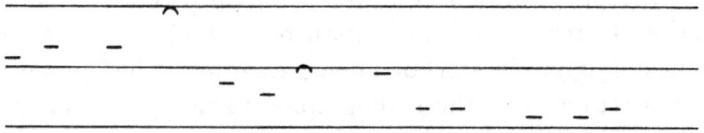

at that time I drank whisky and lemonade + and I would

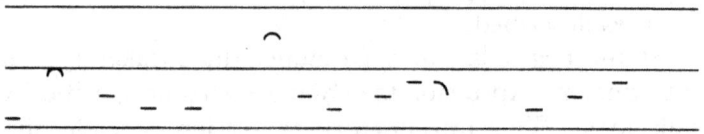

go and ask for whisky and lemonade and I would get

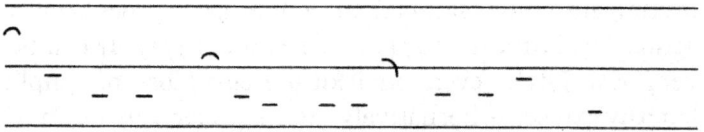

whisky and lemon + because you have to ask for whisky

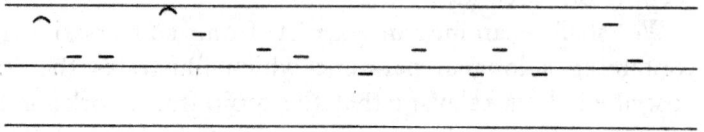

or scotch and seven up + you know + I eventually

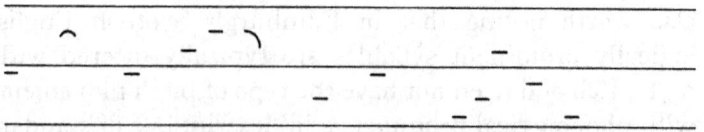

cottoned on to it + but + and they couldn't get over

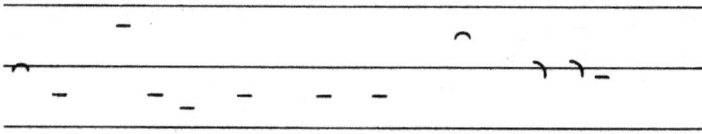

the fact that I didn't like ice in whisky and of course

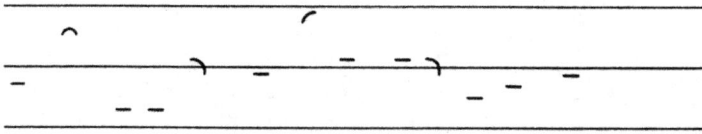

they either gave me ice whether I wanted it or not or

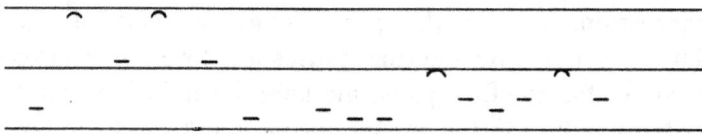

they stacked the glass up + right up to the level that

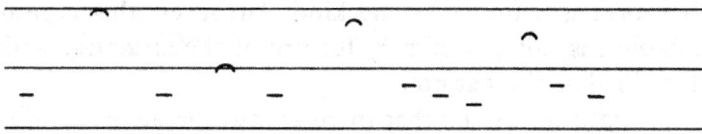

you would normally have if you had ice in your drink

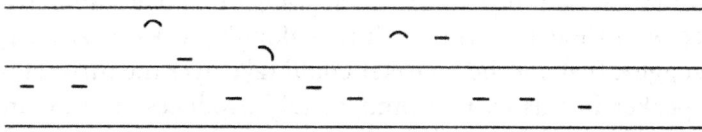

anyway + and consequently I got ploughed + frequently +

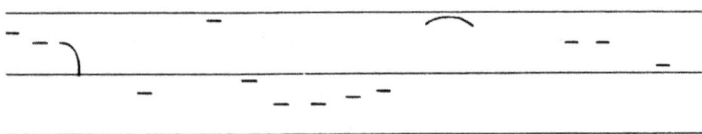

and that's that I + I tended to stick to my drink + +

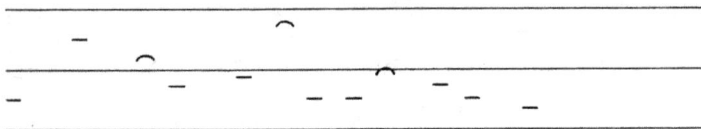

This paratone begins with an introductory expression *my drink*, uttered very high in the pitch range, and closes with the same expression, low in the pitch range, as part of the speaker's summing-up. The internal pauses are brief, none exceeding 0.5 seconds, but the final pause marking the end of the paratone is long (1.6 seconds). Those are the formal markers of the boundaries of this paratone. Of course, there are internal aspects, such as the semantic cohesion within the lexical field established by *my drink*, which could also be appealed to in claiming that this chunk of discourse is a unit of some kind. However, this type of internal cohesion is not a necessary feature of the structural unit we have described as the paratone.

It might be argued that there are two paratones, and not one, in this extract. There appears to be a break where + *but* + is used. Indeed, just prior to *but*, there is what has been described as a 'possible completion point'. The speaker has come to the end of a sentence and pauses. It is a point at which those who analyse conversation in terms of 'turn-taking' (Sacks et al., 1974) would suggest that another speaker could take over the turn. However, the speaker in this extract immediately produces an 'utterance incompletor' – in this case *but*, though any clause connector would do – making, as Coulthard (1977: 56) points out, a potentially complete utterance into an incomplete one. After another brief pause, the speaker continues, using *and* to indicate that what she is going to say is connected to what she has just said. We would not want to describe this possible completion point (or any other which occurs in this extract) as a paratone-boundary. The formal markers, low pitch close plus lengthy pause plus raised pitch introductory expression, are not present. In intuitive terms, we might also say that what follows + *but* + is not on a separate speaker's topic, but continues the talk 'about' 'my drink'.

At the end of this extract, there is an obvious 'completion point'. In 'turn-taking' terms, it is a point at which another speaker is free to take over. However, in this part of the conversation, one speaker clearly 'has the floor' and she is allowed to continue, as shown in extract (17).

(17)   oh apart from once when we went we found em + an Irish bar

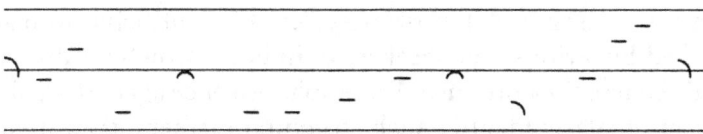

in San Francisco that was famous for its Irish coffees +

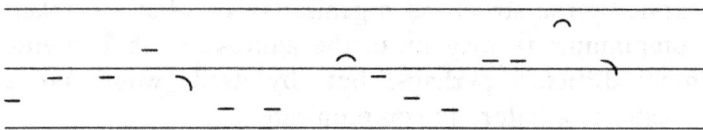

In beginning a new paratone, the speaker marks as intonationally prominent two expressions – *an Irish bar* and *Irish coffees*. In the course of the paratone, she talks about both the bar and the Irish coffee made there. It seems quite reasonable to assume that, when a speaker is organising a 'speech paragraph' which has two connected elements as its foci, both elements can be made phonologically prominent in the introduction. When the speaker closes this paratone, she repeats one of her introductory expressions – *it was very good Irish coffee too* – not particularly low in the pitch range, but followed by a lengthy pause.

Some of the features we have described as marking paratone boundaries in spoken discourse can, of course, have other functions. Although the lengthy pause is also identified by Chafe (1979: 176) as an indication of segmentation in his spoken discourse data comparable to paragraphing in written discourse, the intonational features we appealed to can have other, quite different, functions. Some of these we will discuss in detail in Chapter 5. What we have described is the use of the *combination* of these formal markers by speakers to indicate a shift in what they're talking about. There may be other, more subtle, indicators of topic-shift used by conversationalists which we have ignored. The significance of 'speaker gaze', as described by Kendon (1967) and specific 'body movements' (de Long, 1974) in signalling speaker change in conversation may also be relevant in topic change. The occurrence of different types of 'fillers' such as 'well', 'mmm', 'you know', 'er', and others may also regularly coincide with topic-shifts. We have concentrated, however, on some of the primary, easily identifiable formal markers used by writers and speakers to indicate structural divisions in the discourse they produce. We emphasise once again that, although we can regularly identify such structural markers, their appearance in discourse should not be treated in any way as 'rule-governed'. They represent optional cues which writers and speakers may use in organising what they want to communicate. Failure to mark out explicitly the structural organisation of what a speaker wishes to commmunicate may make the addressee's task of interpretation more difficult, perhaps, but, by itself, would not necessarily constitute a failure to communicate.

3.7 Discourse topic and the representation of discourse content

Although we have tried to illustrate some types of boundary markers which can be identified in both spoken and written text, it is a noticeable feature of reported studies in this area that they concentrate almost exclusively on the analysis of written text. This strong bias in favour of written data is also present in studies of discourse content. In fact, the written data, for which analysis of content is offered, typically consists of sets of sentences which the analyst has constructed. We will point out some of the disadvantages of this approach as we investigate the various methodologies which have been proposed for the representation of discourse content.

A hypothesis underlying much of the work we shall report is that there is a specific connection between 'discourse topic' and 'discourse content'. The former can be viewed as, in some sense, consisting of the 'important' elements of the latter. If the representation of discourse content can be presented as a hierarchy of elements in the discourse, then the top-most elements are natural candidates for treatment as the 'most important' components of the discourse topic. If it can also be shown that people remember these top-most elements better than others, then this might be evidence that what we have 'in our heads' after reading a text are those elements which constitute the discourse topic. In order to evaluate such an approach, we have to consider critically how such representations of discourse content are arrived at.

In recent years many scholars, psycholinguists in particular, have been concerned to produce representations of the semantic content, or information content, of texts. Common to many of these attempts to represent semantic content is a notion of **proposition**, a notion which derives from formal logic but which is used in a very free way in the text-analysis literature, often to include notions which might be better regarded as 'statements' or 'simple sentences'. Whereas in logic the proposition is often held to represent the context-independent, invariant meaning expressed in a sentence (statement), in the text-analysis literature a 'proposition' is often taken to represent a 'once-off' interpretation of a text-sentence as it is used in a context. Lyons (1977: 141) comments on the controversy surrounding the notion: 'Some authors think of propositions as purely abstract, but in some sense objective, entities; others regard them as subjective or psychological . . . Further difficulties are caused by the use of 'proposition' in relation to 'sentence' and 'statement': some writers identify propositions with (declarative) sentences, others identify them with statements, and others with the meanings of (declarative) sentences; and there is little consistency in the way in which 'statement' is defined.'

It is often the case that 'propositions' are represented in the text-analysis literature simply as relationships between a predicate and its arguments, and they are expressed as in (18a):

(18)   John hit Mary

(18a)   Hit (John, Mary)

Here the representation in (18a) is usually taken to be the single proposition which (18) as a text-sentence can be used to express. The analyst decides on the single appropriate interpretation for the sentence by his choice of semantic representation in (18a). We shall point out some of the problems raised by this approach. Another general feature of the text-analysis approach to the notion of 'proposition' concerns the psychological status of the semantic representation involved. For many cognitive psychologists who produce text-content analyses, the propositions contained in their representations are to be treated as what speakers have in their minds after they have read a piece of text. These propositions are treated as conceptual structures. We shall discuss some of the problems involved with this approach. In general, the term 'proposition' as used in the following discussion, is best treated as meaning 'semantic representation'.

One very influential approach to the analysis of the semantic representation of text can be found in the work of van Dijk (1977). Van Dijk's analytic approach has its origins in attempts to produce a 'text-grammar' (cf. van Dijk et al., 1972; van Dijk, 1973), but it has developed to include the representation of discourse content and to relate this 'content' to a notion of 'discourse topic'. Since we have discussed the representation of 'topic' at some length already, we shall approach van Dijk's representation of discourse content via his analysis of how 'topic' is to be characterised.

Van Dijk (1977) sets out to present an explicit formal account of the concept 'topic of discourse'. In his analysis of a piece of written text, van Dijk proposes that the topic can be expressed as a complex proposition which is entailed by the joint set of propositions expressed by the sequence of sentences in the text. It should be emphasised that van Dijk's analysis is based on an underlying semantic representation of the text rather than the sequence of sentences which constitute the text. The semantic representation of a text is its *macro-structure* which defines 'the meaning of parts of a discourse and of the whole discourse on the basis of the meanings of the individual sentences' (van Dijk, 1977: 6). For example, the macro-structure of a discourse fragment consisting of a single, non-complex sentence is the underlying proposition. Van Dijk's illustration of this relationship is reproduced here as examples (19) and (19a), in which (19a) is the semantic representation (i.e. the macro-structure) of the sentence (19).

(19)   Peter is going to Paris next week.

(19a)   [go to (Peter, Paris)] e & next week (e)

(van Dijk, 1977: 137)

Assuming it is possible to produce underlying propositions of this sort for each sentence of a longer piece of text, it should be apparent that the resulting semantic representation will be at least as large as, and even possibly larger than, the piece of text itself. The semantic representation appears to be only a translation (which is incidentally, also an interpretation) of the piece of text into an alternative format. This procedure does not seem to provide a means of identifying 'the topic' of a piece of discourse. The semantic representation cannot be 'the topic'. We certainly do not expect the expression of the topic of a discourse to be longer than the discourse itself. As van Dijk himself points out, 'discourse topics seem to reduce, organize and categorize semantic information of sequences as wholes' (1977: 132). No means of systematically 'reducing' the semantic representation to produce the discourse topic representation is provided. Instead, one is required to return to the piece of text, make up a sentence which appears to summarise the main points in the piece of text, and then translate this sentence into a semantic representation. For an extended piece of text containing five paragraphs, van Dijk produces the sentence (20) and translates it into the semantic representation (20a) which is thereafter treated as the discourse topic.

(20)   A (little) town (called Fairview) is declining because it cannot compete with another town (called Bentonville).

(20a)   town (a) & town (b) [~CANa (compete with (a, b))] (e) & cause (e, f) & [decline (a)] (f).

(van Dijk, 1977: 134)

It ought then to be possible to produce a proof that the complex proposition in (20a) is entailed by the joint set of propositions in the semantic representation of the whole text. The proof would be carried out in terms of formal relationships between propositions. Whether such a proof can in fact be carried out (van Dijk does not provide one) is a matter of concern for logicians rather than linguists.

What must be of concern to linguists interested in notions such as 'discourse topic' is the fact that the formal means of identifying the topic for a piece of discourse claimed by van Dijk is, in fact, an illusion. Neither the topic representation nor the semantic representation of the whole text derive from anything more formal than the analyst's interpretation of what the text means. To produce the discourse topic, van Dijk does nothing more than what schoolchildren are frequently asked to do by their English teacher – produce a single sentence summary for the text under consideration. As any English teacher knows, this exercise is considerably easier with some passages (simple descriptive or narrative) than with others (discursive or explanatory prose) and it inevitably produces a variety of different, though certainly related, interpretations of what must be included in the single 'topic' sentence. (A similar point was made earlier with regard to possible titles for discourse fragments.) At the discourse level, van Dijk provides a means of formalising interpretations of both the joint set of meanings of the sentences in a text and the summarising sentence for the same text, and suggests that a formal relationship of entailment can be shown to exist between those interpretations. At best, this is a formula for determining, not the *topic* of a discourse, but the *possible topics* of a discourse. If we can already determine the possible topics of a discourse without recourse to logic, then the elaborate translation into logico-semantic representations is redundant.

So far we have treated propositions as some type of easily derivable translations for natural language sentences which represent the 'meaning' of those sentences. For many writers, however, including van Dijk (1977), a proposition represents a concept or a conceptual structure, and, in the strong view, the propositional form is the representation in which all knowledge is used and stored. If the representation of a piece of text can be made in terms of propositions which are to be treated as concepts in the reader's mind, then it follows that the discourse analyst must be capable of providing, not just an analysis of a piece of text, but an analysis of the mental representation of that text. That is, the discourse analyst may claim that the product of his analysis is not simply a good account of the facts ('good' in analytic terms such as economy and exhaustiveness), but can go on to claim that the product of his analysis is psychologically 'real'. It is what people have in their heads after they have read a text. Such a claim quite naturally leads to proposals regarding the nature of memory for texts, as in Kintsch's hypothesis that 'the amount of time required to read and remember a paragraph should be proportional to the number of propositions in its base' (Kintsch, 1974: 135).

In support of this type of hypothesis, there is experimental evidence indicating that texts, or even single sentences, are not stored verbatim in memory (see Bransford & Franks, 1971). Indeed, it is a fairly common experience that the content or *gist*, but not the actual words, of a text can be recalled. If the content of a text can be expressed as a base structure consisting of a set of identifiable propositions, then this set can be proposed as the memory representation for the particular text and the basis for what is recalled rather than the actual words. Since language-users do not express themselves in propositional format, it is difficult to test this view of text-recall directly. As an indirect test, Kintsch & Keenan (1973) proposed that two texts which are roughly the same length (in words), but which differ in the number of underlying propositions will require different reading/understanding times. Examples of the material used in this experiment, together with their propositional analyses, are presented as (21) and (22). In each proposition, there is first a relational term, followed by one or more arguments. Propositions can be arguments of other propositions.

(21)   Romulus, the legendary founder of Rome, took the women of
         the Sabine by force.

         1 (TOOK, ROMULUS, WOMEN, BY FORCE)   2
         2 (FOUND, ROMULUS, ROME)   ╱
         3 (LEGENDARY, ROMULUS)   1 ──→ 3
         4 (SABINE, WOMEN)   ╲
                                                           ↘ 4

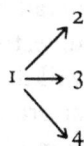

(22)   Cleopatra's downfall lay in her foolish trust in the fickle
              political figures of the Roman world.

1 (BECAUSE, α, β)
2 (FELL DOWN, CLEOPATRA) = α
3 (TRUST, CLEOPATRA,
     FIGURES) = β
4 (FOOLISH, TRUST)
5 (FICKLE, FIGURES)
6 (POLITICAL, FIGURES)
7 (PART OF, FIGURES, WORLD)
8 (ROMAN, WORLD)

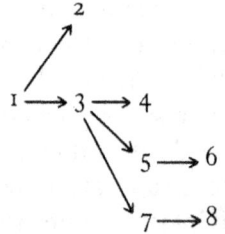

$$1 \longrightarrow 3 \longrightarrow 4$$
$$\nearrow 2$$
$$\searrow 5 \longrightarrow 6$$
$$\searrow 7 \longrightarrow 8$$

Subjects, asked to indicate when they had read and understood the
pieces of text, did indeed take significantly longer with (22) than
with (21). A result, one might say, which confirms the hypothesis.

To the right of the proposition set in both (21) and (22), there is
a representation of the hierarchical relationships claimed to exist
among the propositions. That is, the representation of a text cannot
be treated as only a list of propositions, but must show that some
propositions are subordinate to others. In another experiment in
which subjects were asked to recall what they had read, they
recalled propositions higher up the hierarchy more easily than those
in subordinate positions. This suggests not only that the mental
representation of a text is in the form of a proposition set, but that
there is hierarchical organisation of the set. It may also suggest,
though Kintsch & Keenan (1973) do not make this point, that the
highest proposition in the hierarchy is an obvious candidate for
being considered the 'topic-proposition' of the text. It would then
be possible to describe the topic-structure of a text in terms of the
hierarchy of propositions, thereby accounting for the relationship
van Dijk (1977) wished to express between the proposition representing the 'topic of the discourse' and the proposition set of the
discourse. Each proposition in the proposition set would be defined
as hierarchically subordinate to the topic-proposition.

We have presented the proposition-based analysis of text in some
detail because it has had a considerable influence on the way many
investigators have undertaken text-analysis. In the next section, we
will describe some of the developments of the proposition-structure
approach by other writers, but, first, it is necessary to point out
some basic problems with the approach.

Fundamental to the proposition-based approach to the analysis of discourse is a concentration on the 'content' of a piece of discourse to the exclusion of all else. Kintsch states that, in his analysis, textual and communicative aspects will be ignored. His reasons for this decision may be discerned in the following quotation:

the memory representation of a text is a function of the content of the text, but not of the way in which it is expressed. That is, identical memory representations may be formed for paragraphs that are all members of the same paraphrase set.

(Kintsch, 1974: 107)

An approach which is based on such a view is clearly not a linguistic approach, for it holds that viewing a text as an example of language in use is of no interest. Those aspects of text-structure discussed in Chapter 4, such as 'staging' and 'thematisation', which are crucially to do with how the content is expressed, would consequently have no effect on the memory representation. It is difficult to reconcile this rather strong view with more recent experimental work which has demonstrated that processes such as 'staging' and 'thematisation' have a marked effect on text-recall (cf. Clements, 1979).

Moreover, if a piece of text is used simply as a means of arriving at a discussion of memory representations, would not some non-linguistic object, such as a photograph, be an equally suitable input? The problem with non-linguistic material is that it seems not to lend itself quite so readily to analysis in propositional terms. Is there any non-arbitrary way of expressing the 'content' of a photograph as, for instance, a set of statements? There is a school of thought in cognitive psychology which argues that memory is modality-specific (cf. Paivio, 1971). That is, our memory of what we experience has a different representation according to how we experience it, either visually or auditorily, for example. This would lead to different memory representations for the same 'text' depending on whether it was encountered in the spoken or the written mode. In this view, in direct contrast to that proposed by Kintsch, the way in which a text is expressed does have an effect on the memory representation.

It could be argued, of course, that a proposition-based analysis provides insight into one aspect of the memory representation of a piece of text and that this weaker view should be held with respect to the propositional content of written texts only. Given a basic analysis of the content of a text in propositional terms, the influence of 'staging', for example, might then be incorporated within the analysis of the hierarchical organisation of the propositions involved.

3.8 Problems with the proposition-based representation of discourse content

There exists a fundamental methodological problem with the proposition-based analysis of texts which makes it difficult to apply, in any practical way, in discourse analysis. The discourse analyst has to be able to set about the analysis of pieces of text he encounters in newspapers, journals, novels, textbooks and so on. He cannot restrict his investigation to pieces of text which he constructs for a particular purpose.

In the following quotation, Kintsch first states the outstanding methodological problem which persists for the proposition-based analysis of text and then describes the solution he chooses.

one of the major problems in work of this type is that no algorithmic procedure exists to analyse a given sentence (or paragraph) into its propositional base structure. However, one can start with the proposition-al expressions themselves and translate these into English text.

(Kintsch, 1974: 124)

Kintsch is saying that, despite the appearance of a highly formal and therefore objective type of approach, the proposition-based analysis of natural language texts is inevitably subjective. If the analyst claims to be able to produce the proposition-set for a piece of text, as we noted van Dijk (1977) was claiming, that proposition-set necessarily represents only a single interpretation. It cannot really be tested. It can only be challenged by another analyst saying, 'My semantic representation is different from yours', and no principled means is available for deciding which of the two is correct, or even which is better. There may, in fact, be no such thing as a single correct semantic representation (i.e. proposition-set) for a text (or even, as Chafe (1977a) argues, for a sentence), if that semantic representation is treated as something which people have in their heads.

Moreover, the solution proposed by Kintsch may be an acceptable heuristic in experimental psychology, but it can have only an extremely limited application in discourse analysis. A set of sen-

tences constructed from a set of propositions may indeed demonstrate that the resulting natural language texts have propositional
structure, but the argument has a distressing circularity.

An attempt to find an appropriate relationship between propositions and natural language texts which avoids the claim that the
content of texts is stored in propositional form can be found in
Clark & Clark (1977). They suggest that 'even if information is
represented in forms other than propositions, one might argue that
it must be transformed into propositions before it can take part in
the utilization process or in memory retrieval for the construction
of sentences' (Clark & Clark, 1977: 164). A similar view has been
expressed by Chafe (1977b) in that 'knowledge is not stored
propositionally at all . . . the basic form of store may consist of
individuated events and objects, each with an associated analogic
content . . . until a need to verbalize them makes propositional
decisions necessary' (Chafe, 1977b: 54).

In both these quotations, it is clear that proposition-forming is
taken as part of the process involved in producing sentences. A
proposition then is a partial structuring of what one wishes to
communicate and is part of the verbalisation process. In this sense,
a particular sentence cannot be treated as having a single propositional source. It may have resulted from several quite different
propositions. A simple illustration of this is provided by Allwood,
Anderson & Dahl (1977: 20), reproduced here as (23).

(23)   He is hungry now.

The sentence in (23), said by Josephine about Napoleon sometime
in 1806 expresses a different proposition from the same sentence
used by Krupskaya about Lenin sometime in 1920. It should be
clear that any analysis of the sentences in a text which appeals to the
propositions involved in the production of those sentences will
necessarily have to appeal also to aspects of the context in which
those sentences were produced. The problem of reconstructing the
underlying proposition(s) for a sentence should be quite apparent.
It involves reconstructing the proposition the producer of the
sentence intended the sentence to convey. The discourse analyst
who wishes to present his analysis in propositional terms should
realise, therefore, that his analysis represents not a straight translation from sentence meaning into an alternative format, but an

interpretation of the speaker's / writer's intended meaning in producing the discourse.

Computing the intended meaning of a speaker / writer depends,
as we have already argued, on knowledge of many details over and
above those to be found in the textual record of the speaker's /
writer's linguistic production. If we use this knowledge in the
process of 'understanding' pieces of language, then any analysis
which makes claims about 'understanding' must include that knowledge in its representation. The analyst who produces only a set of
propositions as a representation of what he understands when he
reads the sentences of a text, is failing to make explicit some aspects
of how he reached that 'understanding'. This failure becomes most
apparent if the analyst attempts to use his proposition-based
representation in the computer modelling of language understanding. All the knowledge which the analyst has assumed is not
available to the computer. As Steedman & Johnson-Laird (1980:
111) explain: 'A well-known foible of computers is their literal-
mindedness and intolerance of imprecision.' In order for the
computer to behave as if it 'understands' a piece of text, it must be
provided with a means of analysing the sentences of the text *plus*
some background knowledge which represents the context in which
the text is to be 'understood'. As a result, those working in that
branch of Artificial Intelligence which attempts to model text-
understanding have found themselves undertaking a great deal of
practical discourse analysis. They have not generally considered the
proposition-based analysis of text-content, as proposed by van Dijk
and Kintsch, to be a useful methodology. We shall consider
alternative methodologies used in the computer-modelling of text
understanding in Chapter 7.

3.9 Memory for text-content: story-grammars

Despite the possible objections which can be raised
against the representation of the content of texts as a hierarchy of
propositions, the basic methodology has, with varying degrees of
formality, been used in many discussions of discourse organisation.

The majority of these discussions have been concerned with how
the content of text is processed in comprehension, stored in
memory, and subsequently recalled. Note that such a concern is
quite different from that which commonly underlies most other

investigations in linguistics. The theoretical linguist typically operates with criteria such as economy, consistency and comprehensive-
ness when considering the competing claims of alternative descriptions of linguistic phenomena. In the promotion of a particular
representation-format for the content of text, however, the criteria
are typically to do with the amount and accuracy of recall protocols
(what readers produce as their remembered versions of what they
have read), and reading or 'comprehension' speed.

Thus, although the representations of text-content to be found in
Rumelhart (1975, 1977) and Thorndyke (1977), for example, are
often referred to as 'story-grammars', they are not to be approached
as one would a linguist's proposed 'grammar'. At a basic level, the
notion of a counterexample, for instance, is very difficult to
conceive when dealing with 'story-grammars', since the components are defined so loosely. In a phrase structure grammar which
contains a component labelled 'Noun Phrase', we have a fairly clear
notion of which elements in a sentence are, and which are not, part
of the noun phrase component. We can, in fact, list the set fairly
exhaustively. What would we put on the right of a rewrite arrow
from a component called 'Event'? An exhaustive list of the acceptable forms by which an Event could be realised is difficult to
conceive.

Given this caveat on the status of content representations found
in a story-grammar, let us look at some examples. (For a survey of
different types, see Yekovich & Thorndyke, 1981.) Rumelhart
(1977) presents the tree-structure diagram shown in (24a) as a
representation of how we comprehend the content of the story
fragment (24).

(24)   Mary heard the ice cream man coming down the street. She
         remembered her birthday money and rushed into the house.

Several aspects of this representation should be noted. A pseudo-
propositional format is used to characterise nodes in the diagram.
The nodes are hierarchically organised so that some parts of the tree
are derived from parts higher up. Not all nodes are rewritten and
some nodes may yet be rewritten, presumably depending on what
comes next in the text. A large number of these nodes contain
elements which are not in the text, such as CAUSE and DESIRE.
That is, the diagram in (24a) is not a representation of what is

(24a)

EPISODE(M)

CAUSE(HEAR(M,ICM),DESIRE(M,IC)) TRY(M,GET(M,IC))

OUTCOME(TRY(M,GET(M,IC))=?

TRY(M,BUY(M,IC))

SELECT(M,BUY(M,IC))

BUY(M,IC) CAUSE(BUY(M,IC),C)

?

TRY
(M,GET(M,BMNY)))

SELECT
(M,SPEND(M,BMNY))

SPEND
(M,BMNY)

?

CAUSE
(SPEND(M,BMNY),C')

?

RUSH((M,INTO HOUSE))

SELECT(M,GO(M,INTO HOUSE))

CAUSE(RUSH(M, INTO HOUSE),C")

?

M   = MARY
ICM = ICE CREAM MAN
IC   = ICE CREAM
MNY = MONEY
BMNY = BIRTHDAY MONEY
C,C',C" = CONSEQUENCES

(Rumelhart, 1977:272)

strictly in the text of (24), but is a representation of Rumelhart's interpretation of what steps are involved in our comprehension of the piece of text.

Although there are superficial similarities between Rumelhart's representation and that proposed by Kintsch, described earlier, in that both have proposition-like versions of text-content and a hierarchical relationship between those propositions, the basis of the representations is clearly different. Most noticeably, Rumelhart has incorporated what must be inferences *on the reader's part* with respect to what is in the text. These inferred elements, such as hearing the ice cream van initiating the desire for ice cream, are necessary factors which Rumelhart set out to incorporate in his representation. However, Rumelhart's main aim was not to investigate the nature of such inferences, but to characterise the primary components in the content of simple stories. Accordingly, he compares his hierarchically represented analysis of several very simple stories with his analysis of subjects' summaries of those stories and finds that the summaries typically include components at the top of his hierarchy and leave out components from lower levels.

Developing Rumelhart's analysis of simple stories, Thorndyke (1977) produced a set of hierarchically organised components for narrative discourse. An extract from these 'rules' is shown in (25).

(25)   (1)   STORY → SETTING + THEME + PLOT +RESOLUTION

        (2)   SETTING → CHARACTERS + LOCATION + TIME

        (3)   THEME → (EVENT)* + GOAL

        (4)   PLOT → EPISODE*

        (5)   EPISODE → SUBGOAL + ATTEMPT* + OUTCOME

        (6)   ATTEMPT → $\begin{cases} \text{EVENT*.} \\ \text{EPISODE} \end{cases}$

        (7)   OUTCOME → $\begin{cases} \text{EVENT*} \\ \text{STATE} \end{cases}$

        (8)   RESOLUTION → $\begin{cases} \text{EVENT} \\ \text{STATE} \end{cases}$

        (9) $\left.\begin{array}{r}\text{SUBGOAL} \\ \text{GOAL}\end{array}\right\}$ → DESIRED STATE

      (10) $\left.\begin{array}{r}\text{CHARACTERS} \\ \text{LOCATION} \\ \text{TIME}\end{array}\right\}$ → STATE

(Thorndyke, 1977:79)

Once again, by comparing both recall protocols and summaries with the original simple story (as analysed by Thorndyke), it was generally found that components at the top of the hierarchy were most readily recalled or incorporated in the summaries. It should be noted that in the summary and recall data presented by both Rumelhart and Thorndyke, there are, in fact, quite a few hierarchically low components also included by different subjects.

The conclusions of Rumelhart and Thorndyke are not particularly related to the content of the texts they use, but, rather, emphasise the existence of a story *schema* which readers employ in the comprehension and resulting memory-representation of narrative texts. From the discourse analyst's point of view, there must remain some reservations about the applicability of story-grammars. The notion of a 'schema' is, in fact, an extremely attractive one and we will reconsider it in more detail later (see Chapter 7). However, the type of story-schema proposed by Rumelhart and Thorndyke may be appropriate only for the short, simple, specially constructed stories they use. (There does seem to be a very small set of such stories, since the same stories are used over and over again in many discussions by those claiming to investigate narrative discourse.) If the discourse analyst wishes to investigate naturally occurring stories, particularly those stories which turn up in the course of conversations, he might find the general categories (such as 'setting' or 'episode') useful, but he has been provided with no principled basis for deciding what *linguistic* material comes under one category and not another. The discourse analyst may actually find that an investigation which tells him that a 'story' consists of a setting plus a theme plus a plot plus a resolution has not told him a lot. The analyst may also be a little worried that the 'story-grammar', as formulated, could generate a 'story' which is composed of the beginning of Cinderella, the middle of Little Red Riding Hood and the end of Snow White (see Garnham et al., 1982).

A more important objection from the discourse analyst's point of view to the type of analysis undertaken by Rumelhart and Thorndyke (and this also applies to others such as Mandler & Johnson (1977) and Stein & Glenn (1979) who have investigated narrative texts) is that their decisions regarding the content of the texts they analyse are arbitrary and subjective. The illusion that the decisions are non-subjective is mainly fostered by the extreme simplicity of the texts investigated. The texts are so constructed as to be context-neutral, free of potential ambiguity, and composed of mainly non-complex sentences. The arbitrariness of what is included in the content-structure can be illustrated by the inclusion of one inference, CAUSE (HEAR (Mary, Ice Cream Man), DESIRE (Mary, Ice Cream)), in (24a), when the proposed analysis of the content-structure of a text (24) requires it. However, when the proposed analysis of a story fragment does not have a 'slot' for the instrument involved in an event, for example, the inferred instrument is ignored. Thus, although we can readily infer the use of some instrument (a rope?) in 'the farmer pulled the donkey', we do not find that inference in the representation – PULL (Farmer, Donkey) (see Rumelhart, 1977: 274). We do not suggest that such an inference must be in the analysis. Anyone wishing to apply the analysis, however, must want to know which inferences he may represent and which he may not. Story-grammars, just like Kintsch's proposition-based analysis discussed earlier, do not provide any algorithm for deciding which propositions (or pseudo-propositions) may, and which may not, be taken from a piece of discourse.

3.10 Representing text-content as a network

In our consideration of how text-content has been represented, we have restricted our discussion to those representations which employ the tree-structure metaphor to express the hierarchical relationships existing among components in the text. An alternative representation format, essentially heterarchical, has been proposed by de Beaugrande (1980). The relevant metaphor is computational and has its origins in the sentence-parsing models of Thorne, Bratley & Dewar (1968), developed as Augmented Transition Networks by Bobrow & Fraser (1969), Woods (1970), and many others since (cf. Winston, 1977).

The processing operation which de Beaugrande puts forward is not a translation of encountered text into a hierarchically organised propositional format, but rather a procedural model which establishes a network of relations between elements in the 'text-world'. On one level there is a syntactic procedure which yields a grammatical network, as illustrated in (26a) for the sentence (26).

(26)   A great black and yellow rocket stood in a desert.

(26a)

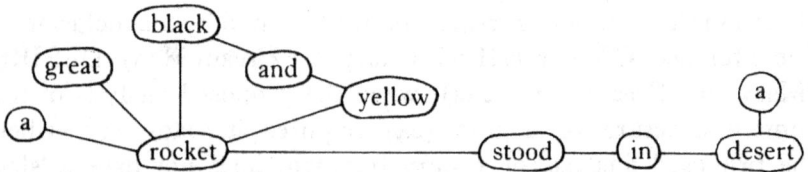

(de Beaugrande, 1980:43)

The relationships between elements, represented by the connecting
links in (26a), are grammatical relations such as 'head-modifier' and
are reminiscent of the non-deep structure relations found in
systemic grammar (cf. Berry, 1975). In parallel with this type of
grammatical network, de Beaugrande (1980: 77) proposes that
there is also a conceptual network. There is a fairly long list of the
'conceptual relations' (e.g. state-of; substance-of; reason-of) which
are required, but the brief illustration in (26b) of the relations
existing in (26) may serve as an indication of how grammatical links
in the network may also be considered conceptual links.

(26b)

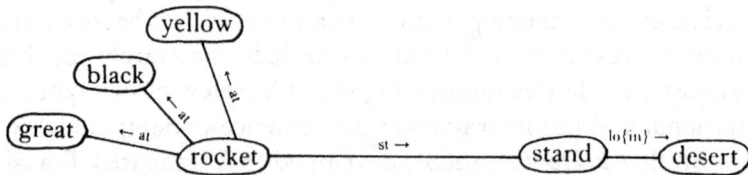

Key at: attribute of; lo: location of; st: state of
(Adapted from de Beaugrande, 1980:43)

It should be apparent that with longer and more detailed texts
the conceptual network will become increasingly more complex.
Although this makes the representation of the text-world model
extremely unwieldy, it may, in fact, be a reasonably accurate

account of a large number of the potential conceptual relations existing within a text. The problem is, as de Beaugrande (1980: 77) points out, that the text-world models he represents are 'idealizations of the actual cognitive entities involved'. It may be that any individual reader may have fewer of the formal conceptual relations in the proposed networks and more of the idiosyncratic, non-formal associative conceptual relations which defy analysis. For example, the description of the rocket in (26) may involve black and yellow stripes for one reader, yet for another be chequered. All de Beaugrande has set out to do is represent the basis (i.e. attribute of) which forms the common factor in those two readers' 'cognitive entities', as derived from the text.

Returning to the notion of 'topic' with which we began this chapter, we can briefly consider de Beaugrande's use of one aspect of his network representation through which he claims to represent 'topic'. The network (27a) of the text fragment (27) shows that one node in the network ('rocket') is shared by all the individual sentences.

(27)   A great black and yellow V-2 rocket 46 feet long stood in a New
         Mexico desert. Empty, it weighed five tons. For fuel it carried
         eight tons of alcohol and liquid oxygen.

(27a)

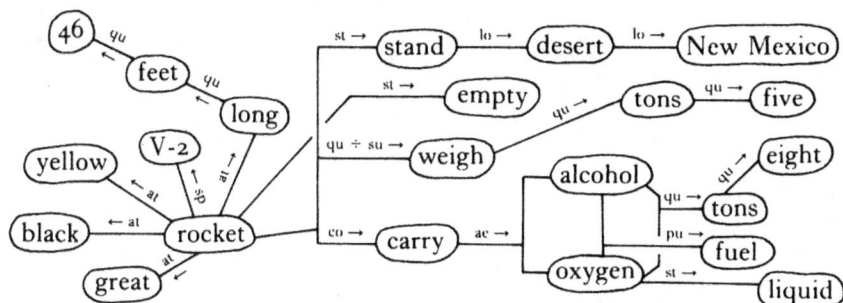

Key ae: affected entity; at: attribute of; co: containment of;
      lo: location of; pu: purpose of; qu: quantity of; su:
      substance of; sp: specification of

(de Beaugrande, 1980:93)

According to de Beaugrande, 'this node-sharing is a graphic correlate of Topic' (1980: 94). Clearly, what de Beaugrande understands as 'topic' is what may be described as a 'topic entity' (see section 4.3). We have already argued that a 'discourse topic' is a much more complex concept. However, de Beaugrande's claim, based on his analysis of simple text, is indicative of how far it is possible to take an extremely limited view of 'topic' when the data studied is so limited.

In fact, we might go further and state that much of the research reported in the literature on issues like 'topic', 'text-structure' and 'text-content' has been restricted to such unrepresentative discourse data that the findings are unlikely to have much wider application in the analysis of discourse. The discourse analyst may glean useful insights into some aspects of simple text from this research, but he cannot forever restrict himself to investigating versions of material like 'The farmer and the donkey' or 'The rocket in the desert'.

One of the issues de Beaugrande (1980: 92) shows an awareness of, but does not investigate, is the fact that 'the heavy use of sentences in comprehension models keeps us from addressing the question of how long a stretch of text people actually process at one time'. It seems unreasonable to suggest that whole narrative texts, for example, are processed in one single sweep. If there are smaller units of discourse, what are their boundaries like, what components do they contain, and how are they internally organised? These are questions we shall attempt to answer in the course of Chapter 5.

4

'Staging' and the representation of discourse structure

4.1 The linearisation problem

One of the constraints on the speaker / writer is that he can produce only one word at a time. When he orders these single words into sentences, and those sentences into texts, he confronts what has come to be called the 'linearisation problem'. He has to choose a beginning point. This point will influence the hearer / reader's interpretation of everything that follows in the discourse since it will constitute the initial textual context for everything that follows. Consider just two types of invented examples. First of all, consider the effect of an identical attributive description being preceded by different evaluative comments:

(1)   a. I can't stand Sally Binns.
        She's tall and thin and walks like a crane.

    b. I do admire Sally Binns.
        She's tall and thin and walks like a crane.

In *a* the attributes *tall and thin and walks like a crane* must be assumed to be unattractive, awkward, ungainly. In *b* those same properties are now endowed with elegance and grace.

Consider next the effect of linear sequencing on the interpretation of events in time where 'the listener can be expected to derive different implicatures from different orderings' (Levelt, 1981: 91):

(2)   a. She married and became pregnant.
    b. She became pregnant and married.

There is, as Levelt reminds us, an *ordo naturalis*, whereby it is assumed that, if there is no cue to the contrary, the first-mentioned event happened first and the second-mentioned event followed it. It is, then, open to the hearer / reader to draw implicatures from that ordering, implicatures which will be constrained by both the content of what is said and stereotypical expectations based on previous experience (cf. discussion in 2.4).

We are familiar, in the field of visual perception, with effects produced by presenting the same stimulus in a different context. A block of colour produced in the centre of a light surround may be perceived as being much darker than that same block of colour presented in the centre of a dark surround. Similarly a line presented in a given context is perceived as being longer than a

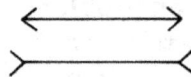

line of the same length which is presented in a different context. In a similar way, understanding of verbal input is processed against the relevant background of the immediately preceding co-text (within, of course, a specified context). The same sequence of words may take on a different 'value' (Widdowson, 1978) when it is uttered in a different co-text. We shall consider this effect, first with respect to the internal structure of messages at the sentence level, and then with respect to the organisation of larger stretches of discourse.

4.2 Theme

We shall discuss the linearisation process at this level only very briefly. This means we are obliged to cut several corners in our discussion. In particular we shall speak of the thematic organisation of the *sentence*. It is important to appreciate, however, that in complex and compound sentences a separate thematic organisation will be assigned to each *clause* (for an extended discussion of processes of thematisation in English, see Halliday, 1967). It is, further, going to be necessary in this section to cite as examples several sets of constructed sentences in order to demonstrate the potentially contrastive effects of different structures.

We shall use the term *theme* to refer to a formal category, the left-most constituent of the sentence. Each simple sentence has a **theme** 'the starting point of the utterance' and a **rheme**, everything else that follows in the sentence which consists of 'what the speaker

states about, or in regard to, the starting point of the utterance'
(Mathesius, 1942). The theme, then, is what speakers / writers use
as what Halliday calls a 'point of departure' (1967: 212). In many
cases (often considered to be the unmarked or neutral cases) the
theme of declarative sentences will be a noun phrase (the grammatical subject), that of interrogatives the interrogative word, and that
of imperatives the imperative form of the verb. In our discussion
we shall focus on simple declarative sentences and consider their
thematic, rather than their syntactic, structure.

It is a striking feature of English, as of many other languages,
that there exists a very wide range of syntactic forms which can be
used by the speaker to convey the same propositional or cognitive
content. Consider a few of the syntactic forms available in English:

(3) a. John kissed Mary.
     b. Mary was kissed by John.
     c. It was John who kissed Mary.
     d. It was Mary who was kissed by John.
     e. What John did was kiss Mary.
     f. Who John kissed was Mary.
     g. Mary, John kissed her.

The same propositional content is expressed each time. In each case
it is asserted that kissing went on and that John did the kissing and
that Mary was the one who was kissed. If the only reason for having
syntactic structure were to permit us to express propositional
content, it is hard to see why there should be such an immense
variety of forms (only a few of which are listed above) to permit the
expression of that propositional content. Why do we find this wide
variety of structures?

A number of different answers to this question have been
proposed. Alice Davidson (1980) suggests 'The more marked the
construction, the more likely that an implicated meaning will be
that which the utterance is intended to convey', where her own
sentence nicely, iconically, demonstrates the deliberate way in
which she is manipulating the syntax to make her point. She
suggests taking the active form as the normal, unmarked, form for
the declarative sentence and claims that the passive may for
example be used to convey a humorous or derogatory effect. So to
the question *'Did John kiss Mary?'* a cautious friend might reply

'Well, Mary was kissed by John.' It is clearly not the case, however, that using the passive necessarily has a marked effect.

From the discourse analyst's point of view, the most wide-ranging and interesting approach must be that which considers the effect of using one sentential form rather than another in the context of discourse. It is clearly the case that (3a–g) could not all function satisfactorily as answers to the same question. A speaker producing these utterances would have different assumptions about the state of knowledge of his hearer, that is about his hearer's presuppositions. Thus, in answer to the question *'What did John do?'*, (3a) seems possible and so does (3e), but the rest seem less appropriate; (3b) seems to be about *Mary* rather than John; (3c) seems to imply that the hearer already knows that someone kissed Mary and identifies *John* as the individual who did it; (3d) seems to imply that the hearer knows that John kissed somebody and identifies the recipient as Mary (and may indeed, with contrastive intonation on *Mary*, indicate that it was Mary rather than somebody else who was the recipient); (3f) similarly assumes the hearer knows that John kissed somebody; (3g) seems more appropriate as an answer to the question *what happened to Mary?*

With simple examples like these, it seems reasonable to suggest that what is primarily at issue is the judgement that the speaker makes about what the hearer believes to be the case with respect to what he wants to talk about. Halliday demonstrates, with an effective example, the dislocating effect on a text of changing the thematic structure. The occasion in each case must be taken as one in which a reporter is announcing on a radio programme what is happening at a reception for three astronauts who have recently completed a successful mission:

(4)   a. The sun's shining, it's a perfect day. Here come the astronauts. They're just passing the Great Hall; perhaps the President will come out to greet them. No, it's the admiral who's taking the ceremony . . .

        b. It's the sun that's shining, the day that's perfect. The astronauts come here. The Great Hall they're just passing; he'll perhaps come out to greet them, the President. No, it's the ceremony that the admiral's taking . . .

This passage was presented by Halliday at a Systemic Workshop in the early seventies. For a similar example see Halliday, 1978.

Here the speaker in *a* simply asserts a sequence of facts and opinions which he thinks will interest his listeners. (We shall not discuss the internal structure of this sequence of assertions, merely note that, having set the scene, he clearly expects to report events as they occur in time, floating opinions when nothing of interest is happening.) This speaker's utterances could be seen as replies to a series of very general questions like *what's going on?*, *what's happening now?* The 'speaker' in *b* on the other hand would have to be imputing a great deal of knowledge to his hearer. The first two clauses appear to answer questions like *what's shining?*, *what's perfect?* The last sentence appears to contradict a belief which the speaker imputes to his listeners, namely that they suppose the admiral will be 'taking' something other than the ceremony. It is hard for the processor to construct a coherent model of what is going on from the text in (b), even though the propositional content is the same as that in text (a) and the cohesive links (see 6.1) are maintained.

The problem Halliday illustrates here is one which is familiar to many writers who pause in the middle of a paragraph, uncertain how to connect the next thing they want to say with the last sentence. It is sometimes possible to force a link with a connector like *however* or *therefore*, but sometimes it is necessary for the writer to recast his proposed sentence, to reorganise the syntactic expression. Whereas in written language we generally only see the finished product, so that we have no indication of where the writer may have made such a correction, in spoken language we can sometimes observe a speaker reorganising what he wants to say and thereby producing a different thematic structure:

(5)   a. (a departmental discussion about spending money)
          X: there was a gift of about £38
          Y: well that isn't a gift + it is earmarked because + well + *the money is* + *in about 1975* some money was . . .

     b. (a former Minister of Transport interviewed after a motor-way accident in fog)
          I'm going to introduce + mm + as a + certainly as a trial a + a measure of segregation + + *this will* – *one cannot* make it compulsory + because of the difficulties of enforcement . . .

     c. (conversation between young woman and her aunt)
          'cause there was *a man in* – *my father*'s in the Scouts . . .

> he's a county commissioner now . . . and eh one of his oldest scoutmasters . . .

In *a* and *b* the speakers appear to have embarked on one structure, which they decide is unsatisfactory, and modify it in midstream to produce a different thematic organisation. In *c* a more extensive reorganisation takes place as the speaker evidently realises that her aunt may not have access to the relevant information that her father is in the Scouts so she stops talking about this 'man', announces that her father is in the Scouts, and then after some local interaction with her aunt, reverts to talking about the man in his role as 'a scoutmaster of her father's'.

Whereas we may not be able to perceive this self-monitoring process at work in written language, it may be demonstrated, by requiring subjects to choose one of a set of possible continuation sentences, that there are preferred thematic sequences, in some genres of discourse at least, which will lead subjects to prefer 'marked' syntactic forms. Thus, given a constructed text like this:

(6)   a. The Prime Minister stepped off the plane.
        b. Journalists immediately surrounded her.
or
        c. She was immediately surrounded by journalists.

There is a preference for *c* as the continuation sentence, rather than *b*. We suppose that this is because readers prefer to maintain the same subject (or *discourse topic entity* – a notion to be developed in the next section). The effect becomes even more striking if there are no competing animates, as in:

        d. She was immediately buffeted by the wind.
or
        e. The wind immediately buffeted her.

The passive (d) seems to be the natural choice here. Given the choice of an active sentence which continues the subject and marks the theme as agent, there is virtual unanimity of preferences for the active form:

        f. All the journalists were immediately smiled at by her.
or
        g. She immediately smiled at all the journalists.

Some recent studies have examined the distribution of some

sentential types in discourse genres of different kinds (see Jones, 1977 and Prince, 1978). It seems clear that some sentential types have a particularly narrow range of distribution. Thus, in expository prose, wh-clefts, in which, as Prince points out, the content of the introductory wh-clause is presupposed information, have a privilege of distribution limited almost exclusively to three functions:

(7) a. introducing the discussion as in:
    What is most striking in the behaviour of newts is ...
    What is particularly worrying about the Cabinet's view of collective responsibility is ...
    What I'm going to talk to you about today is ...
  b. summarising the discussion as in:
    What I have tried to argue then is ...
    What we have been considering is ...
  c. more rarely, to indicate explicit contrast as in:
    You may find peace in the bosom of many religions. What is unique about what Christianity has to offer is ...

We are grateful to Mahmoud Ayad from whose analysis we draw and from whose extensive corpus of wh-clefts we have borrowed these examples.

We have proceeded so far on the simplifying assumption that the left-most constituent in the sentence is the grammatical subject of the declarative sentence. This permits a simple conflation, made by many scholars, of the categories *theme* and *grammatical subject*. Thus, in discussion of discourse one may find the term *theme* rather than grammatical subject used (e.g. in Clark & Clark, 1977). It is important to note that the left-most constituent (as in (3g)) is not always the grammatical subject. It is frequently the case, for instance, in declarative sentences, that adverbs or adverbial phrases may precede the grammatical subject as in:

(8) a. *Late that afternoon* she received a reply paid telegram ...
    (64)
  b. *In one place* Betty saw the remains of the study safe ...
    (64)
  c. *Without hesitating* Betty replied ... (64)
  d. *Then* he went on ... (65)
  e. *In the meantime* she would be the better of professional aid
    ... *An hour later* a pleasant-looking middle-aged woman arrived and took charge. (65)
    (all from Freeman Wills Crofts, *Golden Ashes*, Penguin Books, 1959)

These extracts are from a detective novel which constantly thematises time adverbials (as well as others). The direct link between what has gone before and what is asserted in the main clause of the sentence is then the adverbially expressed relationship. In extracts from a travel brochure we find, predictably, more locational adverbials thematised:

(9)   a. *On some islands* it is best if you . . .
        b. *In Greece and Turkey*, you are met at the airport . . .
        c. *In all other places* we make bookings . . .
        d. *At the centres* where we have our own representatives you . . .
        e. *In some centres* we have local agents . . .
        f. *On a few islands* you have to collect them yourselves . . .

(Aegina Club brochure 1981, p. 3)

In general it seems reasonable to suggest that the constituent which is thematised in a sentence is, in some sense, 'what the sentence is about', regardless of whether or not the constituent is the grammatical subject. When the grammatical subject is thematised, this seems self-evident. Thus in

    (a) Fred borrowed a hammer from John
    (b) John lent a hammer to Fred

sentence (a) seems to be 'about' *Fred* and (b) seems to be 'about' *John*. Where adverbials of time were thematised, as in the examples (8) above, the sentence seems to be 'about' (or, put differently, to be answering the question) 'what happened next?' We shall discuss the implications of this textual structuring in the next section.

Meanwhile, we should note that there is another set of adverbials which are frequently thematised but which do not contribute to the structure of the discourse in the same way. This set includes what we shall call *metalingual comments* in which the speaker / writer specifically comments on how what he is saying is to be taken. He may comment on the structure of what he is saying: *let me begin by, first of all I shall, I shall now turn to, in conclusion, finally*, etc. He may comment on his commitment to belief in what he is saying: *obviously, of course, clearly* as against *perhaps, possibly, supposedly*, etc. He may produce one from a large number of expressions which indicate how the recipient is to 'tag' the content in his memory: *in confidence, between you and me, frankly, briefly*, etc. (For an extended discussion of adverbials of this kind, see Brown & Levinson, 1978.) It is clear that this thematised 'metalingual' comment is not to be integrated with the representation of content which the recipient is constructing. It merely gives him directions, in some cases about the type and structure of mental representation he should be constructing (*Once upon a time* presumably instructs the recipient to construct a fairy-tale model), in some cases about the internal structure of the model (*more importantly*), and sometimes comments on the reliability of what is asserted (*perhaps*).

Sometimes, of course, 'hedges' of this sort are not thematised but inserted within the sentence, or they follow it, as in:

(10)   a. Frankly I don't think he will.
         b. I frankly don't think he will.
         c. I don't think he will, frankly.

It is hard to make judgements on the effect of different placings of adverbials in sentences in isolation. Some hearers feel these variations produce no difference in meaning, others perceive subtle nuances of difference. Like many issues concerning thematisation / linearisation / selection of syntactic structure, this issue is little understood. We shall assume in the rest of our discussion that *theme* is a formal category in the analysis of sentences (or clauses in a complex or compound sentence) and, following Daneš (1974), we shall assume that it has two main functions:

(i)   connecting back and linking in to the previous discourse, maintaining a coherent point of view

(ii)   serving as a point of departure for the further development of the discourse.

4.3 Thematisation and 'staging'

The process of linear organisation which we have been examining, largely at a sentential level in 4.2, produces the same sort of problem for the speaker / writer in organising units larger than the sentence. We may talk in general of **thematisation** as a discoursal rather than simply a sentential process. What the speaker or writer puts first will influence the interpretation of everything that follows. Thus a title will influence the interpretation of the text which follows it. The first sentence of the first paragraph will constrain the interpretation not only of the paragraph, but also of the rest of the text. That is, we assume that every sentence forms part of a developing, cumulative instruction which tells us how to construct a coherent representation.

4.3.1 '*Staging*'

A more general, more inclusive, term than *thematisation* (which refers only to the linear organisation of texts) is 'staging'. This metaphor is introduced by Grimes in a way which seems consonant with our use of *thematisation*: 'Every clause, sentence, paragraph, episode, and discourse is organised around a particular element that is taken as its point of departure. It is as though the speaker presents what he wants to say from a particular perspective' (1975: 323). Grimes is here particularly concerned with how the linear organisation can be manipulated to bring some items and events into greater prominence than others. Thus an initial main clause will, iconically, refer to an important event, while following subsidiary clauses will supply subsidiary information. Other scholars have widened the application of Grimes' staging metaphor. Thus Clements (1979: 287) suggests: 'Staging is a dimension of prose structure which identifies the relative prominence given to various segments of prose discourse.' This definition opens the door to far more than processes of linearisation, and permits the inclusion within 'staging' of rhetorical devices like lexical selection, rhyme, alliteration, repetition, use of metaphor, markers of emphasis, etc. We shall use 'staging' not as a technical term, but as a general metaphor to cover the exploitation of such varied phenomena in discourse.

The notion of 'relative prominence' arising from processes of thematisation and 'staging' devices has led many researchers, particularly in psycholinguistics, to consider staging as a crucial factor in discourse structure because, they believe, the way a piece of discourse is staged, must have a significant effect both on the process of interpretation and on the process of subsequent recall. In 4.3.2 we shall examine some work which relates to discourse 'staging'.

4.3.2 '*Theme*' as main character / topic entity

In this section, we encounter uses of the term *theme* quite different from the formally constrained category which we (following Halliday, 1967) use to refer to the left-most constituent in the sentence or clause. We find *theme* used sometimes to refer to the grammatical subjects of a series of sentences as in this remark by Katz (1980: 26): 'The notion of a discourse topic is that of *the common theme* of the previous sentences in the discourse, the topic carried from sentence to sentence as *the subject of their predication*' (our emphasis). The same term is also used, particularly in the psycholinguistics literature, to refer not to a constituent, but directly to the referent of the constituent. Thus Perfetti & Goldman (1974: 71) write: 'By thematisation we mean the discourse process by which *a referent* comes to be developed as the central subject of the discourse' (our emphasis).

This latter usage leads naturally to an interpretation of *theme* as meaning 'main character'. The discourse process of thematisation referred to by Perfetti & Goldman then leads to the *foregrounding* of a referent, as described in Chafe (1972), whereby a particular referent is established in the foreground of consciousness while other discourse referents remain in the background. The foreground or 'thematised' individual, as Perfetti & Goldman emphasise, may be referred to by a variety of different formal expressions. Thus an individual called *Dr Jones* can be 'thematised' when identified in the discourse by the expressions as *the doctor* or *the surgeon* or *he*, just as well as by the repetition of the expression *Dr Jones*.

Perfetti & Goldman performed a series of experiments (1974) in which they sought to demonstrate the effect on the recall of sentences occurring in a text of using a prompt word referring to a thematised referent, as opposed to using a prompt word referring to a non-thematised referent. They were able to show that a thematised referent occurring as syntactic subject was the better prompt for sentence recall. Such a finding is consonant with the observation that pieces of discourse about a 'main character' are frequently organised into sets of sentences in which the character is referred to by the noun phrase acting as syntactic subject. A good example of this is the thematisation of 'Birdie' in extract (14) in Chapter 3.

Perfetti & Goldman's results may help to explain why one basic organisational method for discourse production involves placing the main referent in subject position. Sets of sentences structured in this way may be easier to remember. This method is favoured by those who prepare encyclopaedic entries, such as (11), in which 'the Nez Perces' are thematised, by obituary writers, as in (12) and by the writers of children's reading books, as illustrated by extract (13). (Expressions used for the thematised referent in each extract are italicised.)

(11)   NEZ PERCES
The Nez Perces continue to bear the name given them by French fur traders, referring to the custom of piercing their noses for the insertion of ornaments. *They* belong to the Sahaptin language family, in contrast to the other peoples of the region, who speak languages of the Shoshonean branch of the Uto-Aztecan stock. *The Nez Perces* number more than 1,500, a reduction of about 2,500 since their first contact with whites. *The great majority* live on a reservation in Northern Idaho: *less than a hundred* live on the Colville Reservation in Washington.
(*Encyclopedia of American Ethnic Groups*, Harvard University Press, 1980)

(12)   *Mr Mitsujiro Ishii*
Mr Mitsujiro Ishii, who as a former Speaker of the Japanese House of Representatives was instrumental in staging the 1964 Tokyo Summer Olympics and the 1972 Sapporo Winter Olympics, died on September 20. *He* was 92. *Ishii* had served as Industry and Commerce Minister and in other cabinet posts under the late Prime Ministers, Shigeru Yoshida, Nobusuke Kishi and Eisaku Sata, before retiring in 1972.
He was speaker of the House of Representatives from February 1967 to July 1969.
(from *The Times*, 25 September 1981)

(13)   *Jack* goes up the beanstalk again.
He comes to the giant's house and *he* sees the giant's wife.
(from *Jack and the Beanstalk*, Ladybird Books, Series 777)

The organisation of stretches of spoken discourse can follow a similar pattern, as shown in extract (14).

(14)   P: did you have any snow + during the holidays
R: there was some actually on + at Hogmanay because we had some friends + *a Greek friend of ours* was visiting us and when *he* left the house + just after Hogmanay + you know *he* had been away about fifteen minutes then *he* rang the doorbell again + *he* said – it's snowing it's snowing + *he* was really excited you know +

If we look at extract (13) as a set of clauses, we can follow a method suggested by Daneš (1974) and represent its structure in the following way:

(15)   Theme$_1$ (*Jack*) – Rheme$_1$ (*goes up the beanstalk again*)
         Theme$_1$ (*he*) – Rheme$_2$ (*comes to the giant's house*)
         Theme$_1$ (*he*) – Rheme$_3$ (*sees the giant's wife*)

In each of the clauses of this piece of discourse the theme, or 'the starting point', is the same. If we wish to claim that the referent 'Jack' is the theme of the discourse, we must be aware that we are basing this claim on the fact that 'Jack' is 'thematised' in each of the clauses in the discourse. It is on the basis of discourses with this type of fixed structure that the term 'theme' seems to have come to be used as a general term in discourse analysis for 'main character' and sentential subject (as well as the left-most constituent).

The possibilities for confusion with this varied use of the same terminology are obvious. We have already said that we shall reserve *theme* for the formally left-most sentential constituent. For the 'main character / object / idea' notion – exemplified by the referents 'Mr Mitsujiro Ishii' in (12) and 'Jack' in (13) we shall use the term writer's / speaker's **topic entity.** In those examples the text was very simply constructed so that the topic entity was formally thematised in each sentence. In the next extract we shall observe that an expression referring to the writer's topic entity is formally the *theme* of some sentences, but not of all sentences. (We shall not examine clauses in non-sentence-initial position, since that would involve a wide-ranging technical discussion of thematisation which we have no space for here, but see Halliday, 1967.)

(16)   *Mr William Serby*

         Mr William Serby who died aged 85 on September 20 was County Treasurer to Buckinghamshire County Council from 1929 to 1961.

         He was commissioned in the Queen's (R. W. Surrey Regiment) in 1915 and served in France until he was wounded in 1916. From 1917 to 1919 *he* served as liaison officer with the French and Russian forces in the North Russian Expeditionary Force.

         In 1926 *he* was appointed County Accountant to the Cornwall C.C.

> During the Second World War *he* commanded the Home
> Guard in Wendover and in later years was actively concerned
> with the work of the R.N.I.B., the Oxford Diocesan Board of
> Finance, the Bucks Historic Churches Trust and in many local
> organisations in Wendover.
> In 1926 *he* married Jean Durns and they had one son and
> two daughters.

(from The Times, 25 September 1981)

Obituaries such as extract (16) provide particularly clear examples of discourses which have only one writer's topic entity
throughout. In this case, it is 'Mr William Serby'. An expression
referring to this individual is thematised for the whole discourse in
the title, and for each of the first and second paragraphs where
expressions referring to him are made the 'starting point' for what
follows. The writer might have continued, as in extract (13) with
expressions referring to the same individual thematised in each
sentence and paragraph. In each of the subsequent sentences and
paragraphs, however, the writer thematises a time-adverbial
phrase. We could say that, although the writer continues with the
same 'topic entity', he organises what he wants to say about this
topic entity according to different (temporally determined) perspectives on the individual concerned. The thematised elements do
not simply produce a chronological list, but provide different
'points of departure' for considering the individual in different
roles.

It might be objected that the term 'topic entity' is unnecessary
and that what we are talking about here is simply our old friend
'topic'. We insist that it is useful to distinguish between the topic
entity / main character notion and the general pretheoretical notion
of 'topic' as 'what is being talked about'. One would hardly want to
say that 'the topic' of an obituary was 'the man' referred to by the
name at the top of the entry, except in speaking in some kind of
shorthand. There are many aspects of 'the man', physical characteristics for instance, which would hardly be considered to be
appropriate aspects for inclusion in an obituary. The 'topic' of an
obituary might be more adequately characterised in some such
terms as 'an appreciation of the noteworthy events and deeds in the
life of X'.

4.3.3 *Titles and thematisation*

We argued in Chapter 3 that the 'title' of a stretch of discourse should not be equated with 'the topic' but should be regarded as one possible expression of the topic. We now wish to propose that the best way of describing the function of the title of a discourse is as a particularly powerful thematisation device. In the title of extract (16), the topic entity was thematised, or, to express the relationship more accurately, when we found the name of an individual thematised in the title of the text, we expected that individual to be the topic entity. This expectation-creating aspect of thematisation, especially in the form of a title, means that thematised elements provide not only a starting point around which what follows in the discourse is structured, but also a starting point which constrains our interpretation of what follows. This point may be illustrated by using part of a text constructed by Anderson et al. (1977: 372), and reproduced here as (17a and b). (We have provided the title in each case.)

(17a)   *A Prisoner Plans His Escape*

Rocky slowly got up from the mat, planning his escape. He hesitated a moment and thought. Things were not going well. What bothered him most was being held, especially since the charge against him had been weak. He considered his present situation. The lock that held him was strong, but he thought he could break it.

The topic-entity of this fragment is the individual named 'Rocky' and, because of the thematised expression in the title, we can read this text with the interpretation that Rocky is a prisoner, in a cell, planning to break the lock on the door and escape. In an exercise which we conducted using this text after which subjects were asked to answer several questions, we found that there was a general interpretation that Rocky was alone, that he had been arrested by the police, and that he disliked being in prison.

When we presented exactly the same questions to another group who read the following text, (17b), we received quite different answers.

(17b)   *A Wrestler in a Tight Corner*

Rocky slowly got up from the mat, planning his escape. He hesitated a moment and thought. Things were not going well.

> What bothered him most was being held, especially since the
> charge against him had been weak. He considered his present
> situation. The lock that held him was strong, but he thought
> he could break it.

In answering questions on this fragment, subjects indicated that
they thought Rocky was a wrestler who was being held in some kind
of wrestling 'hold' and was planning to get out of this hold. Rocky
was not alone in a prison cell and had had nothing to do with the
police. By providing different 'starting points' in the thematised
elements of the different titles, we effectively constrained the way
in which the piece of text was interpreted. (Anderson et al. (1977)
discuss the different possible interpretations of the one piece of text
(without titles) presented in (17a) and (17b) in terms of knowledge
structures or 'schemata' which are activated for the interpretation of
texts. We shall discuss schemata and related concepts in more detail
in Chapter 7.)

Extracts (17a) and (17b) provide a particularly dramatic illustration of the effect of thematisation. There are, of course, many other
easily recognisable thematisation devices used in the organisation of
discourse structure. Placing headings and sub-headings within a
text is a common thematisation device in technical or public-
information documents. It also occurs, you will have noted, in
linguistics textbooks. What these thematisation devices have in
common is not only the way they provide 'starting points' for
paragraphs in a text, but also their contribution to dividing up a
whole text into smaller chunks. This 'chunking' effect is one of the
most basic of those achieved by thematisation in discourse.

4.3.4 Thematic structure

In (8) and (9) we demonstrated the possibility of elements other than the grammatical subject occurring as the formal
theme of the sentence or clause, by considering a set of thematised
adverbial phrases of time which occur in a detective story, and
adverbial phrases of place which occur in a travel brochure. In (11)
we exemplified the structure of an encyclopaedic entry where the
grammatical subject, referring to the writer's topic entity, was
consistently made the theme of succeeding sentences. Then in (16)
we discussed an obituary in which there was an interweaving of

themes which related to the individual, the topic entity, and themes which related to different temporal frames, an interweaving which permitted the writer to represent his topic entity from different temporal perspectives. Here we consider the thematic structure of three further passages:

(18)   *This rug* comes from the village of Shalamazar in the southern Chahar Mahal, but *the design* is woven in many of the villages. *The design* is one of those that fit into several possible categories, involving as it does elements of bird, tree, vase and prayer types. *The prayer mihrab* may be omitted in some cases, but *the vase* is always present, as are the strikingly drawn birds . . . *In rugs of this type* excellent natural dyestuffs are very often found, and *the quality* varies from medium to quite fine. *Outstanding examples* . . .
(P. R. J. Ford, *Oriental Carpet Design*, Thames and Hudson 1981, p. 113)

Observe the sequence:

> This rug (illustrated)
> the design
> The design
> The prayer mihrab ⎱ (details of design)
> the vase   ⎰
> In rugs of this type
> the quality
> Outstanding examples

The thematic organisation here gives a clear identification of

(i)   the writer's topic area
(ii)   the organisation of the paragraph, moving from a particular example of a rug type, through characteristic design, to generalisations about rugs of this type.

The thematic structure of the extracts we have examined so far is relatively helpful to the identification of topic area and the organisation of structure. Other cases are far less clear. Journalistic prose is often far more loosely structured:

(19)   *Due in the bookshops* soon from Faber and Faber is a small paperback which reveals more about the way British television drama is really produced than all the weekend symposiums and university gabfests I've attended in the last ten years. *It* consists of seven chunks, one each from . . . *The title, Ah*

Mischief, comes from Hare's contribution. *He* tells of going nervously to visit . . .

(*The Listener*, 29 April 1982, p. 12)

This set:

Due in the book shops	The title
It	He

makes it clear that the writer's topic area is concern with a book, though the structure of the contribution is much less clearly marked. It is possible, though it would need to be demonstrated, that less clearly marked structure is more difficult for a recipient to process.

The analysis of thematic structure in spontaneous speech provides considerable problems. We have glossed over some of the problems of attribution of thematic structure in written language, and we shall do so again as we encounter spontaneous, conversational speech. Much of what is said is not readily related to the syntactic categories 'sentence' or 'clause' (*contra* Labov (1966) who reported that 'about 75% of utterances in most conversations are well-formed by any criterion (when rules of ellipsis and general editing rules are applied, almost 98% would fall in this category)' cited in Linde & Labov, 1975). In the following extract, an attempt has been made to assign thematic structure:

(20)   *the environment I was living in* was Berkeley + *which* is purely academic + *no it* wasn't purely academic it was em + *it* was basically academic *I* mean *most of Berkeley* is the university + *it*'s like a town + *in which* the university dominates the city + like Cambridge + or Oxford + *the university* is the hub of the city + and *most of the people you* found there kind of ancillary to the university + + em and *you* also got a lot of wasters there *I* mean *people* who dropped out of university and can't bear leaving the place +

The thematic framework here is generally less specific:

the environment I was living in	it
which	in which
no	the university
it	most of the people you
it	you
it	I
I	people
most of Berkeley	

Again it is possible to discern the speaker's topic area but it is not possible to discern the developing organisation of the text by looking at the thematic structure. It is a characteristic of primarily interactional conversational speech in our data that the interactional aspect, marked by *I* and *you*, is frequently thematised (cf. also (2) in Chapter 1, description of a rainbow). This marking gives a clear indication of the speaker's view of what he is using language to do.

Thematic organisation appears to be exploited by speakers / writers to provide a structural framework for their discourse, which relates back to their main intention and provides a perspective on what follows. In the detective story cited in (8), the writer shuttles about, commenting on the activities of a number of different individuals, located in different parts of England and Europe within the space of two pages. The coherence of structure is imposed, partly at least, because locally within the text the author is meticulous in relating events to each other in time. Each new adverbial phrase marks the fact that the scenario has shifted. The relevance of the various activities to each other, or to the plot, is not plain to the reader at this point. He has to trust the writer to restrict himself to the account of relevant activities and his warrant for this sustained trust is that the author goes to such trouble to specify the complex temporal relationships of the activities he describes.

In the travel brochure (9), what is essentially an unstructured list of facts is given structure and arranged into paragraphs on the basis of different geographical locations. It is the different geographical locations, realised in thematic position, which form the framework of the discourse.

Anyone who has ever written an essay is familiar with the problem of where to start the essay, how to relate paragraphs to what has gone before, and how to relate sentences to what has gone before. We all frequently encounter prose where the writer has not paid sufficient attention to thematic organisation. Consider this citation on the wrapping of a Swiss Lemon Oil soap tablet:

(21)   Li-mang is what the Chinese called the citrus lemon tree in 1175 AD and some believe the Mongolians invented lemonade in 1099. Lemons, like other species of citrus fruits, have been cultivated for thousands of years and are native to Southeastern Asia.

There is more than one problem here, but one reason why this text reads rather oddly is because of the thematised *some* in the co-ordinated second clause of the first sentence, following the marked structure in the first clause.

4.3.5 *Natural order and point of view*

We have already mentioned the notion of a 'natural order' for the presentation of a narrative sequence of events. As Levelt (1981) remarks, it is natural to put the event that happened first before the event which followed it. A sequence of events in time, told as a narrative in English, will often be presented in the order in which they happened and, often, with an unstated implication of a relationship in which the second event in some sense follows from the first (e.g. *was caused by*). This type of non-logical inference has been characterised by Horn (1973) as *post hoc ergo propter hoc*. Consider the following passage. Just before it begins, a violent storm has broken, with torrents of rain:

(22) Between where I stood by the rail and the lobby was but a few yards, yet I was drenched before I got under cover. I disrobed as far as decency permits, then sat at this letter but not a little shaken.
(W. Golding, *Rites of Passage*, Faber & Faber, 1980, p. 191)

It is not stated that the narrator is 'drenched' by the rain (rather than by, say, perspiration) or why he wishes to get under cover. It is not made clear why he disrobes or why he finds himself 'not a little shaken'. The normal assumption of an English-speaking reader will be, however, that the series of events are meaningfully related to each other, and he will draw the appropriate inferences that the narrator is drenched by the rain, wishes to take cover from the rain, disrobes because his clothing has been drenched by the rain, and is 'not a little shaken' because of his immediately preceding experience in the violent storm. (For a discussion of inferencing see Chapter 7.) We stress that these inferences will be drawn by an English-speaking reader because it appears that in other cultures there are rather different bases for narrative structures (cf. Grimes, 1975; Grimes (ed.), 1978; Becker, 1980).

It is clearly the case that there are stereotypical orderings in genres other than those which obviously consist of a series of events in time. Thus Linde & Labov report that 97% of the subjects, in a survey in which subjects were asked to describe the lay-out of their apartments, described them in terms of 'imaginary tours which transform spatial lay-outs into temporally organised narratives' (1975: 924). The narrative tour in each case begins at the front door, just as it would if the interviewer were to arrive for the first time at the apartment. A similar alignment with the point of view of the hearer is taken by speakers who are asked to give directions in a strange town. They always begin, co-operatively, from the point where the enquiry is made and then attempt to describe the route as a succession of acts in time. In each of these cases then, there is a 'natural' starting point and the description is an attempt to follow a 'natural' progression. Levelt suggests that by adopting the stereotypical pattern of the culture 'the speaker facilitates the listener's comprehension' (1981: 94) since both speaker and hearer share the same stereotype.

It seems very likely that there are other constraints on ordering in types of discourse which are not simply arranged as a sequence of events in time. Van Dijk (1977) suggests that descriptions of states of affairs will be determined by perceptual salience so that the more salient entity will be mentioned first. He suggests that 'normal ordering' will conform to the following pattern:

(23)   general – particular
          whole – part / component
          set – subject – element
          including – included
          large – small
          outside – inside
          possessor – possessed

                                                    (van Dijk, 1977: 106)

Consider the following extract in terms of van Dijk's proposed constraints:

(24)   [1]It was indeed a horrifying sight. [2]The walls alone stood, bare
          and gaunt and blackened, with cracked and split stone dres-
          sings and gaps where the cornice had been dragged away when
          the roof collapsed. [3]Within were heaps of wreckage, mostly
          brick and stone from internal walls which had fallen, but with
          occasional objects of twisted metal and quantities of broken
          glass. [4]In one place Betty saw the remains of the study safe and

in another three stick-like objects which she eventually classified as the barrels of shot guns.
(Freeman Wills Crofts, *Golden Ashes*, Penguin Books, 1959,
p. 64)

The first sentences describe the *general, whole, large, outside*.
The second sentence moves to the walls, *part, including, large,
outside*. The third sentence moves *inside* and begins to observe
small included objects. The last sentence introduces *small included
particulars*, initially unidentified and then particularised. It seems
reasonable to suggest that, in general, in this descriptive passage the
constraints which van Dijk proposes are adhered to. Suppose the
constraints were not adhered to? It would follow then, that when
the 'normal' ordering is reversed, some 'special effect' (staging
device, implicature) would be being created by the speaker / writer.
Van Dijk suggests that if the normal ordering (general–particular)
is reversed as between (25a and b) the second sentence in (b) will
be taken as giving an explanation for the state of affairs described in
the first sentence:

(25)   a. Peter always comes late. He won't be in time tonight either.
         b. Peter was late again. He never comes on time.

Van Dijk's suggestion is certainly of interest to the discourse
analyst. We should, however, take note of Levelt's warning: 'the
. . . question of how natural order relates to different domains of
discourse, will never be answered exhaustively: there are as many
natural orders as there are things to talk about' (1981: 94).

One obvious constraint on ordering which may override the
'perceptual salience' principle outlined by van Dijk, is the maintenance of a consistent point of view. Fillmore (1981) has noted
that a feature of literary discourse is the effect of a particular
orientation or 'angle of vision' on the way events are presented.
Thus, at the beginning of Hemingway's *The Killers*, the way the
reader has to view the events is determined by the organisation of
the first sentence:

(26)   The door of Henry's lunchroom opened and two men came in.

The 'opening of the door' takes place before the appearance of the
two men. This ordering of events is compatible with the fact that
the men 'came in'. The structure of this fragment reflects the view

of events which a narrator inside the lunchroom must have had. In another of Fillmore's examples, (27) below, the sequential structure of reported events is determined by the order in which they were observed, rather than by their most natural physical sequence:

(27)   The light went on. She was standing by the door.

In literature, the author frequently assigns the role of narrator to one of his characters. The author then has to manipulate the knowledge which the reader needs so that it can be plausibly known to and recountable by the narrator. Several authors have explored the literary possibilities of recounting the same events seen through the eyes of different characters and interpreted differently by them (cf. for two very different literary types, *The Moonstone* by Wilkie Collins and *The Alexandrian Quartet* by Lawrence Durrell). The problem for the author is to create a coherent view of a particular world.

The problem is, of course, one which affects all our production of language. Kuno (1976) and Kuno & Kaburaki (1977: 627) have pointed out that the variation in what they call 'camera angles' has an effect on the syntax of sentences. If the speaker is empathising with one participant in a domestic drama rather than another, the same event may be described for example by sentence *a* or by sentence *b*:

(28)   a. John hit his wife.
        b. Mary's husband hit her.

The speaker's empathy, his sympathy with one point of view rather than another, may also lead to a particular choice of lexis. Consider the following paradigm:

(29)   a. Mary, Queen of Scots, was executed by the English Queen.
        b. Mary, Queen of Scots, was assassinated by the English Queen.
        c. Mary, Queen of Scots, was murdered by her cousin, Elizabeth.

In each case the agent referred to is the same individual, the patient referred to is the same individual, and the agent causes the patient to die. (The cognitive content might be held to be the same.)

However, in *a* the action is reported as a legal process (*executed*) sanctioned by the constitutional monarch (*the English Queen*). In *b* the action is reported as an illegal, politically motivated act (*assassinated*) sanctioned by the constitutional monarch (*the English Queen*). In *c* the action is reported as an illegal, criminal act (*murdered*) performed by a close relation (*her cousin Elizabeth*). In each case the writer reveals a different assessment of the character and motivation of the act. (For a discussion of the wide range of factors influencing lexical choice in discourse, see Downing, 1980.) The question of 'empathy', described by Chafe as arising because 'people are able to imagine themselves seeing the world through the eyes of others as well as from their own point of view' (Chafe, 1976: 54), takes us far beyond the relatively formal investigation of the effects of thematisation into the general area of 'staging' which we return to in the next section.

4.3.6 *Theme, thematisation and 'staging'*

Throughout this chapter we have attempted to draw a distinction between the linearisation problem in terms of the cognitive ordering of events, description, etc. and the linearisation problem in terms of the linguistic means available to the speaker / writer for expressing that cognitive structuring, particularly the thematic organisation of the sentence or clause. The distinction is, however, difficult to maintain for the obvious reason that our only access to the speaker's / writer's cognitive structuring is via the language which he uses to express that structuring.

We have assumed that the notion of 'staging' embraces a much wider field, facets of which we have only briefly discussed. It embraces on the one hand the speaker's / writer's overall rhetorical strategy of presentation which may be motivated by an intention to create suspense, to convince his listener of the truth of what he is saying by adding credible supporting details, to persuade his listener to a course of action, or to shock or surprise. Indeed a speaker / writer may simultaneously have all of these intentions. The 'staging' which the discourse analyst might be concerned with is that which is manifest in the language used. It must be obvious, however, that, whereas the discourse analyst can draw attention to the effect of particularly marked staging, his discussion of the 'effect' of staging, or indeed his abstraction of some particular linguistic forms rather than others, as contributing to that effect, will necessarily be fairly unconstrained, in many ways akin to traditional literary interpretation or rhetorical discussion. Most linguists will feel uneasy at this 'soft' extension in the discussion of discourse. Notwithstanding, it is clear that discourse analysts can contribute to a description of the staging of the following extract:

(30) B: I think if your physical appearance is em sort of neat and + well-controlled and so on this gives at least a superficial + feeling that one's going to give a neat and well-controlled performance

L: that's right·+ do you know I remember something which er points this up very well something that Gill said + and it's now I suppose er + er eight years ago + when + em + what's that Russian chap's name who was here for a while

B: Shaumyan

L: Shaumyan yeah + when he was here + em I gave a seminar on phonetics and the brain + which I later wrote up in Work in Progress but never did anything + with em + to my slight regret + but I – that was the first time I'd ever ventured beyond as it were orthodox phonetics in – in public + em and it was in front of + our department after its first amalgamation I think + and er one or two people from outside were also present + so in very many ways I was before an unknown public + relatively speaking er talking about somewhat unfamiliar territory of a very speculative nature + but claiming expertise + and I remember that one of the things I did was buy a new pair of shoes

We could characterise this as a discussion of the beneficial effects of a good physical appearance on the confidence of someone addressing an audience. Whereas speaker L is certainly saying something about this, we can note that he is presenting a detailed, structured orientation from which his comment on the matter has to be appreciated. He first establishes a particular time co-ordinate relating to a place co-ordinate, selecting a means of fixing the time which involves an element familiar to his interlocutor ('when Shaumyan was here') which may have the effect of reminding his interlocutor of how much younger, less experienced or less confident they were at that past time. The impression is further elaborated by details of what the speaker talked about ('speculative, never-published') and to whom ('not close colleagues but outsiders'). This structured accumulation of elements contributing to a lack of confidence is counterbalanced by a single act of confidence-boosting, presented as the final comment. We could point to the fairly complex syntactic structure of the earlier part of the fragment, with a number of subordinate clauses adding extra detail. We could point to the typically polysyllabic lexis of most of the fragment and the sudden transition to the simple, monosyllabic *one of the things I did was buy a new pair of shoes* with its parallel transition out of professional life into the everyday life of the High Street. We could describe the change of voice quality on that last quoted phrase, the overall raising in pitch; the breathy voice, the effect of smiling.

It is presumably the case that these details noted by the discourse analyst are relevant to his interpretation of the fragment. The problem with a complex fragment of this sort, which has no near-parallels in most of our data, is that we can only bring the most general notions of 'regularity' to bear on it, notions no more specific than those found in any general manual of rhetoric. In the present state of knowledge it seems to us wise to restrict the discussion of general staging processes, in the analysis of discourse, to data which consists of multiple realisations of strictly comparable data like descriptions of apartment lay-outs (Linde & Labov, 1975), re-tellings of narrative events (Grimes, 1975; Chafe, 1979; Chafe (ed.) 1980) or instructions to perform a task (Grosz, 1979; Yule, 1981).

One form of strictly comparable data which is readily available for analysis in everyday language can be found in letter-writing. The 'staging' of letters in terms of what information is represented and how it is thematised depends on the type of letter and the intentions of the writer in writing it. In most letters the basic elements which are thematised are those primary (contextual) features of time, location and addressee which we considered earlier as constituting part of the topic framework. The more formal the letter, the more explicit is the information contained in these thematised elements. If we compare the beginnings of two letters, extracts (31) and (32), we can see that the same type of information is thematised, but the amount of explicit information differs. The inclusion of the addressee's full address in (32) is not, obviously, intended to 'inform' the addressee where he himself lives, but to mark the letter as one of a filed series in which this information is preserved, as a formal letter. The specificity of information in representing the writer's address is one conventional means of marking the 'starting point' for the discourse which follows.

(31)

Stirling, Sunday.

Dear George,

I hope you managed to get home safe and sound through that downpour yesterday. The roads must have been treacherous. . . .

(32)

Davies's Educational Services Ltd.,
66 Southampton Row,
London W C 1B. 4BY

18th August, 1978.

George Yule, Esq.,
Department of Linguistics,
The University,
Edinburgh, 8.

Dear Mr. Yule,

In your letter of the 10th July, 1978, you told me
that you were arranging for me to be sent the ELBA
material in response to my letter of the 3rd March ...

As soon as one begins to investigate the different formats used in letter-writing, general similarities in the type of information thematised are discernible, but the variety of staging considerations to be recognised is extremely large. The envelope, plain brown official or light blue personal, airmail or 'official paid', is just one part of the complex staging which precedes the reading of the actual contents of a letter. Clearly, much of this type of 'staging' is non-linguistic (part of the external context of discourse), but its effect on our interpretation of the text of letters and many other types of discourse should not be ignored.

5
Information structure

5.1 The structure of information

In the previous chapters we have been considering increasingly restricted views of the production and interpretation of discourse. In Chapter 2 we considered the effect of situational context on discourse and in Chapter 3 the effect of different perspectives of topic structure. We devoted Chapter 4 to discussing the effect of linearisation in discourse, how what is presented first limits the interpretation of what follows and how decisions on thematisation provide the overall structure within which the addressee interprets the discourse.

In this chapter we focus in even further, to the smallest units of discourse structure: small local units at the level of phrase or clause. We consider how information is packaged within such small structures and, particularly, what resources are available to speakers and writers for indicating to their addressees the status of information which is introduced into the discourse.

5.1.1 Information structure and the notion 'given / new' in intonation

The serious study of information structure within texts was instituted by scholars of the Prague School before the Second World War. They studied what they called 'the communicative dynamism' of the elements contributing to a sentence, within the framework of 'functional sentence perspective'. (For an overview of this work see Vachek, 1966; Firbas, 1974.)

Many of the insights developed by the Prague scholars were first brought to the attention of Western scholars by Halliday in an extremely influential article published in 1967. Halliday elaborated and developed those aspects of Prague work which related directly to his own interests in the structure of texts. In particular, he adopted the Prague School view of information as consisting of two categories: **new information**, which is information that the addressor believes is not known to the addressee, and **given information** which the addressor believes is known to the addressee (either because it is physically present in the context or because it has already been mentioned in the discourse).

Halliday further followed the Prague School in supposing that one of the functions of *intonation* in English is to mark off which information the speaker is treating as new and which information the speaker is treating as given. In his discussion of information structure, Halliday is particularly concerned to specify the organisation of information within spoken English and to relate this organisation to phonological realisation, especially to intonation. More recently, many scholars have extended the discussion of 'given' and 'new' information to the range of syntactic structures which are held to realise these categories of information. This has resulted in a drift of the meaning of the terms so that their extensions, particularly that of 'given', are now very much wider than Halliday intended them to be and, more importantly, no longer relate to the intonational phenomena which Halliday was concerned to describe. Once again we have a potentially confusing range of meaning associated with one term. We shall attempt to keep the meanings distinct by organising our discussion in the following way. First, we shall outline Halliday's account of information structure and its intonational realisation. (We shall cite, almost exclusively, Halliday's 1967 paper since this is the paper which has most influenced the work of other scholars. Halliday's own position on some of the points we discuss has moved considerably since 1967, cf. Halliday, 1978.) We shall follow this outline with a critique of Halliday's position, and the statement of a somewhat different position, still on information structure as realised in intonation. After that, we shall turn our attention to the syntactic realisation of information structure and, at this point, we shall confront the change in meaning of the terms 'given' and 'new'.

5.1.2 *Halliday's account of information structure: information units*

Halliday assumes that the speaker intends to encode the content of the clause (the basic unit in his grammatical system). In many ways what Halliday views as the 'ideational' content of a clause may be compared with what others have called the 'propositional' content of a simple sentence (see discussion in 3.7). This clause content is organised by the speaker into a syntactic clausal structure, in which the speaker chooses among the thematic options available to him and, in spoken language, the clause content is organised into one or more **information units** which are realised phonologically by intonation.

According to Halliday, the speaker is obliged to chunk his speech into information units. He has to present his message in a series of packages. He is, however, free to decide how he wishes to package the information. He is 'free to decide where each information unit begins and ends, and how it is organised internally' (1967: 200). Thus, given that the speaker has decided to tell his hearer that 'John has gone into the garden with Mary', the speaker may package this information into one chunk as in

(1)   a. John has gone into the garden with Mary

or two or three chunks as in

         b. John – has gone into the garden with Mary
         c. John – has gone into the garden with – Mary

The realisation of this difference in chunking will be discussed in the next section.

The 'internal organisation' of the information unit, relates to the way in which given and new information is distributed within the unit. Characteristically, Halliday suggests, the speaker will order given information before new information. The 'unmarked' sequencing of information structure is taken to be *given–new*. Naturally, information units which are initial in a discourse will contain only new information.

5.1.3 *Halliday's account of information structure: tone groups and tonics*

Information units are directly realised in speech as **tone groups**. (Other descriptions have called units of the same general size 'breath groups', 'phonemic clauses', or 'tone units', cf. Lehiste, 1970.) The speaker distributes the quanta of information he wishes to express into these phonologically defined units.

Tone groups are distinguished phonologically by containing one, and only one, **tonic syllable**. The tonic syllable is characterised as having the maximal unit of pitch on it. (In other descriptions it is called 'nuclear syllable' or 'sentence stress' and is characterised as having maximal moving pitch, maximal pitch height, maximal intensity and / or maximal duration, cf. Lehiste, 1970.) Tone groups, being produced in spoken language, are also related to the rhythm of spoken language (as described in Abercrombie, 1964). In Halliday's terms, each foot begins with a stressed syllable and contains any number of following unstressed syllables. It follows that tone groups must begin with a stressed syllable. Occasionally, the first syllable in the initial foot in a tone group is unstressed. A **silent ictus** (equivalent to a silent 'beat' in music) is then postulated as initial in the tone group. In the following example the tonic is marked by capitalisation, tone group boundaries by //, and the silent ictus by $\wedge$:

$$// \wedge \text{I} / \text{find it incompre} / \text{HENsible} //$$

The tonic syllable functions to focus the new information in the tone group. In the unmarked case, the tonic syllable will focus the last lexical item in the tone group, which will generally be the head-word of the constituent containing new information. Consider the recital by a four-year-old of a fairy story which is very well known to her:

(2)   a. // $\wedge$ in a / far-away / LAND //
      b. // $\wedge$ there / lived a / bad / naughty / FAIRy //
      c. // $\wedge$ and a / handsome / PRINCE //
      d. // $\wedge$ and a / lovely / PRINcess //
      e. // $\wedge$ she was a / really / WICKed / fairy //

The child (no doubt influenced by the read-aloud version which she has heard, which in turn will be influenced by the punctuation of the written version) chunks her story into information units which are realised as tone groups. In tone groups *a–d*, the last lexical item receives a tonic syllable, which marks this as the focus of new information. In tone group *e*, the tonic syllable does not fall on the last lexical item, *fairy*, since the 'fairy' is already given in the preceding co-text and is treated as given by the speaker. The tonic syllable falls on the last lexical item which indicates 'new' information, on *WICKed*.

It is important not to suppose that the status of information is dictated by whether or not an entity has been referred to already within the discourse. As Halliday consistently and correctly remarks: 'These are options on the part of the speaker, not determined by the textual or situational environment; what is new is in the last resort what the speaker chooses to present as new, and predictions from the discourse have only a high probability of being fulfilled' (1967: 211).

Halliday states that there is a close relationship between the realisation of the information unit phonologically, in the tone group, and syntactically, in the clause: 'In the unmarked case (in informal conversation) the information unit will be mapped on to the clause, but the speaker has the option of making it co-incide with any constituent specified in the sentence structure' (1967: 242). (3) is an extract from a transcription presented by Halliday (1967: 201), where the speaker organises his information into phonological chunks, tone groups, which are co-extensive with both clauses and phrases:

(3)   // I had one of those nice old tropical houses // I was very lucky // it was about thirty years old // on stone pillars // with a long staircase up // and folding doors // back on to a verandah //

Compare (2) where the child also organised her story into tone groups which are co-extensive with clause and phrase.

In the next two sections we shall return to a consideration of the following aspects of Halliday's model:

(a)   the nature of the category 'tone group'
(b)   the nature of the category 'tonic'
(c)   the relationship of the information unit to phonological and syntactic categories.

5.1.4 *Identifying the tone group*

It is clear in listening to much unplanned spontaneous speech that speakers produce units which are rhythmically bound together, which are not always readily relatable to syntactic constituents, but which appear to be intended by the speaker to be taken together. It seems reasonable to call these, as Halliday does, 'information units'. If the discourse analyst wishes to characterise the realisation of information units, he needs an analytic system which enables him to recognise these realisations in a reliable and principled manner. In working with speech read aloud, or with previously rehearsed speech, it is often possible to identify tone groups in the stream of speech, particularly as syntactic boundaries regularly coincide with phonological boundaries. However, in unplanned spontaneous speech, there are problems in identifying the tone group by phonological criteria alone. In principle, if tone groups really can be distinguished by phonological criteria alone, it should be possible to identify them from a content-indecipherable, but tone-clear, recording. In practice it is not. The claim, as expressed, is too strong.

Halliday describes the intonational contour of tone groups as being constituted around the tonic syllable: 'Within the tone group there is always some part that is especially prominent . . . The tonic syllable carries the main burden of the pitch movement in the tone group' (1970a: 4). The clear indication is that there is just one strong intonational movement within the tone group. It is possible to find such smoothly articulated intonational contours, but they are comparatively rare. It is usual to find tightly rhythmically bound structures with several peaks of prominence. Brown, Currie & Kenworthy (1980) report a series of experiments in which judges, experienced in teaching Halliday's system, were unable to make reliable identifications of tonics, hence unable to identify tone groups reliably.

If it is frequently difficult or impossible to identify the single peak of prominence round which a tone group is structured, it ought to be possible, in principle, to locate the boundaries of the unit. Halliday does not specify criteria for identifying the boundaries. He does, however, indicate that the boundaries will be, in part at least, determined by the rhythmic structure of the utterance: 'the tone group is a phonological unit that functions as realisation of information structure. It is not co-extensive with the sentence or the clause or any other unit of sentence structure; but it is co-extensive, *within limits determined by the rhythm*, with the information unit' (1967: 203, our emphasis). This insistence on tying the information unit directly to the form of phonological realisation yields some odd-looking information units as in (4).

(4)   // not only THAT but you // didn't know / where to start /
          LOOKing for the / other and a // GAIN as I / say . . .
          (1967: 209)

A similar information unit boundary located in the middle of a
word occurs in another example transcribed by Halliday, cited as
(5) below. These tone group boundaries seem counterintuitive if
they are really to be regarded as the direct encoding of the
boundaries of information units in speech. There are problems,
then, with the identification of tonics and of tone groups in
spontaneous speech. We offer an alternative system of analysis in
5.1.5 and 5.1.7 which, naturally, confronts the same sort of
difficulties, but does, we believe, offer the practical discourse
analyst a more secure basis for the identification of its categories.

5.1.5   *The tone group and the clause*

A problem arises from Halliday's commitment to the
clause as the principle unit of syntactic organisation. In spite of his
assertion that 'in the unmarked case (in informal conversation) the
information will be mapped on to the clause', in his own extended
transcription of conversation, the *phrase* seems a much more likely
candidate:

(5)   // ∧ it was a / *fast* / *line* and // very pleasant to *travel* on // much
          the most / interesting / route to the / *north* // ∧ but for / *some* /
          reason it was ne // *glected* . . . //
                                                      (1970a: 127)

Extracts (2) and (3) (also quoted from Halliday) exemplify the
same phenomenon. The point for concern here is whether in a
model which does not take the clause as the domain of the main
areas of syntactic choice, as Halliday's does, it is helpful or
necessary to identify units which are mapped on to phrases rather
than clauses as 'marked'. If they are 'marked', and the marking
means anything, then some special, implicated, meaning ought to
attach to them. If we simply look at paradigm sentences cited out of
context as in (1a and b), it seems reasonable to suggest that

(1b)   // John // has gone into the garden with Mary //

is in some sense more 'marked' (nudge, nudge) than

(1a)   // John has gone into the garden with Mary //

If, however, instead of using a sentence which is open to 'significant' interpretations quite independently of intonation, we use a less weighted sentence, say (6),

(6)   // the room // is taking a long time to warm up //

the 'marked' significance seems to disappear. It is possible that intonation, together with pausing and other paralinguistic features of voice quality, may contribute to a 'marked' interpretation. It has yet to be shown that presenting phrases, rather than clauses, as information units does contribute to a marked reading. In the absence of such a demonstration, we shall not recognise an unmarked syntactic domain for information units.

If we abandon the clause as the unmarked syntactic domain of the information unit, more follows. You will remember that Halliday suggests that the unmarked structure of information within the information unit will be that *given* information precedes *new* information. This is very plausible if you take the clause (or simple sentence) as the unmarked syntactic domain because you can choose your examples from genres like those illustrated in (11) to (16) in Chapter 4 (obituaries, encyclopaedic entries, etc.) where, indeed, you are likely to find a 'given' form, referring to the topic entity, at the beginning of a clause, which is then followed by new information. Indeed you can sometimes perceive this organisation in snippets of conversation as in (7).

(7)   we didn't see snow till we came up – the motorway

where 'we' is given in the context of discourse. If, however, we look at *phrases* marked out as information units, it is rarely going to be the case that they contain given information, unless the whole phrase is given. (Consider the phrases marked as information units in (2) and (3).) In information units realised as phrases, then, we are more likely to find all new information.

We return to the question of the syntactic unit which realises information structure in 5.2.1.

5.1.6 *Pause-defined units*

A number of people working on intonation in discourse have found a problem with the principled identification of tone groups by phonological criteria alone and have resorted to working with units bounded by pauses in the stream of speech (for example, Chafe, 1979; Brown, Currie & Kenworthy, 1980; Butterworth (ed.), 1980; Deese, 1980).

The use of pause phenomena as a basis for building an analysis of chunking in spoken discourse might, at first glance, seem a rather precarious undertaking. The number and duration of pauses used by a speaker will obviously vary according to his rate of speech. It would be unlikely then, that one particular pause length, say one second, would have a single function for all speakers in all speech situations (a problem familiar to anyone who has worked with any kind of phonological data). However, one obvious advantage of working with pauses is that they are readily identifiable and, apart from the very briefest 'planning' pauses, judges have no difficulty in agreeing on their location. They are, furthermore, amenable to instrumental investigation, hence, measurable. What we might hope to find, in investigating the incidence of pauses, is different types of pauses in some regular pattern of distribution.

In an investigation of this type, it is important to choose the data used in the investigation so that you can generalise across speakers. A further practical point is that you should work initially on data which, you believe, will yield regular units which you will be able to recognise. If you begin by working in this tricky area with uncontrolled 'once-off' data you may find yourself working with data like that exemplified in (8) in which it is hard to discern regularities.

(8)   (numbers indicate pause lengths in seconds)
      a. but (0.8)
      b. as (0.3) is well known (1.1)
      c. it (0.2) very frequently happens that you you'll get a (0.3) co-occurrence of (0.2) an item with (1.0)
      d. a recognised grammatical class (1.0)
      e. erm (0.4) say a class of possessives or a class of (0.7)
      f. erm negatives of one sort or another (0.6)
      g. so that it is (0.4) erm (1.1)
      h. we cannot restrict lexical patterning (0.6)
      i. entirely to items as items (1.1)
      j. erm (0.6)
      k. whatever that may mean in itself may mean (1.2)

This extract from a post-graduate seminar presents a sample of speech very near the beginning of the seminar before the speaker has 'got into his stride'. It is a perfectly familiar phenomenon and one which produces particularly 'dis-fluent' speech. (Even here certain regularities might tentatively be identified. The very brief pauses (0.2–0.3) are barely perceptible. There are four occurrences of pauses immediately adjacent to *erm*, a conventional 'planning marker'. Pauses regularly occur following 'sentence' boundaries (*d* and / or *e*, *h* and *k*).) The analyst makes life considerably easier for himself if he works, initially, with speech where he knows what it is the speaker is trying to say, and where he can make direct comparison across speakers (a methodology exploited for a range of purposes in, for example, Linde and Labov, 1975; Grosz, 1981; Chafe (ed.), 1980; Levelt, 1981).

In a study of the speech produced by twelve pairs of undergraduates, in which one member of the pair described a diagram which he could see, but his listener could not, so that his listener could draw the diagram, we were able to observe the incidence of pauses in comparable speech across a number of speakers. A typical piece of speech produced under these conditions is shown in (9).

(9)   A: halfway down the page (0.3) draw (0.6) a red (0.4)
          horizontal line (0.2) of about (0.5) two inches (16) on eh
          (1.1) the right hand side just above the line (1.9) in black
          (0.1) write ON (3.2)
       B: ON (3.4)
       A: above the line (14) draw (0.2) a black (0.65) triangle (1.0)
          ehm (1.9) a right-angle (0.2) triangle (1.9) starting to the
          left (0.2) of the red line (1.0) about (0.9) half a centimetre
          above it (4.0)

In extract (9) the following pause types, defined in terms of relative length, can be identified.

1.   *Extended pauses* These are long pauses which, in this
      extract, extend from between 3.2 to 16 seconds (which
      occur at points where the speaker has provided sufficient
      information for the hearer to draw or write what has been
      described). We represent such pauses in our transcrip-
      tions by ++.

2.   *Long pauses* These pauses range from 1.0–1.9 seconds in
      this extract. We represent such pauses by +.

3.   *Short pauses* These pauses range between 0.1–0.6
      seconds in this extract. We represent such pauses by –.

We assume that extended and long pauses might be proposed as unit boundaries, whereas the short pauses might be treated as unit-internal. Adopting this view (9) can be presented as (10):

(10)   A. halfway down the page – draw – a red – horizontal line – of about – two inches ++
on eh + the right hand side just above the line + in black – write ON ++
B. ON ++
A. above the line ++
draw – a black – triangle + ehm + a rightangle – triangle + starting to the left – of the red line + about + half a centimetre above it ++

(In 5.1.8 we shall consider the structure of information in data of this sort and in 5.1.7 we shall consider the role of phonological prominence in the same set of data.)

The ranges of pause lengths found across subjects in this data is summarised in (11).

(11)

```
0      0.5     1      1.5     2      2.5     3
```

short   long   extended
pauses   pauses   pauses

We represent pauses as following utterances, as though pauses represented termination markers in the way punctuation represents termination markers. We should note that Chafe (1979), whose work on pauses shows results very similar to ours, indicates pauses as preceding utterances, since he regards the pause length as a function of the amount of planning which the speaker is putting into his next utterance. Chafe reports work in which subjects are asked to retell a series of events which they have seen enacted in a short silent film. Chafe observes 'major hesitations' (equivalent to our 'extended pauses')

. . . at those places in a narrative where paragraph boundaries seem to belong. For example, look at the following portion of one of our film narratives, in which the speaker finishes telling about a boy's theft of some pears and begins telling about some other things that happen subsequently (Speaker 22):

> And as he's holding onto the handlebars he takes off with them
> (1.1) Um – (0.7) then (0.4) uh – (2.1) a girl – on a bicycle
> (1.15) comes riding towards him . . . in the opposite direction.

> . . . *Um–* and *uh–* are lengthened pronunciations of . . . "pause fillers".
> The total amount of time spent hesitating between the end of the first
> sentence and the beginning of *a girl on a bicycle* was 6.25 seconds. We
> have here.clear evidence of some important and time-consuming mental
> processing. (1979: 162)

This view of pauses as indicating the time spent by the speaker
on constructing the following utterance is obviously interesting. In
our discussion of how the discourse analyst may proceed in
analysing discourse we shall take the more sober view of extended
pauses and long pauses as constituting boundaries of phonological
units which may be related to information units.

5.1.7 *The function of pitch prominence*

Halliday makes the simplifying assumption that there is
only one function of pitch prominence, 'the main burden of the
pitch movement', and that is to mark the focus of new information
within the tone group. In fact the limited resources of pitch
prominence may mark a good deal more than this. They are also
exploited by speakers to mark the beginning of a speaker's turn, the
beginning of a new topic, special emphasis, and contrast, as well as
information which the speaker presents as new. In our view,
phonological prominence (which may vary considerably in phonetic
realisation from one accent to the next) has a general *watch this!*
function and, inter alia, is used by speakers to mark new information as requiring to be paid attention to. Phonological non-
prominence is then associated with all the elements which the
speaker does not require the hearer to pay attention to, which will
include not only 'given' information, but also, for example, unstressed grammatical words. (For an extensive discussion of this
point of view, cf. Brown, Currie & Kenworthy, 1980; Yule, 1980.)

We have already remarked (5.1.4) that experienced judges, in a
series of experiments, were not able to identify 'tonics' consistently.
Whereas some judges did show a consistent preference for the last
lexical item in a phrase (which tends to be realised with extended
length), any lexical item which introduced new information in the
discourse was recognised by some of the judges, some of the time,

as 'a tonic'. In an extensive series of instrumental measurements, it was possible to show that the phonetic cues which have traditionally been claimed to mark the tonic (maximal pitch movement, maximal pitch height and maximal intensity) rarely cumulated on one word in spontaneous speech (except in cases of contrast), but tended to be distributed separately or paired, over words introducing new information. Where these maxima competed as cues, judges regularly identified several tonics in short phrases, even two tonics in two-word phrases.

Such a finding is not, of course, inconsistent with Halliday's remark that 'the speaker has the option' of relating the information unit to 'any constituent specified in the sentence structure'. What it does yield, however, is a density of identified tonics, hence tone groups, which is not indicated in any of Halliday's transcriptions of speech, and it certainly destroys the notion of the unmarked relationship between clause (or indeed phrase) and tone group. What it leaves is a notion that any lexical item introducing new information (new entity–noun, new property–adjective, new activity–verb) is likely to be realised with phonological prominence, which is likely to be identified as a 'tonic'.

Many scholars working on intonation, particularly those working on intonation in conversational speech, have abandoned (if they ever held) the requirement that information units, however realised, should contain only one focus, hence be realised with only one tonic (cf., for example, Bolinger, 1970; Crystal, 1975; Chafe, 1979; Pellowe & Jones, 1979; Thompson, 1980). We, too, abandon the notion of a single tonic realising the focus of an information unit. We can now proceed to a more satisfactory representation of our four-year-old's fairy story (12).

(12)   a. in a FAR-away LAND +
         b. there LIVED a BAD NAUGHty FAIRy ++
         c. and a HANDsome PRINCE +
         d. and a LOVEly PRINcess ++
         e. and she was a REALly WICKed fairy ++

We have capitalised the phonologically prominent syllables in this representation. Hereafter we shall represent the phonologically prominent *word* as prominent, disregarding what is, for our present purposes, the irrelevance of the phonological structure of the word. (In this rendering, spoken by a child with a Yorkshire accent, the final word in each information unit, whether or not it is phonologically prominent, is realised on an extended falling tone. Each preceding phonologically prominent word is realised on a less extended falling tone. Had the speaker been a Glasgow speaker, most, if not all, of the falls would have been rises.)

In the study of diagram descriptions, which we have already mentioned (5.1.6), we examined the distribution of phonological prominence with respect to information which we knew was being introduced into the discourse for the first time and with respect to information which we knew had already been introduced. Expressions introducing new information were realised with phonological prominence in 87% of cases as in:

(13) a. draw a BLACK TRIANGLE
      b. draw a STRAIGHT LINE
      c. write OUT in BLACK
      d. there's a CIRCLE in the MIDDLE

Expressions introducing given information were produced without phonological prominence in 98% of cases (the exceptions were contrasts), as in:

(14) (expressions mentioning given information are italicised)
      a. UNDERNEATH *the triangle*
      b. at the END . . . of *this line* write the word ON just ABOVE *the line*
      c. a LINE . . . about TWO INCHES + and ABOVE *it* write ON

How are we to account for the fact that the mention of some entities which we know independently are being introduced into the discourse for the first time are not being marked by the speaker with phonological prominence? Most of these examples apparently arise from the same source – although the entity introduced is certainly a new entity, the form of expression used to introduce it has just been used in the discourse to mention an immediately preceding entity. Thus one speaker mentions 'the triangle' and then introduces a different, new, triangle, speaking with a near monotone, low in her pitch range: *a right-angled triangle like the black one.* We could account for this lack of phonological marking on the grounds that the speaker believes that the hearer is, at the relevant point in the discourse, thoroughly acquainted with the task and expects another triangle to be introduced, that triangles are 'in his consciousness'. Schmerling (1974: 72) suggests that, depending on very general contextual expectations, speakers may choose to mark different aspects of their message as new. Thus, she suggests that a speaker identifying a man in the street to his hearer may produce

This is the DOCTOR I was telling you about

but if the speaker is working in a hospital and talking to another employee he is more likely to produce

This is the doctor I was TELLING you about.

Similarly if you have already been describing one triangle and triangles are clearly 'in the air', you might not choose to mark yet another member of the same class as new. This seems at least a plausible explanation for the phenomenon we observe.

It does, however, lead on to a further and more general observation. This is that we should not expect 100% direct mapping from categories at one level of description into categories at another level of description. We have already observed the curious information units which Halliday is obliged to identify as a result of mapping them directly on to tone groups whose boundaries are determined by the rhythm of speech (see discussion in 5.1.4). It is our general experience in other areas of linguistic analysis that there has to be some accommodation between analytic units at one level of description and those at another. Thus the proposition identified at the level of semantic form is not directly mapped into syntactic units without syntactic residue. The English phonological unit / b / may be identified at a phonological level as a 'voiced bilabial stop', but at a phonetic level its realisation may sometimes be described as 'voiceless' or as 'fricative'. We should not expect things to be different at the level of information structure. It seems reasonable to suggest that information structure is realised partly by syntax (in the thematic structure, i.e. by word order) and partly by phonological systems including phonological prominence and pause. We should expect to find regularities in the realisation of information structure within these systems. We should not, however, be misled by the vast volume of work on the intonation of sentences read aloud, into supposing that there are categorial rules which map information units on to syntactic units which are co-terminous with intonationally and pausally defined units, and that spontaneous speech is somehow defective with respect to this ideal state, hence uninteresting and 'mere performance'. Whereas syntactic structure, rhythmic structure, intonation and pausing may all contribute to the identification of information units in speech, they will not, in all cases, *determine* the boundaries of such units.

As discourse analysts our job is to identify the regularities which do exist in spoken language. At the moment we do not have a fully satisfactory explanation for the distribution of those expressions which introduce new entities but are not marked with pitch prominence. We have to recognise this as an unsolved problem, not dismiss it as mere performance variation.

In the diagram-description data, the conversations produced by the speakers were relatively short – between 150 and 200 words – and the entities they were concerned with were very limited. It is hardly surprising that the few entities, established in such short conversations, should be expected by the speaker to remain accessible to the hearer, especially since the hearer has a visual record of what has been mentioned in the shape of the diagram he is drawing. In longer conversations, speakers may feel they have to reinstate previously mentioned information. We have a record of a conversation in which A tells B about a woman she met on a bus. The conversation drifts on to other topics. About three minutes later, A refers again to the woman, now as *this lady* uttered with phonological prominence. It seems reasonable to suppose that she judges that the referred-to entity is no longer salient in her hearer's memory.

It is important to remember, as Halliday stressed, that it is not the structure of discourse which determines whether information is treated by the speaker as new, and marked with phonological prominence, or treated by the speaker as given, and not marked with phonological prominence. It is, on the contrary, the speaker's moment-to-moment assessment of the relationship between what he wants to say and his hearer's informational requirements. For example, it is not the case that if a speaker has just mentioned a referent he must necessarily repeat it low in pitch, treating it as 'given'. Consider:

(15)

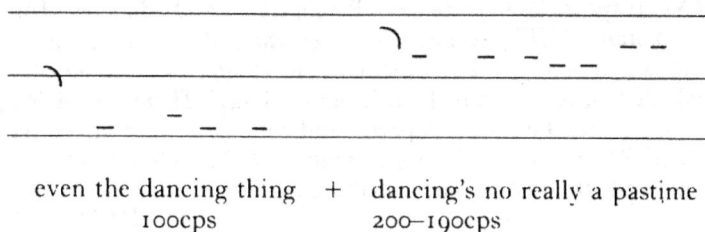

    even the dancing thing   +   dancing's no really a pastime
        100cps   200–190cps

The speaker (Scottish, hence *no* rather than *not*) has been talking about 'dancing', finishes the first comment low in his pitch range, and then embarks on a new aspect of 'dancing', marking the beginning of the new aspect with phonological prominence.

As we have said, we assume that the limited resources of intonation are regularly exploited by the speaker to mark a range of discoursal functions, a range which includes the marking of information as either 'new' or 'given'. With respect to information structure, intonation operates like an on / off switch. The speaker either treats the information as 'new' and marks it with phonological prominence, or he treats it as 'given' and does not mark it with phonological prominence. Reciprocally, from the point of view of intonation, information is regularly allocated to one of two categories which the speaker marks for the hearer. With respect to its intonational realisation, Halliday was absolutely correct in identifying only two categories of information, 'given' and 'new'.

5.2 **Information structure and syntactic form**

In this section we move away from considering information structure in terms of its phonological manifestations and turn to the way in which it is manifested in syntactic form.

5.2.1 *Given / new and syntactic form*

It has often been observed that, in English, new information is characteristically introduced by indefinite expressions and subsequently referred to by definite expressions (where, for the moment, we only consider expressions which introduce new entities into the discourse). The observation was made more than two centuries ago by Harris:

'Tis here we shall discover the use of the two Articles (A) and (THE). (A) respects our *primary* Perception, and denotes Individuals as *unknown*; (THE) respects our *secondary* Perception, and denotes Individuals as *known*. To explain by an example. I see an object pass by, which I never saw till then. What do I say? *There goes A Beggar, with A long Beard*. The Man departs, and returns a week after. What do I say then? *There goes THE Beggar with THE long Beard*. The Article only is changed, the rest remains unaltered.

(Harris, 1751: 215–16)

In (16) we exemplify a range of syntactic forms which have been frequently identified in the literature as expressions referring to given entities. The expression claimed to be 'given' is italicised in each case.

(16) a. 1. Yesterday I saw a little girl get bitten by a dog.
      2. I tried to catch *the dog*, but *it* ran away.
(Chafe, 1972: 52)

   b. 1. Mary got some beer out of the car.
      2. *The beer* was warm.
(Haviland & Clark, 1974: 514)

   c. 1. Mary got some picnic supplies out of the car.
      2. *The beer* was warm.
(Haviland & Clark, 1974: 515)

   d. 1. Yesterday, Beth sold her Chevy.
      2. Today, Glen bought *the car*.
(Carpenter & Just, 1977a: 236)

   e. 1. I bought a painting last week.
      2. I really like *paintings*.
(Chafe, 1976: 32)

   f. 1. Robert found an old car.
      2. *The steering wheel* had broken off.
(Clark, 1978: 310)

   g. 1. What happened to the jewels?
      2. *They* were stolen by a customer.
(van Dijk, 1977: 120)

   h. 1. I saw two young people there.
      2. *He* kissed *her*.
(Sgall, 1980: 238)

   i. 1. (Sag produces a cleaver and prepares to hack off his left hand)
      2. *He* never actually *does it*.
(Hankamer & Sag, 1976: 392)

   j. 1. Look out.
      2. *It*'s falling.
(Carpenter & Just, 1977a: 236)

k. 1. William works in Manchester.
   2. So *do* I.

(Allerton, 1975: 219)

The syntactic forms which are regularly discussed in association with 'given' information include:

A.   (i) Lexical units which are mentioned for the second time as in (16) *a* and *b*, particularly those in definite expressions.

    (ii) Lexical units which are presented as being within the semantic field of a previously mentioned lexical unit as in *c*, *d*, *e* and *f*, again particularly those in definite expressions.

B.   (i) Pronominals used anaphorically following a full lexical form in the preceding sentence as in *a*, *g* and *h*.

    (ii) Pronominals used exophorically (to refer to the physical context of situation) where the referent is present, as in *i* and *j*.

    (iii) Pro-verbals (less commonly discussed) as in *i* and *k*.

The discussions from which these examples are abstracted are concerned with particular syntactic realisations, in constructed sequences of sentences, where some element in the second sentence is held to be in some sense 'given'. We shall return in 5.3 to consider the range of interpretations of 'given' status which underlies these various sequences. For the moment we shall concentrate on the form of expressions which are considered as conventional indications that their referents are being treated by the speaker / writer as 'given'.

In the examples in (16) we find two predominant forms of expression used to refer to an entity treated as given, pronominals and definite NPs. These forms are often treated in the linguistics literature as though they were in free variation. It is clearly important for the discourse analyst to know whether the forms which occur in cited examples have, in fact, the same privilege of distribution in naturally occurring discourse as is attributed to them in invented sequences. If the forms are in free variation, one form should be as appropriate as another in the same context, so, for example, in (16g) the cited form:

(16)   g. 2. *They* were stolen by a customer

might equally well be replaced by a repetition of the sort which occurs in (16b) yielding

g. 3. *The jewels* were stolen by a customer

Are these equally appropriate continuation forms? Are they understood in the same way?

It is clearly possible for the expressions used to 're-identify' a given entity to carry a good deal more information than that in (g3). Donnellan (1978) produces a sequence of forms illustrating this point, cited here as (17).

(17)   a. 1. A man came to the office today carrying a huge suitcase.
         2. It contained an encyclopaedia.

         b. 1. A man came to the office today carrying a huge suitcase.
         2. The suitcase contained an encyclopaedia.

         c. 1. A man came to the office today carrying a huge suitcase.
         2. The huge suitcase carried by the man who came to the office today contained an encyclopaedia.

Donnellan comments 'In some of the cases repetition of information makes the discourse sound like the awkward language of a child's first reader' (1978: 58). If we find (17c) 'awkward', this is presumably because normally, in genres other than children's first readers, speakers do not reiterate so much 'given' information. A question which should interest discourse analysts is 'Under what conditions do these different forms occur?' Can we find instances in discourse of typically different distribution of pronominal forms as opposed to definite NPs?

We can give an answer to this question for one, limited, genre. It is important to be clear from the outset that the distribution we describe for this particular genre may not apply to all other genres. It is important to examine a wide range of data before beginning to make claims about 'typical distribution in English'.

The diagram-drawing data we have already referred to offers a clear advantage to the discourse analyst who is studying forms used to refer to new and previously mentioned entities, since he can distinguish, in his recording of the entire interaction, the occasions on which an entity is introduced for the first time, and the occasions on which an entity is subsequently mentioned. As each new entity expression is introduced, it can be given a numerical subscript, as in (18):

(18)   draw *a line*$_1$ and above *it*$_1$ write *ON*$_2$

As the analysis proceeds through the text, more new entities are introduced, and each succeeding expression introducing a new entity will receive a higher number. Thus in any particular stretch of analysed text, the NP with the highest number attached to it will mention the most recently introduced new entity. NPs with lower numbers attached to them, will be being used to refer to previously mentioned, given, entities as in the extracts in (19).

(19)   a. at the end of *the line*$_2$ draw *a square*$_4$
          b. underneath *the red line*$_4$ write *IN*$_7$
          c. draw *a diameter*$_2$ across *it*$_1$
          d. draw *a straight line*$_5$ across *the circle*$_1$

Note that the expressions mentioning 'given' entities here include a pronominal expression *it*, a simple definite NP *the line* and a definite NP which specifies an identifying property *the red line*. Do all these forms occur in identical environments?

Armed with the method of indexing we have described, we can find out. We can distinguish an expression referring to the most recently introduced entity before the new entity. We shall call this the expression referring to a *current* given entity. Such expressions will always be indexed by the number immediately below that which marks the most recent 'new' expression. Thus in (19c) the expression *it* is used to refer to an entity which was introduced immediately before 'a diameter' was mentioned. Any expression indexed with a number greater than 1 below the number indexing the 'new' expression, we shall call an expression mentioning a *displaced* given entity. In (19 a, b and d) we have instances of 'displaced' expressions: *the line, the red line, the circle*. Consider now extract (20).

(20)   draw *a black triangle*$_1$ ++ underneath *the triangle*$_1$ draw *a red line about two inches*$_2$ ++ and at the right hand side of *this line*$_2$ write *ON in black*$_3$ ++

In the pause-defined unit *underneath the triangle draw a red line about two inches*, the expression *the triangle* mentions a current given entity, current with respect to the 'new' entity introduced by the expression *a red line about two inches*. In the next unit, the expression *this line* mentions the current given entity, current with respect to the 'new' entity introduced by the expression *ON in black*.

With this distinction, current/displaced, established in the analysis, it is possible to check through the data and to examine the realisation forms in each case. In the restricted data we describe here, we find there is not free variation between all the forms we are interested in, as we show in (21).

(21)

	Current	Displaced
the + property + NOUN	3	44
the + NOUN	21	56
pronoun	65	
ellipsis	11	

(In each case the figures represent the percentage of expressions under each head which have this particular form.)

It is clear that expressions of the form *the + property + noun* is used almost exclusively in identifying displaced entities. The simple definite NP, *the + noun*, is used predominantly in identifying displaced entities but is also used identifying current entities. In this data, *pronouns* never occur as expressions identifying displaced entities, only as expressions identifying current entities.

It must be clear that the norms of distribution we state for this limited data may be different in other genres. It should also be clear that the indexing analysis becomes a good deal more problematical when it is applied to richer data, as we shall briefly demonstrate in a discussion of a very different genre, the elliptical written language of a recipe.

(22) *Chicken Korma*

Ingredients

1 roasting chicken, about
  2 lb, cut in pieces
½ lb butter or ghee
1 medium-sized onion
½ teaspoon ground saffron
3 teaspoons ground coriander
  seed
½ teaspoon ground chilli

½ teaspoon mashed garlic
5 oz plain yogurt
1-inch piece of ginger,
  sliced
1 teaspoon cloves, black
  pepper and cummin seed,
  whole
salt to taste

Method

Slice the onion finely, brown in the butter and then place in a
small dish. Put the ground spices into a breakfast cup of water,
add to the fat in the pan and cook for 3 minutes, stirring the
while. Now add the chicken, mix well, see that the meat is just
covered by water and boil for 20 minutes with the lid on the
pan.

   When the liquid has almost evaporated, continue to cook,
but stir the chicken till golden brown.

   Crush the browned onion with a spoon and add it to the
chicken with the yogurt, salt to taste and remainder of the
spices. Add a cup of water, put on the lid and simmer gently
till the chicken is tender. (If the chicken is not quite done and
the liquid has evaporated, add a little more water and cook for
a further period.)

(Harvey Day, *The Complete Book of Curries*, The Cookery
Book Club, 1970, p. 128)

Most 'new' entities are introduced into the discourse in the list of
ingredients. The first mention under *Method* of items which were
introduced in the list of ingredients, regularly takes the form of a
definite lexical expression:

(23a)   *the onion, the butter, the ground spices* (superordinate to those
          mentioned in the list), *the chicken, the yogurt*

We could characterise this writer's preference in discourse organisation as selecting an entity as 'topic entity' for a sequence of events
within a sentence, and then producing no further mentions of that
entity within the sentence, relying on ellipsis as in (23b).

(23b)   Slice *the onion* finely, brown Ø in the butter and then place Ø
          in a small dish.

If we were to try to apply an 'index of mention' to the entities
introduced in this sentence, the analysis would presumably appear
as in (23c).

(23c)   Slice *the onion*$_1$ finely, brown Ø$_1$ in *the butter*$_2$ and then place
          Ø$_1$ in *a small dish*$_3$.

This seems an unsatisfactory representation. Even if we were to
accept the oddity of indexing ellipses, 'holes' in the sentence, the
indexing does not appear to represent in a satisfactory manner what
it is that is being referred to. The object which is 'placed in a small

dish' does not consist simply of 'the onion' but of 'the onion which has been browned in *the butter*'. As soon as data involving change-of-state predicates is studied, the simple indexing of mention which we applied in the diagram-drawing becomes inadequate. We need a much more complex mechanism capable of 'carrying' predicates and, indeed, of sloughing them gradually off, as the discourse proceeds. (We return to the general problem of 'pronominal substitution' and 'substitution by ellipsis' in 6.1.)

Whereas in the diagram-drawing data we had a secure basis for identifying first and subsequent mention which enabled us to draw a confident new/given and current/displaced distinction, this simple approach can no longer apply when we turn to richer data. Nonetheless the analysis developed for the restricted data has served its purpose since it enabled us to draw a principled distinction between 'current' and 'displaced' entity referring expressions. Generalising that distinction to (22) we can observe that displaced entities are regularly referred to by full lexical definite NPs.

In restricted data it is possible for the analyst to ascertain which expressions introduce new entities into the discourse and which expressions are used to introduce entities which have been specifically mentioned before. Once this has been done, the forms of those expressions become available for linguistic description. Observe that our interest does not lie simply in describing the form of the expression, which is obviously of prime interest to the sentence grammarian. Our interest lies in observing the forms *in the context in which they are used*. We want to know how speakers, having a given quantum of information to impart, identify and package that information.

5.2.2 *Information structure and sentence structure*

In the previous section, we examined the form of nominal expressions used to refer to entities on the occasion of their first and subsequent mentions. We pointed out that, as soon as the data becomes richer and involves change-of-state predicates, the secure distinction between first and second mention becomes blurred. It is no longer possible for the analyst simply to count through the mentions in a text and assert of an entity previously mentioned that it is, necessarily, 'given' (a point we also made with respect to (15)). Halliday, as we saw in 5.1.5, has particularly insisted on the importance of taking this view: 'what is new is in the last resort what the speaker chooses to present as new, and predictions from the discourse have only a high probability of being fulfilled' (1967: 11).

In recent years, a number of psycholinguists working on information structure have taken the 'given/new' distinction as expounded by Halliday and applied it to written sentences, often written sentences cited in isolation. Since written sentences have no intonation, these writers assign intonation structure to them. They then rely on the syntactic form of nominal expressions, of the sort we were examining in the last section, and on sentence structure, to determine what, in the sentence, has the status 'new' and what has the status 'given'. They regard the information status as irrevocably assigned by the form of expression used. This approach to information structure has led to a re-interpretation of what is meant by the status 'given', as we shall see below and in 5.3.

Clark & Clark (1977: 93) report an experiment carried out by Hornby (1972). Hornby presented subjects with a series of written sentences read aloud. The sentences are reproduced in (24) as they appear in Clark & Clark's discussion:

(24)   *GIVEN AND NEW INFORMATION*
        Five types of sentences and their given and new information

SENTENCE	GIVEN AND NEW INFORMATION
1. It is the BOY who is petting the cat.	Given: X is petting the cat New: X = the boy
2. It is the CAT which the boy is petting.	Given: the boy is petting X New: X = the cat
3. The one who is petting the cat is the BOY.	Given: X is petting the cat New: X = the boy
4. What the boy is petting is the CAT.	Given: the boy is petting X New: X = the cat
5. The BOY is petting the cat.	Given: X is petting the cat New: X = the boy

The status of the capitalised elements is explained on page 32: 'Sentences signal given and new information by stress or accent on particular words (e.g. Halliday, 1967) . . . The word with the focal stress, or a phrase containing it, always conveys the new information.'

A number of points arise from this presentation. First of all it is not entirely clear whether given / new status is being determined by the sentential form (as the sub-heading to the table suggests) or by the effect of the placing of 'focal stress' on different constituents of the sentences, or by some interaction of these two distinct systems.

Secondly, it somewhat misrepresents Halliday's position to suggest that he takes the view that '*Sentences* signal given and new information' (our emphasis). Halliday repeatedly insists that it is speakers who signal information status.

Thirdly, Hornby and, apparently, Clark & Clark are attributing one focus of information to each sentence. The only sentence in this set which is directly relatable to the Hallidaian clause is sentence 5. All the other sentences are realised in two clauses. In a Hallidaian analysis each of these two clauses would be expected to contain an information focus as is demonstrated in the similar examples discussed in Halliday (1967: 226):

(25) a. // the one who painted the SHED last week // was JOHN//
      b. // JOHN // was the one who painted the SHED // last week //

By analogy we would expect sentence number 3, for example, to be realised with two points of information focus:

c. // the one who is petting the CAT // is the BOY //

Fourthly the term 'given' is no longer being used as an analytic term to describe the status of the referents of expressions within the clause (or tone group), but is being used of the presuppositions attributed to clauses within sentences.

This view of 'givenness' is picked up by other psycholinguists – for instance, Sanford & Garrod, 1981. On page 92 they cite Halliday who, they say, 'goes on to suggest that the "Given–New" partition can apply to any sentence in a discourse and is signalled both in its syntax and intonation. To take a simple example, the sentence "It was Mary who left" seems to break down into Given: "Someone left"; and New: "The someone who left was Mary".' On page 93, they continue 'Now if we go back to our example, we see that this is naturally read as "It was MARY // who LEFT //", meaning that MARY and LEFT are given stress and so treated as New information, whereas "It was" and "who" are not given stress and so treated as Given.' The analysis on page 92 resembles the Hornby / Clark & Clark analysis. The analysis on page 93 owes more to Halliday (though it is doubtful if he would consider *it was* and *who* as being 'treated as Given', cf. 1967: 229ff.). The first analysis is concerned with what is *presupposed* in the 'relative' clause and derives from processes of sentential thematisation, the second analysis is concerned only with the information status of the referents of expressions within the clause, and derives from imputed intonation structure. Both are perfectly reasonable types of analysis of different phenomena, whose categories may interact to produce a particular effect, but they must not be confounded.

In 5.3 we shall see how far this procedure of taking what is 'presupposed' in a sentence, and including it within the category of 'given information', has extended the meaning of the term 'given' in the psycholinguistics literature in such a way that it no longer clearly relates to the way the term is used in the linguistics literature.

5.3 The psychological status of 'givenness'

In this section, we turn from an examination of the forms, intonational and syntactic, which are used by speakers to indicate given / new status, to a consideration of what scholars using these terms have understood by them. How does information come to have the status of 'being treated as given'?

5.3.1 *What does 'given' mean?*

Halliday produced characterisations of given / new, in terms of speaker-expectations, which are capable of being rather narrowly interpreted, as we suspect he intended. 'Given' information is specified as being treated by the speaker as 'recoverable either anaphorically or situationally' (1967: 211) and 'new' information is said to be focal 'not in the sense that it cannot have been previously mentioned, although it is often the case that it has not been, but in the sense that the speaker presents it as not being recoverable from the preceding discourse' (1967: 204). Whereas this characterisation does discriminate between the status of information marked intonationally as 'given' or 'new' by the speaker, it is capable of being interpreted so as to embrace a wider range of other phenomena. As Dahl remarks: 'The concepts of old and new information are used to explain such phenomena in language as intonation, stress and word order and the use of anaphoric devices' (1976: 37).

A scholar who has preserved the narrow interpretation of the status of given information and, indeed, attempted to redefine the term to force a narrow interpretation is Wallace Chafe, in a series of publications (1970, 1972, 1974, 1976). He writes:

> The terminology has been and continues to be misleading to linguists and psychologists who use it. Calling something 'old information' suggests it is 'what the listener is expected to know already'.
>
> (1976: 30)

Chafe insists that given status should be restricted to 'that know-ledge which the speaker assumes to be in the consciousness of the addressee at the time of the utterance' (1976: 30). He develops a series of images, such as 'in the forefront of the mind' (1970: 211) and 'spotlighted in the hearer's attention', in order to try to force home the *here and now* saliency which he attributes to given status at the moment of utterance. He stresses that givenness is a transient status: 'One indisputable property of consciousness is that its capacity is very limited. As new ideas come into it, old ones leave. The speaker's treatment of an item as given, therefore, should cease when he judges that item to have left his addressee's consciousness' (1976: 32). In Chafe's analysis, as in Halliday's, it is perfectly possible for a speaker to say *I saw your father yesterday*, where 'your father' is treated as new, if the speaker judges that the addressee's father is not in the addressee's consciousness at the time of the utterance.

A very different view of givenness is put forward by Herb Clark (in, for example, Clark & Clark, 1977). Clark takes the general view of 'given' status characterised by Chafe as 'what the listener is expected to know already'. Clark & Clark characterise information status thus:

> given information should be identifiable and new information unknown . . . listeners should be confident that the given information conveys information they can identify uniquely. They understand that it is information the speaker believes they both agree on and that the speaker is asserting his beliefs about.
>
> (1977: 92)

This looks very like the characterisation of *presupposition* we provided in 2.1 (cf. also discussion in 5.2.2).

Perhaps the most expansive development of the Clarkian view of given status is to be found in Sanford & Garrod (1981). They propose a processing model which invokes the notion of *scenario* (discussed in 7.6). The scenario may be characterised here as a particular stereotypical configuration of past experience. Thus a courtroom scenario would be stored in memory with attendant typical characters and procedures. Sanford & Garrod suggest (1981: 114): 'The scenario enables referring to individuals to be made in the first instance by a definite noun-phrase, because they are already *given* in the representation.' Givenness is acquired then, not because this status is attributed to information by the speaker / writer, nor because it is salient in the context or previously mentioned in the co-text, but because of its status within the scenario which the language evokes. Thus, if a courtroom scenario is established, a 'lawyer' would form part of this scenario and hence could be treated as 'given'.

It is clear that the concept under discussion here is very different from that discussed by Halliday or Chafe. What is under discussion here has to do with the structuring of background knowledge (cf. 7.6). In a discussion of the sequences presented in (16b and c),

    b. 1. Mary got some beer out of the car.
        2. The beer was warm.
    c. 1. Mary got some picnic supplies out of the car.
        2. The beer was warm.

Chafe comments thus on Haviland & Clark's (1974) experiment, which showed that subjects took longer to process c2 than b2:

> In the first case, where the beer was mentioned in the context sentence, it is indeed given in the target sentence and we would expect that subjects, if they had been asked to read the target sentence out loud, would have pronounced it with low pitch . . . In the second case, where the beer was not mentioned in the context sentence, it is not given in the target sentence and subjects, if they had read it, would have been expected to give it high pitch . . . the basis for the definiteness of *the beer* in the two target sentences is not the same.
>
> (1976: 41)

Chafe goes on to suggest that what Haviland & Clark are concerned with is not *givenness* (as the term is used by Chafe), but *definiteness* (1976: 42). He points out that givenness may coincide with definiteness and often does, but that it is perfectly possible to find combinations of definiteness and newness (as in *c2* above) or as in *I saw the milkman yesterday for the first time for ages* said with no previous mention of 'the milkman' and without one in sight.

There is a great deal of room for confusion between the use of *given* as restricted to the status of information within a tone group (or clause) or extended to include whatever knowledge speakers and hearers share. In the next section we shall explore an attempt by Prince (1981) to develop a new taxonomy of information status, introducing new, and as yet unsullied, terminology.

5.3.2 *A taxonomy of information status*

If we wish to take account of the different views of information status expressed on the one hand by linguists like Halliday and Chafe, and on the other by psycholinguists like Clark & Clark and Sanford & Garrod, we need a richer taxonomy than the simple 'given / new' distinction that we have been working with so far.

Prince (1981) provides the basis for an extended taxonomy. She suggests that we should view a text as 'a set of instructions on how to construct a particular *DISCOURSE MODEL*. The model will contain *DISCOURSE ENTITIES*, *ATTRIBUTES* and *LINKS* between entities' (1981: 235). How is such a model to be constructed?

Prince suggests that the speaker may introduce new entities into the discourse. New entities are of two types. *Brand new* entities are assumed not to be in any way known to the speaker and will typically be introduced into the discourse by an indefinite expression like *a man I know* or *a bus in Princes Street*. The second type of new entity, *unused* entity, is assumed by the speaker to be known to the hearer, in his background knowledge, but not in his consciousness at the time of utterance. Chafe's example *I saw your father yesterday* (1976: 30) would fit into this category, as would expressions like *Chomsky* or *Jackendoff* addressed to a student of linguistics who, the speaker believes, is currently thinking about instrumental phonetics, rather than syntax, for example.

Prince calls her second class of entities *inferrables*. These are entities which the speaker assumes the hearer can infer from a discourse entity which has already been introduced. Thus 'the driver' would be inferrable from the interpretation of the expression *the car*, as long as you have the background knowledge that 'cars have drivers'. There is no difficulty in interpreting the expression *the driver* in (26):

(26)   there was a car approaching the junction + but the driver didn't stop at the give way sign

In Prince's terms, it is an inferrable relationship which enables us to interpret the second sentence in (16c–f) as relating to the first sentence in each case. The class of inferrable entities would include, presumably, those scenario-based entities which Sanford & Garrod (1981: 114) classify as 'given' (e.g. courtroom scenario = lawyer).

The third set of discourse entities is the *evoked* class. There are two types. The first, *situationally evoked*, is salient in the discourse context (for instance 'I' and 'you'). The second is *textually evoked* and is an entity which has already been introduced into the discourse which is now being referred to for the second or subsequent time; (16a and b) exemplify this. 'Evoked' entities are what Halliday and Chafe expect to find speakers treating as 'given'.

We need to introduce a further distinction into Prince's category of *textually evoked entity*. In 5.2.1, we drew a distinction between *current* and *displaced* entities, both of which have already been introduced into the discourse, but where the *current evoked* entity is the one which was introduced as 'new' immediately before the current *new* entity was introduced. Displaced entities were introduced prior to that. This distinction, as we observed in the distribution of realisation forms in data, is justified by the difference in the typical realisation of the two categories.

The combination of Prince's system with our current / displaced distinction yields the following taxonomy of information status:

(27)   *New*   *Inferrable*   *Evoked*
         brand new   situational
         unused   textual – current
                                                          – displaced

In section 5.3.3, we shall first try to apply this taxonomy within the restricted data we have already discussed, and then consider its wider applications.

5.3.3   *The information status taxonomy applied to data*
Within the restricted diagram-drawing data which we
have already referred to in previous sections, it is possible to discern
the different categories of entity identified by Prince, as they are
introduced, and to observe the form of expression used to refer to
them. A synopsis of the outcome of such an analysis is presented as
(28). (Detailed discussion of different aspects of this analysis is to
be found in Yule, 1981 and Brown, 1983.)

(28)   Forms produced to refer to:
          1. NEW ENTITIES
          a. *brand new*   (i)   draw *a black triangle*
                                  (ii) draw *a straight line*
                                  (iii) write *OUT in black*
                                  (iv) there's *a circle* in the middle
          b. *unused*:   no examples in this restricted data

          2. INFERRABLE ENTITIES
                                  (i)   it's right through *the*
                                        middle (circle)
                                  (ii) you start at *the edge*
                                        (triangle)
                                  (iii) with *the right-angle*
                                        (triangle)
                                  (iv) *the corner* (triangle)

          3. EVOKED ENTITIES
          a. *situational*   (i)   in the middle of *the page*
                                  (ii) *you've* got a triangle
          b. *textual – current* (i)   to the left of the red line
                                        about half a centimeter above
                                        it
                                  (ii) there's a black circle . . .
                                        above *it* there's
                                  (iii) draw a line in the middle
                                        and above *it* write ON
                                  (iv) it's a right angle triangle
                                        . . . the bottom line of *the*
                                        triangle
                                  (v)   A. it's in red
                                        B. Ø in red +
          c. *textual – displaced*(i)   draw a black triangle . . .
                                        underneath *the triangle*
                                  (ii) to the left of *the red line*
                                  (iii) *the black one*
                                  (iv) at the base of *the red one*

From a syntactic point of view there are a number of forms of expression available to a speaker from which he can choose when he refers to an entity. We can summarise these informally thus:

(29)   *a*   (+ properties) X
        the   (+ properties) X
        it
        $\emptyset$ (ellipsis)

How are these forms distributed in our data? As you will see, *brand new* entities are regularly introduced by *a (+ properties) X*, where the specification of properties is not always present. The words *IN* and *OUT* in this data are referred to by naming the word – we shall not discuss the issue of names here. *Inferrable* entities are regularly introduced by definite expressions. In this data, inferrable entities include the known properties of circles (*middle, edge, radius, bottom*), of triangles (*apex, angle, side,* and, for some individuals, *right-angles*), of pages (*middle, corner, side, top*), or lines (*end, edge, top*), etc. *Evoked situational* forms are mostly used to mention the page which the hearer is drawing on, the hearer (*you*), and to the red and black pens which the hearer is drawing with.

Most of the expressions used to mention *current textual* entities are 'lexically attenuated', to use Chafe's term, either pronominal or elided, though there are some definite referring expressions. (We ignore here the problem of treating a null anaphor (or ellipsis) as a 'referring expression'. We assume that a structural gap is an instruction to the hearer / reader to fill it.) These entities, which the speaker knows have to be in the forefront of his hearer's consciousness, are referred to with the minimal referring forms. *Displaced textual* entities, on the other hand, are never, in this data, referred to pronominally or elided, but always referred to by a definite referring expression, often accompanied by an identifying property.

We may further note that whereas the expressions relating to *new* and *inferrable* entities are regularly realised with phonological prominence, 'evoked expressions' are not realised with phonological prominence except in a few cases of contrast. The interaction of distribution of syntactic form together with the distribution of phonological prominence significantly contribute to identifying the information status in terms of the taxonomy we have been discussing, as (30) shows.

(30)

	Brand new	Inferr-able	Situa-tion	Current	Dis-placed
a + properties	77				
a − properties	21				
the + properties		29		3	44
the − properties	2	71	58	21	56
pronoun			9	65	
ellipsis			33	11	
prominence +	87	79	2		4
prominence −	13	21	98	100	96

(In each case the figures represent the percentage of expressions under each head which have this particular form. Scores
for phonological prominence show percentage of actually
occurring realisations.)

In 5.2.1 we discussed the striking difference in the characteristic
syntactic form of expressions relating to current and displaced
entities (except for the overlap of simple definite NPs). This
difference appears to confirm the correctness of Chafe's view that
givenness has a very transitory status. In this specifically transactional data, where the speakers introduce a number of similar
entities, a displaced entity may be particularly liable to require
specification of its properties in order to distinguish it from other,
potentially competing, displaced entities. In spite of the increased
specificity of the lexical identification, expressions used for displaced entities in this data are normally uttered without phonological prominence (not associated with an intonational peak), so are
analysable, in Halliday's terms, as 'given'.

It should be pointed out that the interactions from which this
data is drawn are, typically, very short, lasting no more than 3–4
minutes, and that the speaker knows, in each case, that the hearer
has in front of him a physical representation of what has previously
been mentioned, since it is the hearer's business to draw that
representation. It might be claimed that everything which the
hearer has drawn can safely be treated by the speaker as given. It is
relevant to observe that it is only expressions of entities and
properties of entities which have previously been *mentioned* in the
discourse, which are phonologically non-prominent in this data.
Those entities and properties which are classified, following Prince,
as 'inferrables', are referred to with expressions which are phonologically prominent (on intonation peaks) hence, 'treated as new'.

This is in spite of the fact that the speaker is referring to 'ends' of lines, 'corners' of squares, 'angles' of triangles which the speaker knows are not only physically present in the context but have just been drawn there by the hearer. If the speaker has no reason to believe that the hearer is paying attention to these particular entities or properties of entities, he mentions them with phonological prominence. Once again Chafe's metaphors, which insist that the speaker must suppose that what he is talking about is *saliently* present in the hearer's consciousness, if he wishes to treat this information as given, seem particularly apposite.

Prince's taxonomy performs the useful function of distinguishing between what has been treated as 'given' in the linguistics literature ('situationally and textually evoked' mention, in her terms), as opposed to what has been treated as 'given' in the psycholinguistics literature ('situationally and textually evoked' mention *plus* the class of 'inferrables').

There remains, however, a real problem with trying to establish a taxonomy of information structure which can be appealed to in analysis independently of the forms which the speaker produces. Consider again some of the expressions which appear in (22), cited here as (31):

(31)   a. 'Slice the onion finely, brown in the butter and then place in *a small dish*
          b. . . . add to the fat in *the pan*
          c. . . . and boil for 20 minutes with *the lid* on the pan

None of the expressions italicised in (31) mentions an entity which has previously been explicitly introduced in the discourse. In each case this is the first occasion of mention. There is a sense, then, in which the items might all be held to be 'brand new'. On the other hand, it might be argued, the writer may reasonably suppose that this recipe is being read in the context of a kitchen, and he obviously believes that the reader will have in his kitchen the items 'a small dish', 'a pan' and 'a lid'. Is there not a sense in which all of these items are 'inferrables', introduced naturally from the 'kitchen scenario'? The reason why we feel that both of these arguments are misplaced is surely because these objects are not being *treated in the same way* by the writer. How do we know this? Because the forms of expression which he uses to refer to them by are different. The problem is that the only evidence we have of the information status the writer attributes to different entities is the form of the expression which he produces.

5.4 Conclusion

We have tried, in this chapter, to give some indication of the many approaches to the question of 'information structure'. We have examined a range of forms, intonational and syntactic, which are held to be associated with 'new' or with 'given' information status. We have indicated that intonational· prominence is not always associated with the use of an indefinite referring expression, and that lack of intonational prominence is not always associated with the use of a definite referring expression. We could show that indefinite referring expressions need not only be used on first mention (as in *draw a triangle + a triangle in red*) and that some first mentions take the form of definite referring expressions (as in 31b and c). We have pointed out that intonation prominence can be associated with other features of discourse than new information (for instance with contrast and emphasis) and that lack of intonational prominence is sometimes associated with first mention (discussed in 5.1.7). We have also pointed out that sentence form does not seem to determine given / new status, though it may indicate presuppositions on the part of the speaker. If we have to rely on linguistic forms alone to determine information status, it seems that the relevant status will not always be clearly marked and, indeed, if syntactic and intonational forms are both regarded as criterial for 'givenness', that these forms may supply contradictory information to the hearer.

We have compared the use of the term 'given' in the linguistics literature with its use in the psycholinguistics literature and attempted, by making appeal to the taxonomy put forward by Prince, to make clear how the term has been extended in the psycholinguistics literature. We considered whether, in principle, it is possible to establish a taxonomy of information status independently of the forms of expressions used by speakers, and we concluded that it is not possible. It seems that our only safe access to information status is provided by the form of the expressions used by the speaker / writer.

The discourse analyst might very well, at this point, decide to give up the concept of information structure since it is so hard to pin down formally and impossible to pin down independently of formal expressions. We believe that the discourse analyst should avoid this counsel of despair. It is certainly the case, as Halliday has always insisted, that information status is determined, not by the structure of discourse but by the speaker. It is also certainly the case that there are no 'rules' for the specification of 'new' or 'given' status by the speaker. There are, however, regularities. In the diagram-drawing data we have described here, we can observe regularities which permit us to make statements like 'speakers usually introduce new entities with indefinite referring expressions and with intonational prominence' or 'speakers usually refer to current given entities with attenuated syntactic and phonological forms'. We must suppose that it is the exploitation of these regularities *in contexts of discourse* which allows us to assess the information status attributed to an entity by speakers and writers. As discourse analysts, when we examine data which is less rigidly controlled than that which we have analysed in detail in this chapter, we may lean on the regularities observed in the tightly controlled material to formulate an initial analysis. This methodology, which involves extrapolating from controlled data to uncontrolled material, provides a more secure basis for an account of information structure than can be produced by generalisations based only on short constructed sentences.

6

The nature of reference in text and in discourse

In the last chapter we were largely concerned with considering the structure of small formal chunks of language, particularly nominal expressions, and exploring the ways in which particular forms in English have come to be associated with a particular information status. These formal structures constitute cues for the hearer / reader as to how the speaker / writer intends the discourse to be interpreted.

We begin this chapter by considering how large chunks of language come to be interpreted as texts. We examine the formal expressions, some of which were discussed in Chapter 5, which are available to the speaker / writer as cues to signal explicitly how parts of the discourse are to be interpreted, particularly anaphoric expressions. We then go on to consider the central question of what it means to refer in discourse.

6.1 What is 'text'?

We have proceeded in this book with the rather simple account of what constitutes a text which we gave, with accompanying caveats, in Chapter 1. Text, we said, is the verbal record of a communicative event. A number of authors have been concerned to provide a tighter, more formal account of how speakers of English come to identify a text as forming a text (cf. for example van Dijk, 1972; Gutwinski, 1976; de Beaugrande, 1980; de Beaugrande & Dressler, 1981; Halliday & Hasan, 1976.) These authors are concerned with the principles of connectivity which bind a text together and force co-interpretation. In this section we shall give a brief outline of the account provided by Halliday & Hasan (1976) since this is by far the most comprehensive treatment of the subject and has become the standard text in this area.

6.1.1 *'Cohesion'*

Halliday & Hasan take the view that the primary determinant of whether a set of sentences do or do not constitute a text depends on cohesive relationships within and between the sentences, which create **texture**: 'A text has texture and this is what distinguishes it from something that is not a text. . . . The texture is provided by the cohesive RELATION' (1976: 2). Cohesive relationships within a text are set up 'where the INTERPRETATION of some element in the discourse is dependent on that of another. The one PRESUPPOSES the other in the sense that it cannot be effectively decoded except by recourse to it' (1976: 4). A paradigm example of such a cohesive relationship is given (1976: 2):

(1)   Wash and core six cooking apples. Put them into a fireproof dish.

Of this text they say: 'It is clear that *them* in the second sentence refers back to (is ANAPHORIC to) the *six cooking apples* in the first sentence. This ANAPHORIC function of *them* gives cohesion to the two sentences, so that we interpret them as a whole; the two sentences together constitute a text' (1976: 2).

Halliday & Hasan outline a taxonomy of types of cohesive relationships which can be formally established within a text, providing cohesive 'ties' which bind a text together. We shall only briefly outline these here.

A familiar type of explicitly marked cohesive relationship in texts is indicated by formal markers which relate what is about to be said to what has been said before – markers like *and*, *but*, *so* and *then*. Halliday & Hasan provide an extended, often illuminating, discussion of the relationships indicated by such markers, together with an extended taxonomy. The taxonomy of types of explicit markers of conjunctive relations is exemplified in (2).

(2)   a. additive: and, or, furthermore, similarly, in addition
       b. adversative: but, however, on the other hand, nevertheless
       c. causal: so, consequently, for this reason, it follows from this
       d. temporal: then, after that, an hour later, finally, at last

It is, of course, not the case that any one of these formal markers stands in a simple one-to-one relationship with a particular cohesive relation: *and*, for example, can occur between sentences which exhibit any one of the four relationships mentioned in (2). Neither is it the case that the posited relationships cannot be held to exist in the absence of formal markers. Consider the following extract from a letter:

(3)   We ended up going for a drink and then a meal in a Bernie's Inn. Returned chez Jane for coffee and talk. Bed about midnight.

Although the sequential nature of the events is only explicitly pointed to by the *then* between *going for a drink* and *a meal in a Bernie's Inn*, it is clearly implied, though not stated, in the subsequent sequence of events. Halliday & Hasan recognise that 'it is the underlying semantic relation . . . that actually has the cohesive power' (1976: 229), rather than the particular cohesive marker. Nonetheless, they insist that it is the presence of the cohesive markers which constitutes 'textness'.

The cohesive relationship which particularly interests them is that which they discuss under the headings *reference, substitution, ellipsis* and *lexical relationships*. Since their use of the term *reference* is particular to them, we shall immediately substitute for it the term *co-reference* (reference in a more orthodox interpretation will be discussed in 6.2). Co-referential forms are forms which 'instead of being interpreted semantically in their own right . . . make reference to something else for their interpretation' (1976: 31). These forms direct the hearer / reader to look elsewhere for their interpretation. Where their interpretation lies outside the text, in the context of situation, the relationship is said to be an **exophoric** relationship which plays no part in textual cohesion (1976: 18). Where their interpretation lies within a text, they are called **endophoric** relations and do form cohesive ties within the text. Endophoric relations are of two kinds: those which look back in the text for their interpretation, which Halliday & Hasan call **anaphoric** relations, and those which look forward in the text for their interpretation, which are called **cataphoric** relations. These relationships are exemplified in (4):

(4)   *Types of co-reference relation*

    a. *exophora*:   Look at that. (*that* = _____)
    b. *endophora*:
        (i) anaphoric – Look at the sun. It's going down quickly.
                (*It* refers back to *the sun*.)
        (ii) cataphoric – It's going down quickly, the sun.
                (*It* refers forwards to *the sun*.)

In the last two examples, the relationship of co-reference was illustrated as holding between a full lexical expression *the sun* and a pronominal expression *it*. The same relationship can also be posited to hold between other forms as exemplified in (5). (In each case the co-reference relationship exemplified here is anaphoric, hence endophoric.)

(5)   a. Repeated form: *The Prime Minister* recorded her thanks to the Foreign Secretary. *The Prime Minister* was most eloquent.
    b. Partially repeated form: *Dr E. C. R. Reeve* chaired the meeting. *Dr Reeve* invited Mr Phillips to report on the state of the gardens.
    c. Lexical replacement: *Ro's daughter* is ill again. *The child* is hardly ever well.
    d. Pronominal form: *Ro* said *she* would have to take Sophie to the doctor.
    e. Substituted form: Jules has *a birthday* next month. Elspeth has *one* too.
    f. Ellided form: Jules has *a birthday* next month. Elspeth has too.

In the last two cases the structure itself, 'the fundamental relation between parts of a text', (1976: 143) forces the reader, when he encounters substitution or ellipsis, back into the text to look for a previous expression to substitute, in the case of substitution, or to provide, in the case of ellipsis. (It should be stressed that ellipsis is a formal notion which does not simply apply to anything which happens to be left unsaid, see Halliday & Hasan, 1976: 142ff., and a particularly helpful discussion in Matthews, 1982: 38ff.) Halliday & Hasan see these two types as involving 'relatedness of form' whereas the other examples involve 'relatedness of reference' (1976: 304), which provides 'continuity of lexical meaning' within a text (1976: 320).

Cohesion within a text can of course be provided by relationships other than those involving co-reference, which are the ones we have chosen to illustrate. Cohesion may be derived from lexical relationships like hyponymy (*daffodil* is a hyponym of *flower*), part–whole (*arm* is part of *a man*), collocability (*Monday* relates to *Tuesday*), by further structural relationships like clausal substitution (Sarah is very fond of Rachel. *So* am I), comparison (*My thumb* is stronger than *that hammer*), by syntactic repetition (We *came in*. They *came in*), by consistency of tense, by stylistic choice (*The gentleman encountered an acquaintance* vs *The guy met up with this bloke he knows*) and so on. Some aspects of cohesion are exemplified in (6).

(6)　　　Lord Melbourne, who was Prime Minister when Victoria became Queen in 1837, did not like birdsong and could not distinguish a woodlark from a nightingale. He preferred the singing of blackbirds anyway; best of all he liked the cawing of rooks and could watch them for hours as they circled at sunset. Victoria was surprised by this: she disliked their grating and insistent calling.

　　　　　　　　　　(Marina Warner, *Queen Victoria's Sketchbook*,
　　　　　　　　　　　　　　　　Macmillan, 1979, p. 77)

We can observe a number of co-referential chains:

(7)　　　a. Lord Melbourne – Prime Minister – Ø – He – he – Ø
　　　　　b. Victoria – Queen – Victoria – she
　　　　　c. rooks – them – they – their

We can also observe chains of lexical collocation:

(8)　　　a. birdsong – woodlark – nightingale – blackbirds – rooks
　　　　　b. birdsong – singing – cawing – calling

There is an instance of an adversative marker (*anyway*), comparison (*preferred, best of all*), a pronominal expression referring back to the content of the previous clause (Victoria was surprised by *this*), consistent tense, and repeated negative structure (*did not, could not*). We might add the effect of the special punctuation marks (;) and (:) which indicate a relationship between what has been said and what is about to be said, just as verbal markers of conjunctive relations do.

Most texts will reveal some cohesive structuring of this kind. Two main questions need to be asked. First, is such cohesion necessary to the identification of a text? Secondly, is such cohesion sufficient to guarantee identification as a text? A subsidiary question which follows on from the second question is: if a text is identified by these criteria, will they guarantee textual coherence?

Is it necessary for a text to reveal at least some of the features of cohesion which we have been discussing in order for it to be identified as a text? Halliday & Hasan appear to suggest that it is. They acknowledge that the notion of cohesion needs to be 'supplemented' by a notion of 'register' (appropriateness to a particular context of situation) but, they say:

the concept of cohesion accounts for the essential semantic relations whereby any passage of speech or writing is enabled to function as a text. We can systematize this concept by classifying it into a small number of distinct categories . . . Each of these categories is represented in the text by particular features . . . which have in common the property of signalling that the interpretation of the passage in question depends on something else. If that 'something else' is verbally explicit, then there is cohesion. There are, of course, other types of semantic relation associated with a text which are not embodied in this concept; but the one that it does embody is in some ways the most important, since it is common to text of every kind and is, in fact, what makes a text a text. (1976: 13)

An important distinction needs to be drawn, which many students adopting Halliday & Hasan's approach have failed to draw, and which Halliday & Hasan themselves are somewhat ambivalent about, as this quotation reveals. This is the distinction between the 'meaning relations' which hold between items in a text and the explicit expression of those 'meaning relations' within a text. This is a distinction which we have already mentioned in our discussion of conjunctive relations: 'it is the underlying semantic relation . . . which actually has the cohesive power'. Few would dispute that it is necessary that such relations be postulated within a discourse which is capable of being interpreted coherently. What is questionable, however, is whether the explicit *realisation* of these relations is required to identify a text as a text. Halliday & Hasan appear to insist that such explicit realisation is necessary when they make statements like 'A text has texture, and this is what distinguishes it from something which is not a text' (1976: 2), and 'cohesive ties between sentences stand out more clearly because they are the ONLY source of texture' (1976: 9). In such statements they seem to be talking of verbal elements which appear in the verbal record, not of underlying semantic relations.

It is, of course, easy to find texts, in the sense of contiguous sentences which we readily co-interpret, which display few, if any, explicit markers of cohesive relations. Apart from the much-quoted constructed example:

(9)   A: There's the doorbell.
        B: I'm in the bath.

we shall quote several more:

(10)   a. Thank you for your comments about voicing. I will even-
           tually get back to that lesson.
                                            (beginning of letter)
        b. Just to test the water I made one telephone call yesterday,
           to a leading British Publisher with offices in New York.
           There was immediate interest in *Clear Speech*.
                                            (letter from a literary agent)
        c. Once again I lie awake in the small hours tormented by my
           social conscience. Sometimes it is the single mothers,
           sometimes the lower classes or disadvantaged Highland
           sheep farmers, but today it is the homeless.
                                            (entry from Auberon Waugh's *Diary*)

In each case, we suggest, there is no explicit marking of relationships between the first and second sentences. Nonetheless, a
normal reader will naturally assume that these sequences of sentences constitute a text (since we are presenting them as if they
were) and will interpret the second sentence in the light of the first
sentence. He will assume that there are 'semantic relations' between
the sentences, in the absence of any explicit assertion that there is
such a relationship (see discussion of 'missing links' in 7.8). It
seems to be the case then that 'texture', in the sense of explicit
realisation of semantic relations, is not criterial to the identification
and co-interpretation of texts.

We turn now to the second question we posed: is formal cohesion
sufficient to guarantee identification as a text? An obvious test here
would be to take any narrative text and, leaving the first sentence
(to play fair, and identify the participants), scramble the next few
sentences. Does what follows constitute a text? Do readers find it
easy to interpret the newly constituted collection of sentences? All
the formal expressions of cohesive relationships will still remain
intact. Consider the following passage.

(11)   [1] A man in white clothes, who could only be the surviving
          half-breed, was running as one does run when Death is the
          pace-maker. [2] The white figure lay motionless in the middle
          of the great plain. [3] Behind him, only a few yards in his rear,
          bounded the high ebony figure of Zambo, our devoted negro.
          [4] An instant afterwards Zambo rose, looked at the prostrate
          man, and then, waving his hand joyously to us, came running
          in our direction. [5] They rolled on the ground together. [6]
          Even as we looked, he sprang upon the back of the fugitive and
          flung his arms round his neck.
          (reorganised in the order 1, 3, 6, 5, 4, 2, this passage is taken
          from Sir Arthur Conan Doyle's *The Lost World*, 1912)

Clearly, formal cohesion will not guarantee identification as a text
nor, to answer our subsidiary question, will it guarantee textual
coherence.

In order to reconstitute this 'text' (11) without the original
sentence-order arrangement given above, the reader may indeed
use some of the formal expressions of cohesive relationships present
in the sentences, but he is more likely to try to build a coherent
picture of the series of events being described and fit *the events*
together, rather than work with the verbal connections alone.

A convincing example of the inadequacy of cohesive ties across
sentences as a basis for guaranteeing 'textness' has been provided by
Enkvist (1978: 110) and is quoted here as (12).

(12)   I bought a Ford. A car in which President Wilson rode down
          the Champs Elysées was black. Black English has been widely
          discussed. The discussions between the presidents ended last
          week. A week has seven days. Every day I feed my cat. Cats
          have four legs. The cat is on the mat. Mat has three letters.

Enkvist points out that there is the 'semblance' of cohesion because
of the *Ford–car, black–Black, my cat – cats* types of connections,
but that we would prefer not to call this concatenation of sentences
a coherent text. (We might note in passing that extract (12) provides
a good exemplification of why the structural formula $S + (S)^n$, is of
little use in the characterisation of text (cf. Östman, 1978).)

The reader may, in fact, have found that, on reading through
(12), he did try to make connections across the first few sentences
and was more than willing to believe that the next sentence would
provide the element(s) which would allow a coherent interpretation
of the whole set. This expectation that contiguous sentences, with

some cohesive ties, will form a coherent text can be exploited by authors to achieve a particular effect. Consider the following set of sentences from the beginning of a novel.

(13)   Through the fence, between the curling flower spaces, I could see them hitting. They were coming toward where the flag was and I went along the fence. Luster was hunting in the grass by the flower tree. They took the flag out, and they were hitting. Then they put the flag back and they went to the table, and he hit and the other hit. They went on, and I went along the fence. Luster came away from the flower tree and we went along the fence and they stopped and we stopped and I looked through the fence while Luster was hunting in the grass.

When we encounter this first paragraph in William Faulkner's *The Sound and the Fury*, we treat it as a text and, if required, could point to a number of cohesive ties existing across sentence boundaries. But, to return to the question posed earlier, do these cohesive ties lead us to a coherent interpretation of what we have read? They do not, for the simple reason that the author has, in fact, withheld some crucial information (facts about the world described) which we need in order to arrive at that interpretation. It may also be worth noting that some of the cohesive ties which exist in this text (e.g. between *hitting, the flag* and *the table*) can only be identified as such once the reader has been informed that a game of golf is being described. That is, the source of the formal cohesion is, in a sense, outside the text and should not be sought in the words-on-the-page.

It is critically important to distinguish between the 'underlying semantic relation' which we shall go on to discuss, in rather different terms, in the rest of this chapter and in Chapter 7 and those formal realisations which are available to, but not necessarily utilised by, the speaker / writer in constructing what he wants to say.

We shall assert that hearers and readers do not depend upon formal markers of cohesion in order to identify a text as a text. As Halliday & Hasan correctly remark: 'we insist on interpreting any passage as text if there is the remotest possibility of doing so' (1976: 23). Where language occurs contiguously in time and space, we attempt to co-interpret. However, we are constrained in these attempts very powerfully by the conventional presentation of the text. We do not, for example, simply read across the horizontal line of a newspaper ignoring the vertical columns. It is possible to find highly cohesive 'texts' if you read across columns of advertisements or sports reports, for example:

(14)   Flat / house 3–5 bedrooms, nice sunny lounge, double bed
                condition unimportant,   room with fitted wardrobes,
                willing to decorate.   all carpets included.

                             Evening News (Edinburgh), 23 June 1982)

It would, however, seem contrary to attempt to co-interpret such a 'text'. We take account of columns, closeness of lineation, type of print (etc.) in processing written texts, and of voice quality, intonation and pausing in processing spoken language. Within chunks of language which are conventionally presented as texts, the hearer/reader will make every effort to impose a coherent interpretation, i.e. to *treat* the language thus presented as constituting 'text'. We do not see an advantage in trying to determine constitutive formal features which a text must possess to qualify as a 'text'. Texts are what hearers and readers treat as texts.

In the next sub-sections we shall return to several points in the treatment of coreference by Halliday & Hasan where, in this section, we have simply reported their position without comment.

6.1.2 *Endophora*

We want in this section to question the correctness of the exophora / endophora distinction drawn by Halliday & Hasan (at least as it applies to structures other than those involving formal substitution, e.g. *one, do, so*, etc.). You will remember that exophoric co-reference instructs the hearer to look outside the text to identify what is being referred to. Endophoric co-reference instructs the hearer / reader to look inside the text to find what is being referred to. If you look back at the analysis of (6) you will see that the first endophoric chain contains elliptical reference, pronominal reference, lexical substitution and eventually comes out at *Lord Melbourne*. This initial referring expression presumably enables the reader to refer to that 'Lord Melbourne' whom he knows about from general background knowledge. The implication is that, however far into the text the reader reads, subsequent reference to 'Lord Melbourne' must always be resolved by going back up through the chain of reference to the original expression which alone has the power to allow the reader to escape from the text and relate what he is reading about to the real world. Halliday & Hasan write:

Note, finally, that it is characteristic of 3rd person forms that they may be cumulatively anaphoric. One occurrence of *John* at the beginning of a text may be followed by an indefinitely large number of occurrences of *he, him* or *his* all to be interpreted by reference to the original *John*. This phenomenon contributes very markedly to the internal cohesion of a text, since it creates a kind of network of lines of reference, each occurrence being linked to all its predecessors up to and including the initial reference.

(1976: 52)

The view expressed here appears very much the view of an analyst who has worked and reworked relatively small chunks of text which are all capable of being displayed on a single page. Consider for a moment what it would mean for the normal human processor. Consider first the position of a listener. You may meet a friend who will tell you how oddly a person he met in a pub behaved. He may tell you a long series of events, always referring to this individual subsequently as *he*. At the end of this rich imaginary account do you believe that you would still be able to recall the exact form of the original referring expression? If you are unable to recall the exact form, does it follow that you have not been able to interpret what you have been told? Any given individual introduced into a conversation may be identified by a very large number of referring expressions. It seems highly unlikely, in the scenario we suggest here, that hearers would retain in memory the original expression. Similarly if you are reading a novel and encounter a new character introduced on the bottom of one page, and you turn over the page and find this individual subsequently referred to as *he*, it is equally unlikely that it is necessary for you to travel back each time through the anaphoric chain to the original *expression* to be able to achieve a reference. As a processing model this must be implausible. As an occasional strategy for working out who did what in a series of events, or for checking back when one gets 'lost' in the course of reading something, it may be quite reasonable. But this procedure cannot be the norm.

We shall suggest that it seems more likely that the processor establishes a referent in his mental representation of the discourse and relates subsequent references to that referent back to his mental representation, rather than to the original verbal expression in the text. If this view is correct, the distinction between endophoric and exophoric co-reference becomes much harder to draw. In both cases, we must suppose, the processor has a mental representation. In the one case he has a mental representation of what is in the world, in the other he has a mental representation of a world created by the discourse. In each case he must look into his mental representation to determine reference.

6.1.3 *Substitution*

Halliday & Hasan adopt a very straightforward model of co-reference. They assume a simple **substitution** view where an expression may simply be replaced by another in the text. (They are not alone in this view. There is a general approach to the analysis of text which is called 'substitutional text linguistics', see Harweg, 1978.) Consider their comment on text (1), reproduced here as (15):

(15)   Wash and core six cooking apples. Put them into a fireproof dish.

'It is clear that *them* in the second sentence refers back to (is ANAPHORIC to) the *six cooking apples* in the first sentence' (1976: 2). We commented on a similar example in the last section in discussing the endophoric chain relating to 'Lord Melbourne'. If we are interested in how readers proceed through such a text, and as discourse analysts we should be, we have to ask whether the expression *them* in the second sentence really simply refers to the *six cooking apples* in the first sentence. As Källgren remarks: 'The content of a text is not merely an enumeration of referents; an important part of the content is the relations that the text establishes between the referents' (1978: 150). Whereas it is indeed those same 'six cooking apples' which are at issue in the second sentence, it is relevant to note, and for the reader to understand, that they have undergone a change of state. Whereas in the first sentence they were pristine apples, straight from the supermarket, in the second they are 'washed and cored'. Their *description* has changed. In order for the reader to understand this, he is unlikely to base his interpretation, as Morgan (1979) points out, on the substitution principle. Consider a more violent, constructed example:

(16)   Kill an active, plump chicken. Prepare it for the oven, cut it
        into four pieces and roast it with thyme for 1 hour.

Presumably the *identity* of the chicken is preserved, at least until it
is dismembered, but its description has certainly changed. A reader
who simply went back up the endophoric chain and substituted the
expression *an active plump chicken* for the *it* in the last clause
would, in a significant sense, have failed to understand the text.

Since recipes involve particularly rapid and obvious changes of
state, we shall re-examine here part of the recipe presented already
in Chapter 5 as (22).

(17)   Slice the onion finely, brown in the butter and then place in a
        small dish. Put the ground spices into a breakfast cup of water,
        add to the fat in the pan and cook for 3 minutes, stirring the
        while. Now add the chicken, mix well, see that the meat is just
        covered by water and boil for 20 minutes with the lid on the
        pan.
            When the liquid has almost evaporated, continue to cook,
        but stir the chicken till golden brown. Crush the browned
        onion with a spoon . . .

You will remember that the list of ingredients included an onion,
butter, etc. We shall examine some of the points in the text,
particularly where ellipsis occurs, which, following Halliday &
Hasan, are taken as instructions to the reader to look for a previous
expression to substitute within the text.

(17a)   brown Ø in the butter and then place Ø in a small dish

The object to be browned is, clearly, the 'sliced onion', the object to
be placed in a small dish is 'the sliced, browned onion'. It has to be
possible to associate changes of state with the referent and to carry
them (or some of them) through the discourse. How else can we
explain the appearance of the expression *the browned onion* in the
last sentence which we quote here? (We are unable to explain why it
is the predicate *browned* which surfaces rather than *sliced*, since we
have not examined this phenomenon in detail.) However, the
reappearance of identified entities with different descriptions
attached to them does suggest that we need some model of
processing which allows entities to accumulate properties or to
change states as the discourse progresses. (It would be a poor
reader of *David Copperfield* who failed to realise at the end that the

hero was no longer the infant whom he was introduced to at the beginning.) Consider another example of structural ellipsis which instructs the reader to look for an antecedent expression in the text:

(17b)   Now add the chicken Ø

'*Add*' is a verb which takes two arguments, add A to B, so we must supply whatever it is that 'the chicken' is added to. What is this to be? It seems that 'the chicken' needs to be added to 'the fat in the pan which has had onions cooked in it and removed from it (hence, tastes of onion), to which has been added ground spices mixed in a breakfast cup of water and cooked for three minutes while being stirred'. There is no simple textual antecedent. It would be folly for the reader to suppose he could add the chicken to the originally mentioned unmelted 'butter'. Now consider one lexical expression:

(17c)   When *the liquid* has almost evaporated

What 'liquid' is this? Clearly it is not simply the only previously mentioned liquid, which is 'the water'. This 'liquid' contains not only the elements which were mentioned under (17b), but also the juices which have been extracted from 20 minutes' worth of boiling the chicken in that mixture, the tastes which result from that process and, moreover, a concentration of the original taste since much of 'the water' has almost evaporated. In short, if the reader plans to invest in a computerised cook which will prepare meals from recipes, he should avoid the model which operates on a cohesion-type program.

We have attempted to exemplify some problems of the cohesion-view in one type of discourse (recipes) where the problems can be graphically illustrated. The points we have made, however, are not confined to recipes. The following two examples, one from a textbook, the other from a public notice, are presented to demonstrate that substitution cannot take place on a strict replacement of an anaphoric form by an antecedent. Such a replacement would have to take place under a constraint of syntactic identity, so the adjective *anecdotal* in (18) will not fit the slot occupied by the pro-form *one*.

(18)   The child may set the pace. Since the literature is mostly anecdotal, we don't mind offering *one* of our own . . .
                    (from de Villiers & de Villiers, 1978: 206)

In the following example, we must assume that 'it' is an 'act of vandalism' which should be reported:

(19)   STOP   BUS   VANDALS
         by reporting *it* at once
         to the driver or conductor
                    (sign displayed in Edinburgh buses)

Any adequate model of discourse description must be able to accommodate the various connections which do exist in texts (17), (18) and (19). The 'cohesion' model does not. It is, however, only fair to point out that Halliday & Hasan are not concerned to produce a description which accounts for how texts are understood. They are, rather, concerned to examine the linguistic resources available to the speaker / writer to mark cohesive relationships. Their examination of these linguistic resources is rich, interesting and insightful. It is important, however, that the discourse analyst should be clear just what it is that Halliday & Hasan are doing and should not assume that the account of textual relations produced as a *post hoc* analysis of the structure of a completed text should necessarily be revealing about how a processor working 'on-line' as the discourse unfolds experiences that discourse.

6.2 Discourse reference

The traditional semantic view of reference is one in which the relationship of reference is taken to hold between expressions in a text and entities in the world, and that of co-reference between expressions in different parts of a text. We shall present an alternative account of the co-reference relation, paying particular attention to pronouns, in section 6.3. In the traditional approach, the term 'reference' is used, together with 'sense', to discuss lexical meaning. The meaning of a lexical item, such as *chicken*, is partially determined by its sense, that is, the component properties of 'animate', 'feathered', etc., and also determined by its reference, that is, the set of objects in the world to which the expression can be correctly applied. Lyons (1977: ch. 7) provides a detailed account of the background and issues involved in this distinction and suggests that the term 'reference' is better replaced by the term 'denotation' in considerations of lexical meaning. We shall follow his practice and say that, in discussions of lexical semantics, it may prove useful to claim that a lexical item (strictly speaking, a lexeme) has *sense* (component properties of meaning) and *denotation* (a set of objects to which it can correctly be applied). This distinction is also generally covered by the terms 'intension' and 'extension', more commonly found in formal semantics, though there are technical differences which we shall not discuss here (cf. Lyons, 1977: 207ff.). The term *reference* can then be taken out of discussions of lexical meaning and reserved for that function whereby speakers (writers) indicate, via the use of a linguistic expression, the entities they are talking (writing) about.

A further distinction made by Lyons (1977: 182) is worth noting. It is often considered important in formal semantics that the expression used to refer to an entity must, in its description, be true of the entity. That is, if an individual is referred to by the expression *the king of England*, then the description contained in this referring expression must be true of the individual in order for correct reference to take place. However, 'correct' reference in this sense is not normally the criterion by which language-users operate when they refer to individuals in discourse. If a speaker and hearer believe that the man who is married to the present queen of England is, indeed, *the king of England*, then the speaker can, on some occasion, successfully refer to the individual by using that expression. In fact, it need not even be the case that the speaker believes the description to be true, but rather that he believes that, by using this expression, he will enable his hearer to pick out the intended referent. Thus, the concept which interests the discourse analyst is not that of correct (true) reference, but *successful reference*. Successful reference depends on the hearer's identifying, for the purposes of understanding the current linguistic message, the speaker's intended referent, on the basis of the referring expression used.

This last point introduces the notion of 'identifying the speaker's intended referent' which is of crucial importance in any consideration of the interpretation of referring expressions in discourse. Despite the fact that, in some analyses, the idea is put forward that some linguistic expressions have unique and independent reference, we shall insist that, whatever the form of the referring expression, its referential function depends on the speaker's intention on the particular occasion of use. On what does the hearer base his identification of the speaker's intended referent, and what forms do referring expressions take?

6.2.1 *Reference and discourse representations*

An idea which has surfaced at various points in the course of this book (see sections 3.7; 5.3; 6.1.2) is that of a 'discourse representation'. This idea has not been pursued at length for the practical reason that, at the moment, we have no way of describing discourse representations in any limited way. There is a sense in which this whole book is about what must be accommodated within a description of a discourse representation. Briefly, let us say that an analytic distinction can be made between what is in the world and what we might describe as the representation in the mind of a person of what is in the world. This latter concept we can treat as the individual's representation, or model, of the world. (In an individual's representation, there may be entities, such as 'Santa Claus' or 'the tooth fairy', whose existence in the world at large may not be easily attested.) More to the point, in paying attention to a particular piece of discourse, as a sample of experience of the world, the individual may build a specific representation of this particular experience of the world which, of course, will be integrated, to a degree, within his more general representation of the world. This specific representation, or model, arising from a particular discourse, we can characterise as the individual's *discourse representation*. (The alternative term, 'discourse model' is used by some analysts, for example Webber (1978, 1981), to capture a similar concept.)

Given this extremely simple version of what a discourse representation might be, we can go on to suggest that when a writer (speaker) produces a piece of discourse, it will be based on his individual representation of a particular state of affairs. The reader (hearer), as he receives the discourse, will normally try to build a representation (his model) of the state of affairs communicated by the speaker. This basic one-way version of discourse communication is quite obviously an abstraction away from the complex interaction which actually takes place between speakers' versions of hearers' versions of speakers' versions (and so on) of representations, in normal discourse situations. However, this basic version should allow us to see that there is likely to be an inherent mismatch between what is in the speaker's representation and what is the hearer's representation. At best, the hearer is likely to arrive at a representation which is only partially similar to the speaker's and which, moreover, can only ever be a partial reflection of the so-called 'actual' state of affairs which existed in the world. A strong version of this view would be that 'humans understand what is said to them in terms of their own knowledge and beliefs about the world' (Schank, 1979: 400).

When a speaker, on the basis of his representation, uses an expression to pick out an individual entity, he will typically take into consideration those features of his hearer's developing discourse representation which he can depend on the hearer being able to use in identifying the intended referent. Many of those features have been outlined in the earlier chapters of this book. The assumption of a similar general experience of the world, sociocultural conventions, awareness of context and communicative conventions are some of the relevant features. The hearer, for his part, will also generally assume that the speaker is operating with those assumptions (unless he indicates otherwise) and will base his identification of the intended referent on an interpretation of the linguistic expression (or sign) which is consistent with those features which are the basis of the world created by his developing discourse representation.

The use of the term 'identification' in this discussion should be treated with some caution. It is presumably rather a rare occurrence that a hearer's identification of an individual entity in his representation will be an exact replica of that which exists in the speaker's representation. Much of the time, the hearer's 'entity representation' may simply be of a form such as 'the entity X which the speaker referred to by means of the linguistic expression Y'. This can be illustrated with an example from an earlier extract, quoted here as (20).

(20)   My uncle's coming home from Canada.

The 'identity' of the individual described as *my uncle* may have a large number of properties ('called Jack', 'bald', 'smokes cigars', etc.) in the speaker's representation, but, for the hearer, there may only be an identity in terms of 'the individual referred to as the speaker's uncle'. This 'identity' may, of course, accrue properties, such as 'is coming home from Canada', in the course of the discourse, or even non-predictable properties deriving, by analogy, from the hearer's version of what type of entity an 'uncle' typically turns out to be.

Generally, then, the hearer will build a representation of the discourse which will contain representations of entities introduced by the speaker through the use of referring expressions. Clearly, in order for the hearer to do this, he must operate with (and believe that the speaker is also operating with) some regular notion of what types of expressions, under what conditions, are used to refer to entities.

6.2.2 *Referring expressions*

There is a vast literature in philosophy and linguistics on the nature and status of expressions which can, or cannot, be used to refer. Since much of the debate revolves around issues of truth, existence and uniqueness, and concerns itself with single system sentences, cited in isolation from any communicative context, the controversies may appear rather esoteric to the practical discourse analyst. After all, the discourse analyst is largely concerned, in his investigation, with data which is the product of the *actual* use of linguistic expressions in a definable context for a particular purpose, rather than the *potential* use of such expressions. In the course of this book, we have presented a large number of data extracts from which we may draw some examples of referring expressions.

There are some indefinite expressions such as *a man, a rainbow, a beautiful girl, a line*, which, as we pointed out in Chapter 5, are typically used to introduce entities into the discourse. In each of these examples, we can say that the speaker intends the hearer to recognise that there is an individual entity referred to by the expression used. It does not seem to be a necessary condition of this type of introductory reference that the hearer should be able to 'identify uniquely', in any strict sense, the individual referred to. There are, of course, recognisable circumstances in which an indefinite expression is unlikely to be taken as a referring expression. From an earlier extract, we can cite the following example.

(21)   My father was a stonemason.

We would not wish to suggest that the speaker is referring to two distinct individuals by the expressions *my father* and *a stonemason* and asserting that these two individuals were, in fact, the same person. Rather, the indefinite noun phrase is being predicated of the subject noun phrase in much the same way as other descriptive expressions (e.g. *left-handed*) are. So, one of the circumstances in which indefinite noun phrases are *not* used as referring expressions is when they appear as the complement of the verb 'to be'.

The other generally recognised condition in which indefinite noun phrases may not be treated as referential is when they appear in linguistic contexts which are, according to Quine (1960), 'referentially opaque'. Referential opacity can occur after certain verbs, such as *look for* and *want*. The classic examples take the following form:

(22)   Marion is looking for a rubber.

(23)   Virginia wants a new job.

It may be that, in uttering these sentences on a particular occasion, a speaker does have a 'specific' referent in mind. That is, the analysis would be that there is a (particular) rubber which Marion is looking for. However, the indefinite expression, *a rubber*, could be used to mean 'any rubber', and in this 'non-specific' reading, it is not being used referentially. (See Lyons, 1977: 187ff. for a more extended discussion of the 'specific–non-specific' distinction.) It may be that the so-called 'ambiguity' of sentences like (22) and (23) arises because they are cited without contexts. We would suggest that, in the analysis of naturally occurring discourse, the analyst will have clear contextual or co-textual cues to guide his assignment of referential or non-referential use to these indefinite expressions. He may also be able to appeal to phonological or more general paralinguistic clues in deciding when other indefinite expressions, such as *someone, something*, are being used to refer to a particular individual or not. That is, in uttering the sentences in (24) and (25), the speaker can indicate, intonationally, for example, that it is his intention to refer to a specific individual.

(24)   Someone (and I know who) won't like this proposal.

(25)   Someone (and I don't know who) has stolen my bicycle.

The use of proper names as referring expressions is generally a less controversial issue. Examples from previous extracts are *Rosanna Spearman, Mr Bennett, Elizabeth, old man McArthur* and *Plato*. It is sometimes suggested that proper names are used to identify individuals uniquely. We would add the caveat that they may be so used only in specific contexts. It is easy to see why a name like *Elizabeth*, used to refer to an individual, must depend, for its referential assignment, on an identification of a particular individual in a particular context. There are, after all, a large number of Elizabeths in the world. Some proper names, however, are taken to have a unique referent, regardless of context, and *Plato* is probably a good example. This view is extremely misleading. We might say that there is an overwhelming tendency to treat the proper name *Plato* as being used to refer to the Greek philosopher, but that contextual considerations can override this tendency. In a rather trivial way, a person can obviously refer to her child, her dog or her boat as *Plato*, given the existing socio-cultural conventions for naming entities. In a more subtle way, following a suggestion by Nunberg (1978), we can note the use of the linguistic expression *Plato* to refer to an entity other than the Greek philosopher, as in (26).

(26)   Plato is on the bottom shelf of the bookcase.

It is clearly not the individual, but rather some publication of his writings, which is being referred to. Note that this assignment of reference depends, for the reader, on the type of predicate attached to the referring expression. We shall discuss this point in greater detail in section 6.3.3. Since we can use proper names with this extended referential function, it would be unwise to maintain that they have any uniquely identifying function.

We should also point out that proper names can, as we noted with indefinite expressions, be used with a descriptive, and so non-referential, function. Such uses are generally signalled by the presence of either the definite or indefinite article, as in (27).

(27)   Young Smith is the Plato of the fourth form.

A final observation on the use of proper names as referring expressions is to do with the 'role-related' aspect which we have already mentioned in Chapter 2. Individuals in the world do not have single, unvarying names, or even titles, and so the use of a proper name to refer to an individual will typically pick out an individual in a particular 'role'. An individual can be referred to as *Professor Young, Mr John Young, John*, etc. on different occasions by different speakers. Successful reference, in context, may depend crucially on selecting the most appropriate 'name' with which to identify an individual for a particular hearer or audience.

The most generally discussed type of referring expression is the definite noun phrase. Examples from extracts elsewhere in this book are *the matron, the priest, the red triangle, the white figure, the browned onion, the trolley,* and *the man who took the photographs.* Such expressions are clearly discourse-specific in their referential function and, as we demonstrated in Chapter 5, have a distinct distribution in some types of discourse. The paradigm uses of definite noun phrases are in subsequent reference to an entity which has already been mentioned in an earlier part of the discourse or to salient objects in the physical context. A related use is in reference to entities which Prince (1981) describes as 'inferrables' (*a car – the driver*), a concept which we will discuss in greater detail in section 7.8 later. For an extended consideration of the sources of 'definiteness', the reader is referred to Christopherson (1939), Hawkins (1978), and the contributions in van der Auwera (1980).

We shall mention here only one or two of the interesting features of definite noun phrases, since many of the issues relating to definite reference have been covered, in connection with more general discourse processes, elsewhere in this book (see sections 2.3; 5.2.1; 7.8). One widely discussed point made by Donnellan (1966) is that some definite noun phrases, even as subjects of their sentences, may be used 'non-referentially'. The distinction Donnellan draws is between a situation in which one refers to a specific individual by using an expression such as *the killer* and an alternative situation in which one uses the expression *the killer*, not for a specific individual, but meaning 'whoever did the killing'. The first use Donnellan says is 'referential', the second he describes as 'attributive'. Thus, in Donnellan's 'attributive' use of a definite noun phrase, the intention of the speaker is not necessarily referential. Perhaps a good illustrative example of Donnellan's point is the first sentence of a newspaper article, presented as (28), which appeared during a manhunt after a policeman had been shot.

(28)   The gun-crazy double killer being stalked in a forest may be forcing a hostage to feed and hide him.

(*Daily Mirror*, 28 June 1982)

Donnellan's argument is aimed at the prerequisite, in some philosophical approaches to the analysis of definite descriptions, that the expression used must pick out a single individual in the world in order for the reference to be correct (i.e. true). The lengthy description in (28) does not, strictly speaking, do this, since the individual so described may not be identifiable at all. No one knows if the definite noun phrase picks out an individual, called Jim Miller, for example. The individual, 'whoever he is', is only discussable in terms of the 'attributes' known about him. This distinction, though offering some insight into how some definite descriptions come to be formed (i.e. via 'attributes'), is actually of only limited interest in the analysis of discourse reference. The discourse analyst, like the hearer (and the reader), is continually having to accept that definite expressions used by a speaker (or writer) are intended to refer to an individual in the world. In listening to a story which begins as in (29), the hearer generally cannot assess whether the expression *the man* 'correctly' picks out an individual in the world, or not.

(29)   Last night a man and a girl came to the house collecting for charity. The man acted pretty drunk . . .

The working assumption, however, is that, for the purposes of the discourse at hand, the speaker intends to use the expression *the man* to refer to an individual and, moreover, as Searle (1969) points out, intends that the hearer recognise that intention. We could say exactly the same of the writer of (28). In the analysis of discourse, Donnellan's 'attributive' uses will generally be treated as intended references. Although they may not pick out an individual 'in the world', they will pick out (or even establish) an individual in the hearer's representation of the discourse.

The idea that hearers pick out speakers' intended referents, on a fairly loose interpretation of what 'attributes' are included in the definite descriptions, is certainly necessary to account for an interesting set of examples presented by Nunberg (1978, 1979).

Working from Quine's (1960, 1969) notion of 'deferred ostension', Nunberg claims that we frequently succeed in referring by using a definite noun phrase which contains a description that has a specific relation to the intended individual referent. The hearer's knowledge of this specific relation is assumed. Thus, a restaurant waiter going off duty might say (30) to his replacement.

(30)   The ham sandwich is sitting at table 20.

Clearly, no analysis which requires a direct relationship between the literal meaning of referring expressions and the properties of the referent will ever account for successful communication via sentences of this type. Even more interesting is Nunberg's suggestion that the same waiter could equally well point at a ham sandwich and say (31).

(31)   He is sitting at table 20.

We shall discuss this and other uses of pronominals in section 6.3. Nunberg's point is that such uses of definite noun phrases as referring expressions are not restricted to 'quasi-metaphorical' examples like (30). They are fairly normal in the sentences presented here in (32) and (33).

(32)   a. The chicken pecked the ground.
          b. The chicken with bean sauce was delicious.

(33)   a. The newspaper weighs five pounds.
          b. The newspaper fired John.

In (32a) we would normally understand *the chicken* to be a reference to the type of bird and in (32b) to the type of meat. In (33a) *the newspaper* is an edition or copy of the publication and in (33b) it is the company or even the publisher. Nunberg's argument is directed against a purely semantic account of reference and for a functional or pragmatic account. We have already indicated our support for such a view. An important point made by Nunberg is that our interpretation of expressions such as *the chicken* and *the newspaper*, when used referentially, is based on our pragmatic knowledge of *the range of reference* of such expressions, which is, on a particular occasion of use, strictly constrained and 'determined by the nature of the predication, and by the conversational context' (1978: 31). We would say that these factors influence the hearer's (reader's) representation of discourse entities, not only for definite descriptions and proper names, but, more crucially, when pronominals are encountered in discourse. Before going on to consider the referential function of pronouns in discourse, let us consider a particularly effective example of how an unusual set of definite noun phrases is used to refer, anaphorically, to a group of individuals.

(34)   Turbaned ladies hobbled towards the cathedral, scuffing the
         dust with feet too splayed and calloused to admit the wearing
         of shoes. Their cottons were printed with leaves and lions and
         portraits of military dictators. They hauled themselves into the
         teak pews . . . [Six intervening paragraphs describe others
         arriving at the cathedral and the beginning of the service.]
             At the Credo, the ladies sighed, heaved their thighs and got
         to their feet. Letters, lions, leaves and military dictators
         rustled and recomposed themselves.
                         (Bruce Chatwin, *The Viceroy of Ouidah*, Picador,
                                                       1982, pp. 14–15)

The 'range of reference' of the expressions *letters, lions, leaves* and *military dictators* is, isolated from this text, large, yet the effect of the predicate, *rustled and recomposed themselves*, and the co-text, yields an immediate (and entertaining) discourse representation for the reader of who these *ladies* are, with respect to the 'ladies' already described, and the motions they are going through.

6.3   **Pronouns in discourse**

From a formal point of view, pronouns are, as we demonstrated in Chapter 5, the paradigm examples of expressions used by speakers to refer to 'given' entities. Pronouns are typically uttered with low pitch in spoken discourse and, as such, are types of referring expressions which, in Chafe's terms (1976), are phonologically and lexically 'attenuated'. Because of their lack of 'content', they have become the crucial test-case items for any theory of reference. After all, to what does the expression *it* refer, in isolation? The fact that there is no reasonable answer to this question has led many linguists to suggest that a pronominal such as *it* is not actually a referring expression, but can only be used co-referentially, that is, within a text which also includes a full nominal expression. The relationship between the full nominal expression and the pronominal expression is then described as an antecedent-anaphor relation, as we have noted already in section 6.1.1. The occasional use of pronouns in situations such as (35) is treated as an example of deixis and virtually dismissed as unrelated to the more serious business of determining how anaphoric pronominals receive their interpretation. (An exception to this general tendency is Lyons (1979) who argues, convincingly, that the anaphoric use is derived from the more basic deictic use of pro-forms in the language.)

(35)   (A large dog approaches A and B. A says to B:)
         I hope it's friendly.

In other treatments, the use of *it* in (35) is described as an example of 'pragmatically controlled anaphora' (cf. Hankamer & Sag, 1977; Partee, 1978; Yule, 1979). In this use of the term 'anaphora', the requirement of an antecedent expression in the text is not considered crucial. In this sense, 'anaphora' covers any expression which the speaker uses in referring on the basis of which the hearer will be able to pick out the intended referent given certain contextual and co-textual conditions. For obscure historical reasons, the term 'anaphora', as it is generally used, is restricted almost exclusively to 'pronominal referring expressions'. We will follow this practice throughout this section. One other aspect of the treatment of pronouns, or anaphors, should be noted, because it determines the nature of the discussion which follows. Both theoretical and experimental work on pronouns has concentrated almost exclusively on the interpretation, and not the production, of pronouns. This probably reflects the general fact that, as Tyler (1978: 227) observes, 'most of the linguistic literature is written from the hearer's point of view'. Thus, in our consideration of existing views and analyses of pronouns in discourse, we shall be primarily interested in determining what is required in an adequate account of the interpretation of pronouns in discourse.

6.3.1 *Pronouns and antecedent nominals*

It is initially quite a plausible notion that the interpretation of the pronoun in (36) is arrived at by a simple process of replacing *it* with *my hair*, as in (36a).

(36)   I've just had my hair curled and *it* looks windblown all the time.

(36a)   *My hair* looks windblown all the time.

Such a view has been described already in section 6.1.2, and is normally expressed in terms of the pronominal 'referring back' to its antecedent nominal (cf. Carpenter & Just, 1977a: 236), or in terms of the pronominal 'substituting for' the antecedent (cf. Tyler, 1978: 336). This general view has been characterised as the 'pronominal surrogate hypothesis' by McKay & Fulkerson (1979). They demonstrate, in an experimental situation, that it is not the case that 'the nature of the antecedent completely determines the interpretation of the pronoun' (1979: 661). We attempted to show with Halliday & Hasan's *six cooking apples – them* example, (15), that the substitution concept was misleading. We argued that if a 'change of state' predicate is attached to a nominal expression, then subsequent pronominals must be interpreted in terms of that predicate. The experimental work of Garvey et al. (1975) and Caramazza et al. (1977), using what they call 'verbs of implicit causality', lends support to this argument.

We might suggest, then, that a better analysis of *it* in extract (36) would involve not only the antecedent nominal expression, but also the accompanying predicate, as shown in (36b). (Throughout this discussion we indicate only the *salient* predicates required in interpretation. There are, of course, many other predicates which could be listed each time a pronoun is represented in this way.)

(36b)   *My hair which I've just had curled* looks windblown all the time.

Notice that the nature of the entity to which *looks windblown* applies is different in (36b) from that in (36a).

In support of this view, there is Chastain's observation that, in some discourses, 'the descriptive content of the anaphorically connected singular terms accumulates over time' (1975: 232) (see also the full representations listed for discourse anaphors in Webber, 1978).

6.3.2 *Pronouns and antecedent predicates*

The representation proposed in (36b) for the pronoun in (36) may seem to make the information carried by a pronoun unnecessarily complex. There is evidence, however, that speakers' use of pronouns is indeed influenced by the predicates attached to antecedent nominals. Extracts (37) and (38) are presented as two examples.

(37)   There's two different ladies go up to the whist and both have a wig and *they*'re most natural.

(38)   Even an apprentice can make over twenty pound a week and *they* don't get much tax [taken] from that.

The correct interpretation of the reference of *they* in (37) depends on the hearer's understanding that there are two wigs and not one, as the nominal antecedent (*a wig*) by itself would suggest. In (38), there is a similar problem, with a singular nominal antecedent and a plural pronoun. By itself, the expression *an apprentice* might be interpreted as introducing a particular individual into the discourse. However, when interpreted in the context of the predicate *can make over twenty pound a week*, it has to be taken, not as a particular individual, but as *any* individual from a set of individuals to whom the lexical expression *apprentice* can be applied. The choice of subsequent pronoun (e.g. *he* or *they*) then simply reflects the speaker's perspective on whether he is considering a typical individual or a set of such individuals. The speaker of (38) chooses the latter. Examples (37) and (38) present a grammatical mismatch in terms of number agreement between antecedent nominal and subsequent pronoun. Extracts (39) and (40), both taken from descriptions of traffic accidents, seem to present a mismatch in terms of gender agreement.

(39)   There's a car going up the road and *he* comes to a crossroads.

(40)   The second car hasn't got time to avoid the person who swerved away to avoid the car that was pulling out and *he* hits *it*.

In example (39), the hearer is clearly required to infer that a car moving along a road must have a driver and that it is this inferred driver who the *he* is used to refer to. Example (40) presents a more complex problem. Despite the presence of both a human and a non-human antecedent for *he* and *it*, the most natural interpretation of what happened requires us to match the grammatically 'human' pronoun with the 'non-human' antecedent, and the 'non-human' pronoun with the 'human' antecedent. Such assignments appear to be made on the basis of the roles of the two referents with regard to an antecedent predicate and a consequent predicate (i.e. X hasn't got time to avoid Y and X hits Y).

Whatever the proper explanation for the natural assignment in (40), it certainly does not seem to be on the basis of an antecedent nominal / anaphoric pronominal substitution relationship.

6.3.3 *Pronouns and 'new' predicates*

In considering the basis for determining referents from pronouns, we have concentrated so far on examples where some type of nominal antecedent does exist in the discourse prior to the occurrence of the pronoun. The inadequacy of the substitution approach is even more apparent in those situations where a pronoun occurs in a discourse with no antecedent nominal at all. It may be of interest to consider such examples in terms of their 'given/new' structure, as described in Chapter 5. That is, the speaker may structure his message in such a way that some 'new' information is attached to a 'given' element (i.e. a pronoun), intending to provide the hearer with a 'given / new' interpretive procedure. However, the hearer may have to reverse that procedure and use the 'new' information to decide what the 'given' referent must have been.

The use of the pronoun *she* near the end of extract (41) provides one example of this process.

(41)   (Talking about the First World War) I used to go about with a chap – I don't know whether he's still alive now or not – but – there was nine – ten – eleven in the family altogether – two girls – and nine boys – and *she* lost eight sons one after the other

In example (41) there is no linguistic expression which could be treated as the direct antecedent for *she*. Of course, we can propose that if the speaker is talking about a *family* and there is a female referent (*she*) who *lost eight sons*, then we can infer that it is 'the mother' the speaker is referring to. Notice that, if the hearer does follow this procedure, then he is using 'new' information to determine a 'given' referent.

Example (41) raises a serious problem for any analysis of pronouns as conveying 'given' information which depends on a referential assignment via information in the preceding discourse. Unfortunately, one of the most influential views of how we process pronouns in discourse, the 'given – new strategy' of Clark & Clark

(1977), is based on a dependency of this sort. In the following extracts from conversational discourse, the examples of pronouns used to realise 'given' information should 'serve as an address directing the listener to where "new" information should be stored' (Haviland & Clark, 1974: 520).

(42)   one of our main jobs in the Botanics is writing on the flora of Turkey + *they* . . .

(43)   I have a cousin who's very deaf + and she can't hear Jessie + because Jessie speaks too loudly + you see *she* . . .

(44)   Oh I was on the bus and + *he* . . .

We think it should be obvious that in none of these fragments, (42)–(44), is there a situation in which 'listeners can be confident that the given information conveys information they can identify uniquely' (Clark & Clark, 1977: 92). Rather, there is, on each occasion, more than one potential referent for the pronoun. The interpretation of the reference of these pronouns depends on what is predicated of them, and is not solely determined by information in the preceding discourse. The reader can, of course, make predictions about the referential assignment of these pronouns on the basis of extracts (42)–(44) alone. Those predictions can be confirmed (or not) by consideration of the subsequent predicates, as shown in (42a)–(44a).

(42a)   one of our main jobs in the Botanics is writing on the flora of Turkey + *they* don't have the scientists to do it.

In this example, it seems that the speaker has assumed that, if he is talking about a country, he can refer to a group of people in that country without having to assert explicitly that 'Turkey has people in it'. If that is a required inference on the hearer's part, then it can only take place after the hearer has heard the 'new' predicate attached to the pronoun *they*. We might also note that, if 'the people of Turkey' are part of the extended domain of reference of an expression such as *Turkey*, then yet another psycholinguistic processing claim regarding pronouns is undermined. Sanford & Garrod (1981) claim that 'pronouns can never be used to identify implied entities in the extended domain of reference'. Clearly, they can, as in extract (42a) and again in (44a).

Extract (43a) exhibits a resolution problem similar to the one described in example (40) earlier, where it is not a case of a missing antecedent, but of a choice between competing antecedents.

(43a)   I have a cousin who's very deaf + and she can't hear Jessie + because Jessie speaks too loudly + you see *she* shouts at her

Given the 'new' predicate in (43a), the hearer can choose the most likely referent for the *she*, probably on the basis of the 'roles' filled by the two participants in the situation.

(44a)   oh I was on the bus and + *he* didn't stop at the right stop

Just as a car involved in a car crash is most likely to have a driver, as in (39), so too is a bus carrying passengers. It may be, of course, that there is only a limited set of such 'situations' in which pronouns can be used to refer to implied entities. If that is the case, then it is our job to characterise the limited set, rather than describe the processing of pronouns as if the set did not exist (e.g. Clark & Clark, 1977) or to claim that such processing *never* takes place (e.g. Sanford & Garrod, 1981).

Examples (42)–(44) have been presented as illustration of the fact that we need to take 'new' predicates into account when assigning an interpretation to some 'given' elements, such as pronouns in discourse. These examples may also provide support for a point made earlier in section 6.2.1, that speakers' and hearers' representations of a discourse are unlikely to be perfect matches. If a hearer has to construct, from what the speaker says, an interpretation of the most likely intended referent, then interpreting pronouns may present special problems. Speaker D, in the following conversational fragment, indicates (with his question) the problem he is having with determining one of speaker C's intended referents.

(45)   (both speakers are looking at a photograph in a book)
        C: it's quite an interesting book actually + *he* was a surgeon and photographer +
        D: a surgeon and photographer?
        C: the man who took the photographs
        D: oh I see I see

It may be, of course, that, unlike speaker D in extract (45), we do not always indicate when we have failed to identify the speaker's intended referent. It is difficult, however, to imagine what type of evidence (other than an indication by one of the participants of confusion) we could reliably use to characterise such potential failures on other occasions, e.g. in examples (37)–(44).

6.3.4 *Interpreting pronominal reference in discourse*

On what does the hearer base his interpretation of the referent of a pronoun in discourse? We have suggested in this section that he may have to use his knowledge of (some of) the elements listed below.

an antecedent nominal expression

and / or   an antecedent predicate expression
and / or   an implicit antecedent predicate
and / or   the 'roles' of antecedent nominal expressions
and / or   the 'new' predicates attached to the pronoun

We have also noted in section 5.2.1 that, in some types of discourse, pronouns are most typically used to refer to 'current' entities. It may be that hearers can use this type of regularity as a basis for their referential assignments. That is, in extract (46), the hearer can interpret the pronoun *it* as a reference to the 'current entity' (*the square*) and not to the 'displaced entity' (*the page*), even though the grammatical categories (number and gender) do not provide distinguishing clues.

(46)   in the middle of the page there's + a square + quite large +
        and near the bottom of *it* + there's a number five + in red

Alternatively, in other types of discourse, there may be an overwhelming tendency to reserve pronouns for reference to 'topic entities' in the discourse, as we noted in section 4.3.2. In extract (47), the hearer can interpret all uses of feminine gender pronouns as references to the main character (*the woman*) and not to the subsidiary character (*the old lady*).

(47)   when the woman arrives at the checkout counter + there's an
        old lady following *her* + and + *she* pays for all the goods
        except for + the bottle in *her* bag + I think + outside the
        supermarket the + the old lady catches *her* up + and produces
        the bag − the bottle and + I think *she* must have been charged
        with shoplifting +

These last two strategies of reference-resolution suggest that the proper direction of future research in this area should not be limited to further investigations of how people interpret pronouns in decontextualised sentence pairs, but rather should be based on more naturally occurring discourse of different types. We hope that our presentation of some of the complexities involved in the interpretation of pronominal reference will stimulate such research and discourage the reader from accepting any simplistic 'substitution' view of the function of pronouns in discourse.

7
Coherence in the interpretation of discourse

7.1 Coherence in discourse

One of the pervasive illusions which persists in the analysis of language is that we understand the meaning of a linguistic message solely on the basis of the words and structure of the sentence(s) used to convey that message. We certainly rely on the syntactic structure and lexical items used in a linguistic message to arrive at an interpretation, but it is a mistake to think that we operate only with this literal input to our understanding. We can recognise, for example, when a writer has produced a perfectly grammatical sentence from which we can derive a literal interpretation, but which we would not claim to have understood, simply because we need more information. Extract (1), the first sentence of a novel, may provide an illustration of this point.

(1) Within five minutes, or ten minutes, no more than that, three of the others had called her on the telephone to ask her if she had heard that something had happened out there.
  (Tom Wolfe, *The Right Stuff*, Bantam Books, 1981)

The novelist is, of course, leading his reader to read on and find out just what the first sentence, though literally complete, has only partially described.

At the opposite extreme, we can point to linguistic messages which are not presented in sentences and consequently can't be discussed in terms of syntactic well-formedness, but which are readily interpreted. Our lives are full of such 'fragments', as in extract (2) from an Edinburgh University notice board and extracts (3) and (4) from newspaper advertisements.

(2) Epistemics Seminar: Thursday 3rd June, 2.00 p.m.
  Steve Harlow (Department of Linguistics, University of York).
  'Welsh and Generalised Phrase Structure Grammar'

Although it is not stated, literally, in this discourse fragment, we know that Steve Harlow (and not a person called Epistemics Seminar) will give a talk (and not write or sing or show a film) with the title shown in quotation marks; in the University of Edinburgh (no, not York, that's where he comes from); on the nearest 3rd June to the time of the notice being displayed, and so on.

(3)   Self Employed Upholsterer
        Free estimates. 332 5862.

(4)   Find the Ball. Win a House. Page 4.

If we encounter (3), we are expected to understand that the source of the advertisement is the *upholsterer* and that he or she will provide *free estimates* of the cost of upholstery work which the reader may need to be done. It is not a random assortment of words and numbers. Although it is not stated in (4), we should expect that on *page 4* of the newspaper, there will be a competition with the task determined by the first sentence and the prize detailed in the second. Despite the imperative forms, the required interpretation of the first two sentences involves the first as a condition for the second.

We might say that, in addition to our knowledge of sentential structure, we also have a knowledge of other standard formats in which information is conveyed. We also rely on some principle that, although there may be no formal linguistic links connecting contiguous linguistic strings, the fact of their contiguity leads us to interpret them as connected. We readily fill in any connections which are required.

This last point we have already mentioned in connection with the assumption of **coherence** which people bring to the interpretation of linguistic messages. Yet, the assumption of coherence will only produce one particular interpretation in which the elements of the message are seen to be connected, with or without overt linguistic connections between those elements. On the assumption of coherence, extract (3) could be interpreted as an advertisement by someone looking for an upholsterer. There is nothing in the literal message to discourage such an interpretation. There are several things in the *reader*, however, which lead him to avoid this interpretation. The most important of these is the reader's (or hearer's) effort to arrive at the writer's (or speaker's) *intended* *meaning* in producing a linguistic message. We have already appealed to this notion in our discussion of discourse reference in Chapter 6. More formal arguments in support of this view of interpreting meaning can be found in Grice (1957) and Schiffer (1972).

On what does the reader base his interpretation of the writer's intended meaning? In addition to the assumption of coherence, the principles of analogy, local interpretation and general features of context, already discussed in Chapter 2, there are the regularities of discourse structure outlined in Chapters 3 and 4, and the regular features of information structure organisation detailed in Chapter 5. These are aspects of discourse which the reader can use in his interpretation of a particular discourse fragment. Yet, the reader also has more knowledge than knowledge of discourse. He knows for example, that *Steve Harlow* is much more likely to be the name of a person than *Epistemics Seminar*. This is a form of conventional socio-cultural knowledge. He also knows that the purpose of the linguistic message, its function in communicative terms, is that of an announcement and not a warning (or a promise, or whatever) partly because of its location, partly because of its form, and partly because of the same socio-cultural knowledge that leads him to know what are, and what are not, usual names for people. He may, of course, have some highly specific local knowledge, deriving from the fact that he is a linguist, has met Steve Harlow, knows of his interest in Phrase Structure Grammar and so on. On the basis of this, he may infer that Steve Harlow is going to use the Welsh language to exemplify certain aspects of Phrase Structure Grammars in the way that Gazdar (another element of specific local knowledge) has done with English. With such an inference, the reader may be said to have gone beyond the discourse-producer's intended message. As we shall demonstrate, however, there is a wide range of possible inferences made by readers in interpreting discourse and it is not always easy to determine which were intended by the text-producer and which were not.

We have isolated three aspects of the process of interpreting a speaker's / writer's intended meaning in producing discourse. These involve computing the communicative function (how to *take* the message), using general socio-cultural knowledge (facts about the world) and determining the inferences to be made. We shall discuss these in more detail in the course of this chapter and consider proposals which have been made to account for these aspects of discourse understanding.

7.2 Computing communicative function

As we pointed out in Chapter 1, there has been a long tradition among social anthropologists and ethnographers studying the language of speech communities of assuming that speakers convey both social and propositional meanings when they produce particular utterance forms in particular contexts. (For relatively early work in this tradition, see Malinowski, 1935.) In recent years there has been a development of interest in the 'social interaction' aspect of language use. Much of this work has been carried out by sociolinguists who have attempted to describe how an utterance can 'count as' a social action such as a greeting or a promise or, in the case of extract (2), an announcement rather than a warning. We shall consider some brief examples used to support the view that utterances must be treated as 'actions' of different types and review the theoretical and descriptive frameworks developed in support of this approach.

Labov (1970) argues that there are 'rules of interpretation which relate what is said to what is done' and it is on the basis of such social, but not linguistic, rules that we interpret some conversational sequences as coherent and others as non-coherent. As an example of a non-coherent conversational sequence, Labov quotes the following example of a doctor talking to a schizophrenic patient, from Laffal (1965: 85).

(5)   A: What's your name?
         B: Well, let's say you might have thought you had something
            from before, but you haven't got it any more.
         A: I'm going to call you Dean.

Labov points out that the recognition of coherence or incoherence in conversational sequences is not based on a relationship between utterances, but 'between the actions performed with those utterances'. Other analysts have attempted to develop this point, frequently basing their discussions on examples such as (6) and (7).

(6)   A: What time is it?
         B: Well, the postman's been already.

This example, quoted in Brown & Levinson (1978: 63), is used to show that the assumption of rationality on B's part leads us to assume that he is providing an answer to the question asked, and so on to the conclusion that the time is past 11 a.m., for example. The next example is taken from Widdowson (1979a: 96) and illustrates a coherent piece of conversational discourse which exhibits no cohesive links between the two sentences involved.

(7)   A: Can you go to Edinburgh tomorrow?
        B: B.E.A. pilots are on strike.

Widdowson claims that B's reply is to be taken as a negative answer to the question, because the strike will prevent the speaker flying to Edinburgh. This is clearly one interpretation of the speaker's intended meaning but we could also suggest others; for example, that the speaker intends a 'don't know' response because he is not yet sure whether he will try some alternative transport. Whatever the intended meaning, we are in no doubt that B's utterance *counts as* a response and not just a gratuitous statement about the way the world is.

The use of some linguistic elements, such as the conjunction *because* (*'cause*) in the following two extracts, would be claimed to be explainable only in terms of an utterance-as-action analysis.

(8)   A: but you'd have telephones around
        B: mm – oh yes . . . I've had the telephone since nineteen
           thirty eight (hmm) oh they were on a long while I think
           before that
        A: 'cause there was a man in . . .

(9)   What's the time, because I've got to go out at eight?

Example (8) is taken from a recorded conversation which was presented more fully as (12) in Chapter 3. Example (9) is quoted in Levinson (1980: 8). The second example was used by Levinson to demonstrate that a conjunction like *because* is not only used to connect two clauses in a complex sentence. It can also be used to introduce the reason for asking a question, as in (9), or for introducing a particular subject into a conversation, as in (8). In other words, the structure of the above examples is not that normally associated with *because* as a logical connector (P because Q), but is as follows:

        I mention / ask   P   because   Q.

Consequently, our understanding of examples (8) and (9) is based, not on an interpretation of the sentences-on-the-page, but on our assumption that a reason is being expressed for an *action* performed in speaking. The action, and the reason for it, are to be identified by virtue of their location within a conventional structure of spoken interaction. This conventional structure provides an account of how some utterances which are apparently unconnected in formal terms (lack cohesion) may be interpreted within a particular genre of spoken interaction, say conversation, as forming a coherent sequence. Widdowson (1978: 29) presents the following example:

(10)   A: That's the telephone.
        B: I'm in the bath.
        A: O.K.

Widdowson suggests that it is only by recognising the action performed by each of these utterances within the conventional sequencing of such actions that we can accept this sequence as coherent discourse. The conventional sequencing may be presented as in (11):

(11)   A requests B to perform action
        B states reason why he cannot comply with request
        A undertakes to perform action

Such a representation yields a description of conversational discourse as a form of social interaction. A similar analysis could be applied to a series of gestures, as in (12):

(12)   (domestic evening scene: husband and wife watching television)
        A indicates by pointing and tapping his ear that he can hear the telephone
        B points to the cat asleep on her lap
        A shrugs and gets up

The analysis of the *interaction* can be made without taking account of the language employed by the speakers. It is typical of many discussions of discourse structure which rely on an analysis of sequences of actions, that rather little attention is paid to the linguistic aspects of the realisations of these actions. In discussing discourse structure in these terms, Coulthard (1977: 7) argues that 'the structure, or constraints on the next speaker, cannot be expressed in *grammatical* terms . . . the linguistic *form* of the utterance is almost irrelevant' (original emphases). A rather similar view is taken by Sinclair & Coulthard (1975: 13): 'the level of language function in which we are centrally interested is . . . the level of the function of a particular utterance, in a particular social situation and at a particular place in a sequence, as a specific contribution to a developing discourse'. Sinclair & Coulthard are concerned to examine the structure of discourse in classroom interaction. They identify five discoursal categories: lesson, transaction, exchange, move, act. Whereas it is, in principle, possible that they could identify some forms of utterance which characterise the boundaries of a lesson (59–60), it is clear that no forms which are unique to 'lessons' exist. 'Lesson' is clearly a sociologically determined category rather than a linguistically determined category. The 'discoursal' category 'transaction' is described thus (1975: 25):

(13)   a. there must be a preliminary move in each transaction
        b. there must be one medial move, but there may be any number of them
        c. there can be a terminal move but not necessarily.

It is clear that the structure represented here would cover a 'transaction' like that represented in (11) which, as we showed in (12) may equally well be used to discuss the structure of non-linguistic social interaction. The categories 'exchange, move and act' can be demonstrated to apply satisfactorily to an analysis of a non-linguistic interaction like a tennis match. They could be used to describe 'the winning of a point' / 'the service' or 'the volley' / and 'the act of serving' or 'the act of hitting a backhand return', respectively. This breadth of application may yield categories which are useful in the investigation of structure in social behaviour, and certainly illuminates the incidence of distributions of propositionally contentless items like *well* and *now*. It is not clear, however, that this creation of a complex taxonomy serves to illuminate our understanding of how participants in an interaction understand what the speaker means by what he says as well as a general appeal to Grice's maxims and the principles of analogy and local interpretation would do.

A more promising approach to the problem of social meaning

from the discourse analyst's point of view, is offered by a consideration of that area of conversation analysis which investigates **turn-taking**. The most influential work in this area is reported in Sacks et al. (1974), Schegloff (1968), Schegloff & Sacks (1973), Jefferson (1972, 1973), and, more recently, in Schenkein (ed.) (1978). The aim of this type of analysis of conversational discourse is to identify the regularities of conversational structure by describing the ways in which participants take turns at speaking. There are some easily identifiable regularities in the ordering of those two-turn units described as **adjacency pairs**. These can take the form of Greeting–Greeting, as in (14) or Question–Answer as in (15).

(14)	A: Hello.	(15)	A: How are you?
	B: Hi.		B: Fine.

With this type of data, the notion of the 'turn' as a unit of analysis seems quite reasonable. However, most conversational data consists of more substantial 'turns' in which several utterances can occur, or in which the basic adjacency pair organisation is difficult to determine. In extract (16), we might suggest that some of the interrogative forms function as both answers and questions, and that the final declarative form is not, in fact, an answer to any of the questions.

(16)	George:	Did you want an ice lolly or not?
	Zee:	What kind have they got?
	George:	How about orange?
	Zee:	Don't they have Bazookas?
	George:	Well here's twenty pence + you ask him

The structure of this extract could be partially characterised as a *sequence*, following a suggestion by Schegloff (1972) that the adjacency pair structure can be disrupted by an 'insertion sequence' which delays the answer-part to one question-part of a pair until another answer to a different question has been provided. This is intuitively reasonable, but the immediate question which springs to mind is how does the analyst determine when an interrogative form counts as a question in an adjacency pair, or as a part of an insertion sequence, or even, as an answer? This type of question is never really raised by those undertaking the analysis of **conversational interaction**, largely because little attempt is made to discuss the relationship between linguistic form and the interactive functions proposed. As Coulthard (1977: 92) points out, the work of Sacks, Schegloff & Jefferson produces many interesting insights into the workings of conversation, but the analytic methodology and categories employed remain so informal and imprecise that they are difficult for others to use in any practical way. The most that the discourse analyst might gain from the conversational interaction approach to an example such as (7), quoted earlier in this chapter, is that its coherence partially depends on our expectation that, according to the adjacency pair formula, what follows a question should be treated as an answer to that question. This may seem a rather obvious point to make, but it is exactly the type of point that, because of its obviousness, is rarely made explicit in the analysis of language. It captures one important aspect of how we assume that two formally unconnected utterances placed together form a coherent piece of discourse. They do so because there is an assumed coherent structure to discourse over and above the more frequently described structure of sentential form.

7.3 **Speech acts**

In 7.2 we discussed approaches to the identification of social meaning in terms of the activity performed by a speaker in uttering, with respect to analyses which identify actions in terms of the conventionally structured sequences in which they occur. In this section we turn to discuss the notion of **speech act** which has developed from the work of linguistic philosophers.

Speech act theory originates in Austin's (1962) observation that while sentences can often be used to report states of affairs, the utterance of some sentences, such as (17) and (18) must, in specified circumstances, be treated as the performance of an act:

(17)   I bet you sixpence it will rain tomorrow.

(18)   I name this ship the *Queen Elizabeth*.

Such utterances Austin described as 'performatives' and the specified circumstances required for their success he outlined as a set of 'felicity conditions'. More precisely, utterances such as (17) and (18) are examples of *explicit* performatives which are not just a specialised group of ritual sentence forms, but are a subset of the utterances in the language which can be used to perform acts.

Another subset are utterances which can be described as implicit performatives, as in examples (19) – (22):

(19)   Out!

(20)   Sixpence.

(21)   I'll be there at 5 o'clock.

(22)   Trespassers will be prosecuted

None of these examples contains a performative verb, but (19) can be used by a cricket umpire to perform an act of dismissal, (20) by a card-player to make a bet, (21) by anyone to make a promise and (22) by a landowner to issue a warning. By extension, it became possible to suggest that in uttering any sentence, a speaker could be seen to have performed some act, or, to be precise, an **illocutionary act**. Conventionally associated with each illocutionary act is the *force* of the utterance which can be expressed as a performative such as 'promise' or 'warn'. Austin also pointed out that, in uttering a sentence, a speaker also performs a **perlocutionary act** which can be described in terms of the effect which the illocutionary act, on the particular occasion of use, has on the hearer.

This is an extremely brief summary of the basic elements in what has been developed since Austin, by Searle (1969, 1979) and many others, as Speech Act theory. Searle (1975) also introduces a distinction between direct and indirect speech acts which depends on a recognition of the intended perlocutionary effect of an utterance on a particular occasion. Indirect speech acts are 'cases in which one illocutionary act is performed indirectly by way of performing another' (1975: 60). Thus, example (23) can be seen as, at one level, a question about the hearer's ability, but, at another level, a request for action.

(23)   Can you speak a little louder?

A sentence such as (23), though interrogative in form, is conventionally used, as Searle points out, to make a request. For a recent survey of the outstanding issues in Speech Act theory, see Levinson (1980, forthcoming).

The principle interest of Speech Act theory, for the discourse analyst is, as we suggested in 7.2, that it provides an account of how some apparently formally unconnected utterances go together in conversational discourse to form a coherent sequence. There are, however, a number of general problems with the application of Speech Act theory in the analysis of conversational discourse. An important practical drawback is expressed by Levinson (1980: 20) in the following terms: 'If one looks even cursorily at a transcribed record of a conversation, it becomes immediately clear that we do not know how to assign speech acts in a non-arbitrary way.' The problem with identifying speech acts should not necessarily lead the analyst to abandon their investigation. Rather, it should lead the analyst to recognise that the way speech acts are conventionally classified into discrete act-types such as 'request', 'promise', 'warn', etc. may lead to an inappropriate view of what speakers do with utterances. From the speaker's point of view several sentences (or syntactic chunks) strung together may constitute a single act. Thus, a fairly extended utterance may be interpreted as a warning or as an apology. On the other hand, one utterance may perform several simultaneous acts. Consider the following utterance of a husband to his wife:

(24)   Hey, Michele, you've passed the exam.

He may be 'doing' several things at once. He may be simultaneously 'asserting', 'congratulating', 'apologising' (for his doubts), etc. As it is presently formulated, Speech Act theory does not offer the discourse analyst a way of determining *how* a particular set of linguistic elements, uttered in a particular conversational context, comes to receive a particular interpreted meaning.

7.4 Using knowledge of the world

We might say that the knowledge we possess as users of a language concerning social interaction via language is just one part of our general socio-cultural knowledge. This general knowledge about the world underpins our interpretation not only of discourse, but of virtually every aspect of our experience. As de Beaugrande (1980: 30) notes, 'the question of how people know what is going on in a text is a special case of the question of how people know what is going on in the world at all'.

We suggested, in Chapter 2, that the interpretation of discourse is based to a large extent on a simple principle of analogy with what we have experienced in the past. As adults, we are liable to possess

quite substantial amounts of background experience and knowledge. How do we organise all this knowledge and activate only
limited amounts when needed? We shall consider proposed answers
to this question in section 7.6. Before we investigate this area, we
shall try to clarify how this view of discourse-understanding via the
use of 'world-knowledge' stands in relation to the view of literal
interpretation via the 'words-on-the-page'.

7.5 Top-down and bottom-up processing

One metaphor for the way we process and comprehend
discourse comes from computational modelling of language understanding. We can think of our processing of incoming discourse as
the combination of (at least) two activities. In one part of the
processing, we work out the meanings of the words and structure of
a sentence and build up a composite meaning for the sentence (i.e.
bottom-up processing). At the same time, we are predicting, on
the basis of the context plus the composite meaning of the sentences
already processed, what the next sentence is most likely to mean
(i.e. **top-down processing**).

Since the main thrust of analysis in general linguistics has been
towards developing a grammatical description of sentence form and
meaning, any view taken on the processing of sentences has tended
to be primarily of the 'bottom-up' type. A similar view can be found
in some **Artificial Intelligence** (AI) approaches to linguistic data,
in which the aim of the research is to develop a *parser* to analyse
acceptable English sentences. In both these approaches, a sentence
containing a grammatical error is rejected, rather than given a
plausible interpretation. If a machine with a fully operational
sentence grammar of English was presented with the following text
(25) to parse, it would tend to come to a halt very quickly and
return a 'non-grammatical' or 'unacceptable' reading for the sentence in the second line. The grammarian or AI researcher who
designed the machine's program would be pleased with this result
because, after all, the machine has fulfilled its designated function
admirably.

(25)   *Slim is beautiful*
        Many reasons are there for peaple to want a slim body. All
        become very lighter and lighter but it's very diffecult to held a
        normally weight.

Nowadays, in our country, Sweden, there is so well of all sort of eating that man light come to big overweight. What to doing?

(We are grateful to Gunnel Melchers of the English Department, University of Stockholm, who brought this text to our attention.)

However, human processors, unlike the machine parser, do not reject ungrammatical text, they try to interpret it. We suspect that the reader has a reasonable interpretation for the writer's intended message in the discourse fragment (25). What enables the human processor to do this? A partial answer to this question is that the human processor does indeed 'parse' the sentences of the encountered text. It would be absurd to suggest that when we read the first line of (25) we do not attempt to build (i.e. from the bottom-up) some composite meaning for the three-word string on the basis of its structure and the meaning of the lexical items involved. At the same time, however, we suggest that the reader is also operating a top-down interpretive strategy which creates expectations about what is likely to come next in the text. (In Chapter 4 we demonstrated how effectively titles provide an interpretive point of departure for texts.) It is the predictive power of top-down processing that enables the human reader to encounter, via his bottom-up processing, ungrammatical or mis-spelt elements in the text and to determine what was the most likely intended message.

An immediate question arises. If we believe that bottom-up processing operates with rules of the sort presented in descriptions of sentential syntax and lexical semantics, what is the basis of top-down processing? A part of the answer to this question was presented in Chapter 2 where we suggested that discourse context creates expectations relating to discourse content. Another part of the answer is that once we start processing a discourse fragment we do not treat it as the first piece of discourse we have ever encountered. We have our experience of having processed other, perhaps very similarly titled, discourse fragments before. We can also draw on our experience of the way the world is – our background knowledge. Yet, as has been noted already, we amass colossal amounts of 'knowledge' and 'experience' in our lives. If top-down processing depends on our activating only a small part of this background knowledge at a time, then there must be some way in which that knowledge is organised and stored to allow easy access. Attempting to represent the way in which background knowledge is held in mental storage has been the goal of a substantial amount of research in recent years.

7.6 Representing background knowledge

There have been several attempts to provide convention-al or stereotypic representations of 'knowledge of the world' as a basis for the interpretation of discourse. These representations, found in psychological and computational approaches to discourse understanding, are mainly used to account for the type of predict-able information a writer / speaker can assume his hearer / listener has available whenever a particular situation is described. Given one particular situation, such as a restaurant scene, the writer / speaker should not have to *inform* his reader / hearer that there are tables and chairs in the restaurant, or that one orders and pays for the food consumed therein. Knowledge of this sort about res-taurants is generally assumed. In representations of this knowledge, conventional aspects of a situation, such as the tables and chairs in a restaurant, can be treated as **default** elements. These default elements will be assumed to be present, even when not mentioned, unless the reader / hearer is specifically told otherwise. A good example of our ability as readers to provide default elements automatically was demonstrated in the consideration of the recipe text, (22) in Chapter 5.

It is a feature of these knowledge representations that they are organised in a fixed way as a complete unit of stereotypic knowledge in memory. Thus, knowledge of a restaurant scene is treated as being stored in memory as a single, easily accessible unit, rather than as a scattered collection of individual facts which have to be assembled from different parts of memory each time a restaurant scene is mentioned. This aspect of knowledge representation is generally in line with a related characteristic of the approaches we will describe, insofar as they all treat discourse understanding as a processing of information in memory. Riesbeck (1975), for exam-ple, boldly asserts that 'comprehension is a memory process'. Understanding discourse is, in this sense, essentially a process of retrieving stored information from memory and relating it to the encountered discourse. An important direction of the research in this area has consequently been towards finding the best storage concept for handling the pre-existing conventional knowledge. It should be noted that with this emphasis on the form of 'storage', little attempt has been made to demonstrate how the information stored in memory is *learned*. If it should turn out to be the case that the way we use stored knowledge is in some way determined by how we come to have that knowledge, then it is possible that the concept of a fixed storage system will have been rather misleading.

The emphasis on storage of knowledge-of-the-world is most apparent in computational approaches to discourse understanding. In order to provide a computer with the background knowledge required to 'understand' discourse, many workers in Artificial Intelligence attempted to create large, fixed data-structures, or memories, in which knowledge was organised and stored. It quickly became apparent that generalised knowledge about the world was too large and too diffuse to be incorporated, in any encyclopaedic fashion, within the computer's memory. The answer, for some AI investigators, was to produce specialised knowledge structures for coping with discourse requiring a particular type of knowledge. That is, knowledge-of-the-world could be incorporated if the 'world' was an extremely limited one. A 'world' consisting of a fixed number of coloured blocks and other shapes is one example (see Winograd, 1972), and that of a travel agent called GUS, arranging flights in California, is another (see Bobrow et al., 1977). It then became possible to think of knowledge-of-the-world as organised into separate but interlinked sets of knowledge areas which, taken together, would add up to the generalised knowledge that humans, in comprehending discourse, appear to use. This is intuitively a very reasonable idea since, when we read a piece of text, we presumably only use that limited subset of our knowledge which is required for the understanding of that text. In other words, when we read a story involving a visit to the dentist, we use our knowledge of dentist-visiting, but not normally our knowledge of typing a letter or going to a birthday party – that is, unless some part of the text also requires that other particular subset of our knowledge to be involved.

We shall consider two AI proposals for dealing with the organisation of knowledge in memory, those relating to **frames** and **scripts**. We have selected these two because they have been very influential in considerations of how discourse is understood, and because they are generally representative of a very large body of research in this area. (For more general discussions of this research, see Wilks, 1977; Winston, 1977; Findler (ed.), 1979; Metzing (ed.), 1979.)

We shall also consider some related attempts in psychological research to provide ways of representing knowledge stored in memory and how it relates to discourse processing. The emphasis in this area is typically less storage-oriented and more concerned with how background knowledge is used in on-line processing. We will briefly discuss **scenarios** and the much more widely used term **schemata**. The idea of **mental models** is also discussed. Although there appear to be many different terms employed by different researchers, there is a very large area of overlap in what these different terms are used to describe (see Tannen, 1979). It should be recognised that, generally, the use of different terminology and considerations of different types of knowledge in these various research areas do not represent sets of competing theories. The different terms are best considered as alternative metaphors for the description of how knowledge of the world is organised in human memory, and also how it is activated in the process of discourse understanding.

7.6.1 *Frames*

One way of representing the background knowledge which is used in the production and understanding of discourse can be found in Minsky's *frame-theory*. Minsky proposes that our knowledge is stored in memory in the form of data structures, which he calls 'frames', and which represent stereotyped situations. They are used in the following way:

When one encounters a new situation (or makes a substantial change in one's view of the present problem) one selects from memory a structure called a *Frame*. This is a remembered framework to be adapted to fit reality by changing details as necessary.

(Minsky, 1975)

It should be noted that Minsky's discussion is not primarily an investigation of linguistic phenomena (much of it is concerned with visual perception and visual memory) but is directed towards a way of representing knowledge. Since one kind of knowledge is knowledge of a language, then there are frames for linguistic 'facts'. For example, Minsky draws an analogy between a frame for a room in a visual scene and a frame for a noun phrase in a discourse. Both frames have obligatory elements (wall / nominal or pronominal) and optional elements (decorations on the walls / a numerical determiner). The basic structure of a frame contains labelled *slots* which can be filled with expressions, *fillers* (which may also be other frames). For example, in a frame representing a typical HOUSE, there will be slots labelled 'kitchen', 'bathroom', 'address', and so on. A particular house existing in the world, or mentioned in a text, can be treated as an *instance* of the house frame, and can be represented by filling the slots with the particular features of that individual house. Formulated in this way, a frame is characteristically a fixed representation of knowledge about the world. Some AI researchers state this point explicitly: 'I take a frame to be a static data structure about one stereotyped topic' (Charniak, 1975: 42). Others view the frame as a computational device which not only stores data, but is capable of implementing programs, that is, 'for organising the processes of retrieval and inference which manipulate the stored representations' (Hayes, 1979).

At a very general level, the notion of a 'frame' provides an attractive metaphor for thinking about discourse understanding as, at least partially, 'a process of fitting what one is told into the framework established by what one already knows' (Charniak, 1979). Thus, if you receive a postcard telling you where you should go to register your vote in a local government election, your 'understanding' of this received information can be described in terms of a 'voting-frame', perhaps, which has a slot for 'voting-place'. The specific locational information (*St Bernard's Centre*) on the card instantiates the stereotypic locational information slot in your knowledge frame. Similarly, when you look at the rest of the discourse on this postcard you see further evidence of information pertaining to your 'voting-frame', as in (26).

(26)   When you go the polling station tell the clerk your name and address.
        (Lothian Regional Council Election Poll Card, May 1982)

The definite noun phrases derive from the same 'voting-frame', in that your stereotypic knowledge of voting provides for a place to vote (*the polling station*) and an official (*the clerk*) in that place. In other words you do not have to be informed that there is such a thing as a *polling station* and that a *clerk* will be there. The producer of this piece of discourse expects you to have this knowledge, and Minsky's frame-theory provides an account of how this expectation influences the discourse produced.

There is, however, a problem with this rather neat account of how the piece of discourse in (26) is understood. If it is indeed the case that the producer of this discourse expected the reader to process it on the basis of a stereotypic voting-frame, then one might ask why he produced the discourse at all. If you do not have to be informed of the existence of the polling station and the clerk, because you have stereotypic knowledge of these things, then why do you have to be informed of the actions you should perform? Surely your voting-frame has stereotypic actions as well as stereotypic entities. If that is the case, then you need not be given the information in (26) at all. It is an unfortunate, but nevertheless logical outcome of a frame-theory version of how we use our stored knowledge, that it predicts that a lot less human discourse should occur than actually occurs. There are many situations in which discourse is produced where the intended audience can be expected, but not guaranteed, to have stereotypic knowledge of what is to be communicated. Discourse producers, like the writer of (26), make their discourse reflect this fact, and present the information in a form which serves as a reminder for those who already know and as an instruction for those who do not.

A second, unresolved problem for what Wilks (1979) describes as 'frame-using systems', concerns the fact that, when an understander system uses a text cue to activate a frame, there may be several frames activated. Remember Minsky's proposal that 'when one encounters a new situation, one selects from memory a structure called a frame'. Consider the following new situation which presented itself at the beginning of a newspaper article.

(27)   The Cathedral congregation had watched on television monitors as Pope and Archbishop met, in front of a British Caledonian helicopter, on the dewy grass of a Canterbury recreation ground.

                              (*The Sunday Times*, 30 May 1982)

The problem should be immediately obvious. Is a 'Cathedral' frame selected? How about a 'television-watching' frame, a 'meeting' frame, a 'helicopter' frame, a 'recreation-ground' frame? These questions are not trivial. After all, it probably *is* necessary to activate something like a 'recreation-ground' frame in order to account for the definite description *the grass* mentioned in the text. Yet a substantial part of such a frame, possibly incorporating a large number of sub-frames covering endless aspects of our stereotypic knowledge of 'recreation', would have no function in our understanding of this piece of text. As Wilks (1979: 153) says, 'many frames are called, but few can be chosen'.

Despite these problems, and criticisms that frame-theory is 'little more than a cumbersome convention for the listing of facts' (Dresher & Hornstein, 1976: 357), the basic concept of frames as structured repositories for our conventional knowledge has provided a useful working model for analysts, not only in AI, but also in sociology (e.g. Goffman, 1974) and linguistics (e.g. Fillmore, 1975; Gensler, 1977).

7.6.2 *Scripts*

The notion of a script was developed by analogy with Minsky's frame, but 'specialised to deal with event sequences' (Schank & Abelson, 1977). The script concept was used by Abelson (1976) to investigate the relationship between attitudes and behaviour but, when applied to text understanding, it incorporates a particular analysis of language understanding proposed by Schank (1972) as **conceptual dependency**.

Schank set out to represent the meanings of sentences in conceptual terms by providing, for any sentence, a conceptual dependency network called a *C-diagram*. A C-diagram contains concepts which enter into relations described as dependencies. There is a very elaborate, but manageable, system of semantic primitives for concepts, and labelled arrows for dependencies which we shall not describe here (see Schank 1972, 1973, for detailed discussion). We shall simply consider one of Schank's sentences and his non-diagrammatic version of the conceptualisation underlying that sentence. Examples (28) and (28a) are taken from Schank (1973).

(28)   John ate the ice cream with a spoon.

(28a)   John ingested the ice cream by transing the ice cream on a
          spoon to his mouth.

The term 'transing' is used here to mean 'physically transferring'. See Schank
(1973) for a fuller discussion.

One benefit of Schank's approach should be immediately clear.
In his 'conceptual' version (28a) of the sentence (28), he has
represented a part of our understanding of the sentence which is not
explicit in the sentence-on-the-page, that the action described in
(28) was made possible by 'getting the ice cream and his mouth in
contact' (1973: 201). In this way, Schank incorporates an aspect of
our knowledge of the world in his conceptual version of our
understanding of sentence (28) which would not be possible if his
analysis operated with only the syntactic and lexical elements in the
sentence.

In a development of the conceptual analysis of sentences,
Riesbeck & Schank (1978) describe how our understanding of what
we read or hear is very much 'expectation-based'. That is, when we
read example (29), we have very strong expectations about what,
conceptually, will be in the x-position.

(29)   John's car crashed into a guard-rail.
         When the ambulance came, it took John to the x.

Riesbeck & Schank (1978: 252) point out that our expectations are
conceptual rather than lexical and that different lexical realisations
in the x-position (e.g. *hospital, doctor, medical centre*, etc.) will all
fit our expectations. Evidence that people are 'expectation-based
parsers' of texts is provided by the fact that we can make mistakes in
our predictions of what will come next. The example (9) from
Chapter 2: *John was on his way to school*, which first suggested
John was a schoolboy, then later, that he was a teacher, is a good
illustration of this point. Riesbeck & Schank provide the following
example:

(30)   a. We went on a hunting expedition.
         b. We shot two bucks.

In our conceptualisation of this 'text', we no doubt have rifles and
bullets and dead animals. We would expect the text to continue in
this vein. But when we come to the third sentence (30c), we find

that our predictions were wrong and have to go back and re-fashion our conceptualisation,

    c. That was all the money we had.

In analysing stories, Riesbeck & Schank supplement the conceptual analysis of sentences with a more general understanding device described as a *script*, which has a function similar to a Minskyan frame. Whereas a frame is generally treated as an essentially stable set of facts about the world, a script is more programmatic in that it incorporates 'a standard sequence of events that describes a situation' (1978: 254). (For a detailed discussion, see Schank & Abelson, 1977.) One application of a script is in the 'understanding' of newspaper stories about car accidents. Evidence of a computer's 'understanding' of such stories through the application of the script procedure is presented in the capacity to answer questions about a story. Given the story in (31), the computer can answer the questions which follow. Note that the answer to question 1 requires the machine to decide that *the passenger* and *David Hall* are the same individual and that the answer to question 2 is the result of an inference that if a person is treated and released from hospital, then he is *hurt* or *slightly injured*.

(31)   Friday evening a car swerved off Route 69. The vehicle struck a tree. The passenger, a New Jersey man, was killed. David Hall, 27, was pronounced dead at the scene by Dr Dana Blanchard, medical examiner. Frank Miller, 32, of 593 Foxon Rd, the driver, was taken to Milford Hospital by Flanagan Ambulance. He was treated and released . . .

    Q1: Was anyone killed?
    A1: YES, DAVID HALL DIED.
    Q2: Was anyone hurt?
    A2: YES, FRANK MILLER WAS SLIGHTLY INJURED.

These answers may seem trivially successful to a human understander, yet they would not normally be a product of any analysis which operated on only the syntax and lexis of the sentences in the text. In very simple terms, it is not stated in the text that Frank Miller was hurt, so how does the computer (or any other processor) come to know this? It uses a limited subset of its knowledge of the world applied to the piece of text it encounters. Riesbeck & Schank suggest that we do the same, and that their expectation-based analysis presents 'a viable theory of how humans process natural language' (1978: 290).

Criticism of the claims of Schank and his co-authors could be made in similar terms to those against Minsky, noted earlier. That is, if scripts are stereotypic event-sequences, then would a stereotypic car crash be described at all, since we already have the information in our scripts? The problem of idiosyncratic scripts – e.g. Schank's daughter asking if he was going to get a new key chain to go with his new car (Schank & Abelson, 1977: 68) – is touched on, but not considered at length. It may be, of course, that we all have more idiosyncratic scripts than stereotypic ones.

One very specific and serious criticism of Schank's conceptual-dependency theory has been made by Dresher & Hornstein, (1976). Schank states the following condition on the well-formedness of conceptualisations:

A C-diagram that contains only the sententially realised information will not be well-formed conceptually. That is, a conceptualisation is not complete until all the conceptual cases required by the act have been explicated.

(1972: 569)

Dresher & Hornstein quite justifiably point out that such a condition is a recipe for endless conceptualisations. If we bring *John's mouth* into the conceptualisation of sentence (28), quoted earlier in this chapter, do we not also bring in *John's hand, his fingers, his arm muscles, his thought processes*, and so on, to arrive at a *complete* conceptualisation? This is a serious criticism and raises a problem which exists for virtually every attempt to incorporate world-knowledge in the understanding of discourse. We can see how *some* extra-linguistic knowledge is involved in our understanding, or our conceptualisation, of sentences and we can propose ways of incorporating that knowledge in our analysis. What we have difficulty with is restricting that knowledge to only the relevant details required in the understanding of particular sentences on particular occasions. The outstanding problem for Schank's theory (and for Minsky, too, as we noted earlier) is to find a *principled* means of limiting the number of conceptualisations required for the understanding of a sentence. In more general terms, we require a principled way of constraining the expansion of any analysis which incorporates extra-linguistic knowledge in its account of the understanding of linguistic data.

Despite this general criticism of the theoretical principles involved in using 'scripts', some empirical research has shown that treating scripts as 'action stereotypes' (Bower et al., 1979) for people's knowledge of routine activities can produce experimental results to support the views of Schank and his collaborators. Bower et al. (1979) found that when they asked subjects to recall texts involving routine activities (e.g. Going to a Restaurant, Grocery Shopping, Visiting a Doctor), their subjects tended to confuse in memory actions that were stated in the text with actions implied by the 'script'. They also found that, when presented with scrambled texts which caused script-actions to be out of predictable sequence, subjects recalled the texts with script-actions in their canonical order. There is, then, some evidence that the script-concept may have some psychological validity, over and above its function as an organisational device in computer data storage. Further evidence is provided by Sanford & Garrod (1981) who base their notion of *scenario* very much on Schank's script concept.

7.6.3 *Scenarios*

Sanford & Garrod (1981) choose the term *scenario* to describe the 'extended domain of reference' which is used in interpreting written texts, 'since one can think of knowledge of settings and situations as constituting the interpretative scenario behind a text'. Their aim is to 'establish the validity of the scenario account as a psychological theory' (1981: 110) in opposition to the proposition-based theory of Kintsch (1974) which we described earlier in Chapter 3. According to the proposition-based approach, the existence of *a waiter*, for example, in the mental representation which a reader has after reading a text about *Going to a Restaurant*, depends entirely on whether a waiter was explicitly mentioned in the text. According to the scenario account, a text about *Going to a Restaurant* automatically brings *a waiter* slot into the representation. As evidence that certain 'role' slots are activated in scenarios, Sanford & Garrod show that substantial differences are recorded in the reading times for the target sentences in the following two conditions:

(32)   a. *Title: In court*
         Fred was being questioned.
         He had been accused of murder.

    Target: The lawyer was trying to prove his innocence.

         b. *Title: Telling a lie*
         Fred was being questioned.
         He couldn't tell the truth.

    Target: The lawyer was trying to prove his innocence.

In condition *a*, with the *In court* scenario activated, reading times for the target sentence containing *The lawyer* were substantially faster than in the *b* condition where a non-specific scenario had been activated.

Sanford & Garrod emphasise that the success of scenario-based comprehension is dependent on the text-producer's effectiveness in activating appropriate scenarios. They point out that 'in order to elicit a scenario, a piece of text must constitute a specific *partial description* of an element of the scenario itself' (1981: 129). These points and the structure of the examples in (32) lend support to our view, expressed already in Chapter 4, that effective staging, particularly thematisation, facilitates the processing of text. One function of thematisation at the text level may be to activate a particular scenario representation for the reader.

We should emphasise that Sanford & Garrod's claims relate to the ease or speed with which texts based on a coherent scenario can be processed. They do not suggest that texts for which a single scenario structure is not immediately available cannot be processed. Their scenario-based approach would encounter just as many problems as the frame-based approach if applied to the 'Pope meets Archbishop' text presented as (27) in Chapter 7. Their suggestion would no doubt be that such texts take longer to process.

Most of the textual material discussed by Sanford & Garrod is in the form of very brief constructed text which is designed for use in the controlled studies of the experimental psychology laboratory. In fact, this is a general feature of the 'texts' which appear in the work of psychologists investigating knowledge representation. Although Sanford & Garrod prefer the term 'scenario', they indicate that their notion of text-processing involving pre-existing knowledge representations has much in common with other studies in which the term *schemata* is more generally used. If there is a difference between the use of these two terms, it appears to be that scenarios are situation-specific (At the Cinema; In a Restaurant), whereas schemata are much more general types of knowledge representations.

7.6.4 Schemata

We have already discussed one area of discourse studies, that related to story-grammars (cf. section 3.9), in which appeal was made to the existence of a particular type of *schema*. For the proponents of story-grammars, there exists a socio-culturally determined story-schema, which has a fixed conventional structure containing a fixed set of elements. One of these elements is the 'setting' and an initial sentence of a simple story (e.g. *All was quiet at the 701 Squadron base at Little Baxton*) can instantiate the setting element. It should be pointed out that, although a simple story may instantiate many elements in the story-schema, it is not suggested that the story has the schema. Rather, it is people who have schemata which they use to produce and comprehend simple stories, among many other things (e.g. place-descriptions in Brewer & Treyens (1981)).

Schemata are said to be 'higher-level complex (and even conventional or habitual) knowledge structures' (van Dijk, 1981: 141), which function as 'ideational scaffolding' (Anderson, 1977) in the organisation and interpretation of experience. In the strong view, schemata are considered to be deterministic, to predispose the experiencer to interpret his experience in a fixed way. We can think of racial prejudice, for example, as the manifestation of some fixed way of thinking about newly encountered individuals who are assigned undesirable attributes and motives on the basis of an existing schema for members of the race. There may also be deterministic schemata which we use when we are about to encounter certain types of discourse, as evidenced in the following conversational fragment.

(33)   A: There's a party political broadcast coming on – do you want to watch it?
        B: No – switch it off – I know what they're going to say already.

However, the general view taken of schemata in the analysis of discourse is much weaker. Rather than deterministic constraints on how we must interpret discourse, schemata can be seen as the organised background knowledge which leads us to *expect* or predict aspects in our interpretation of discourse. In fact, Tannen (1979: 138) uses the description 'structures of expectation' (adopted from Ross, 1975) to characterise the influence of schemata on our thinking. In Tannen (1980), there is also evidence that such expectations influence what type of discourse we produce. After watching a film (with no dialogue), a group of American subjects described in great detail the actual events of the film and what filming techniques had been employed. In contrast, a group of Greek subjects produced elaborate stories with additional events and detailed accounts of the motives and feelings of the characters in the film. Different cultural backgrounds can result in different schemata for the description of witnessed events.

This effect is not, however, caused by different cultural back-grounds alone. Anderson et al. (1977) presented a constructed text, partially repeated as (34), to a group of female students who were planning a career in music education and also to a group of male students from a weight-lifting class. Both groups had very similar cultural backgrounds, but would be predicted to have different 'interests'.

(34)   Every Saturday night, four good friends get together. When Jerry, Mike, and Pat arrived, Karen was sitting in her living room writing some notes. She quickly gathered the cards and stood up to greet her friends at the door. They followed her into the living room but as usual they couldn't agree on exactly what to play. Jerry eventually took a stand and set things up. Finally, they began to play. Karen's recorder filled the room with soft and pleasant music. Early in the evening, Mike noticed Pat's hand and the many diamonds . . .

(Anderson et al., 1977: 372)

The reader will no doubt have activated some discourse analysis 'schema' by now and have expectations that the female group with musical interests would interpret the passage as describing a musical evening. That is exactly what Anderson et al. found. They also found that the male, weight-lifting, group preferred an inter-pretation in which the passage described some people playing cards rather than musical instruments. Anderson et al. suggest that people's personal histories, and interests (and sex, perhaps) contribute to the creation of 'higher-level schemata which cause them to "see" messages in certain ways' (1977: 377).

Both Tannen and Anderson derive their concept of 'schema' from the writings of Bartlett (1932). Bartlett believed that our memory for discourse was not based on straight reproduction, but was constructive. This constructive process uses information from the encountered discourse, together with knowledge from past experience related to the discourse at hand, to build a mental representation. That past experience, Bartlett argued, cannot be an accumulation of successive individuated events and experiences, it must be organised and made manageable – 'the past operates as an organised mass rather than as a group of elements each of which retains its specific character' (1932: 197). What gives structure to that organised mass is the schema, which Bartlett did not propose as a form of arrangement, but as something which remained 'active' and 'developing' (1932: 201). It is this 'active' feature which, combined with the experience of a particular piece of discourse, leads to the constructive processes in memory. The subject whom Bartlett (1932: 77) describes as remembering a story about 'two young men going down a river to hunt seals' in terms of 'two brothers going on a pilgrimage' has actively constructed the remembered discourse.

This 'active' aspect of Bartlett's proposed schemata is not generally a feature of other knowledge representations (e.g. frames) we have been considering. In some uses of the term 'schemata' by other writers, the 'active, developing' aspect is not promoted. For example, Rumelhart & Ortony propose that 'schemata represent stereotypes of concepts' (1977: 101). They present a schema for FACE which has subschemata for EYE, MOUTH, etc., which seems to have a lot in common with the slot and filler features of a frame. Their schema for FACE might best be described as a **prototype** for the various human objects called 'faces', in much the same way as Rosch (1973, 1977) and Rosch et al. (1976) suggest there are prototypic representations for natural and semantic categories like 'tree' and 'bird'. Viewed in this way, a schema is a fixed 'data structure'. Indeed, Rumelhart & Ortony propose schemata for linguistic knowledge which are very similar to the language frames of Minsky (1975). They propose that the GIVE schema has three variables, a giver, a gift and a recipient, which are analogous to the 'cases' described by Fillmore (1968). They are clearly suggesting that schemata have fixed structures, containing set elements.

It may be, of course, that our background knowledge is organised and stored in some fixed schemata, together with some other, more flexible schematic structures. In whatever way they are represented, schemata seem to present the discourse analyst with one way of accounting for discourse production and interpretation which does not take place *ab initio* on each occasion. Like frames, scripts and scenarios, they are a means of representing that background knowledge which we all use, and assume others can use too, when we produce and interpret discourse.

The problems we noted with frames and scripts and scenarios are, however, also present for schematic representations. The selection and integration of schemata in the processing of a non-constructed piece of text such as (27) presents a substantial management problem. Given the proposals in the literature for how knowledge may be represented, future research must be aimed at devising heuristics for the *selection*, on a particular occasion, of the *relevant* partial representation (and no more) that is required for the local interpretation of discourse fragments. In so doing, this research will necessarily also have to devise controls on stereotypic knowledge representations which allow them to recognise 'weird' events which nevertheless fit the stereotype format. If an understander system decides that John ate a steak after reading the following text, then it has failed to 'understand' what most human processors understand about this particular restaurant scenario.

(35)   John is pretty crazy, and sometimes does strange things. Yesterday he went to Sardi's for dinner. He sat down, examined the menu, ordered a steak, and got up and left.

(from Kaplan, 1981: 131)

7.6.5 *Mental models*

A view of how we interpret discourse (and experience) which does not appeal to stereotypic knowledge or fixed storage systems has been put forward by Johnson-Laird in a series of papers. Johnson-Laird (1981a) argues against an approach to the meaning of sentences which depends on a decomposition of word-meaning having to take place. An example of a decomposition view is that of Katz & Fodor (1963) where the 'meaning' of *man* is decomposed into *human, adult, male.* The conceptual dependency type of analysis used by Schank (1972), discussed earlier, is another example. Johnson-Laird proposes that we are indeed capable of decomposing word-meaning, but that we do not typically do so in our normal understanding of sentences. He suggests that a sentence like (36) receives an immediate interpretation which makes sense to most people as praise for the book.

(36)   This book fills a much needed gap.

Upon further analysis, however, we can work out that the sentence is actually saying that it is the gap, not the book, which is needed. To account for this everyday non-analytic process of comprehension, Johnson-Laird proposes that we use words in a sentence as 'cues to build a familiar mental model' (1981a: 122). A mental model is a representation in the form of an internal model of the state of affairs characterised by the sentence. We should note that although such models are not described as stereotypic, the term 'familiar' is rather smuggled into the description without any account of what 'being familiar' is based on. There are, moreover, theoretical problems with the concept of an 'internal' model, which Johnson-Laird (1981a: 117) acknowledges. However, he notes that the experimental evidence on instantiation (cf. Anderson & Ortony, 1975; Anderson et al., 1976; Garnham, 1979) supports a view of understanding via mental models, rather than via the decomposition of word meaning. When subjects were asked to recall a sentence like (37), Anderson et al., found that the word *shark* was a much better recall cue than the word *fish*.

(37)   The fish attacked the swimmer.

Johnson-Laird accounts for this finding by suggesting that readers interpreted the sentence by constructing a mental model in which the relevant event and entities were represented. We should note that this is, at least, a text-specific model, since it is very easy to imagine texts in which the term *fish* would not bring *shark* to mind at all.

Johnson-Laird (1980, 1981b) specifically appeals to the ideas of model-theoretic semantics in support of his notion of mental models. In formal semantics, a model structure can be used to represent a possible state of affairs at a particular point in time and space which can correspond to the 'meaning' of a sentence (cf. Thomason (ed.), 1974; Partee (ed.), 1976). We shall not describe formal model-theory in any greater detail here, except to point out that it is not intended as a psychological account of meaning or understanding. As Johnson-Laird observes, model-theory relates language to the world, but not by way of the human mind. What a psychologically interesting model-theory has to be concerned with is that 'in so far as natural language relates to the world, it does so through the mind's innate ability to construct models of reality' (Johnson-Laird, 1981b: 141). These *models* of reality are, of course, representations of the way the world is. They may differ from one individual to the next. This is unavoidably the case when such models are the result of a listener's (or reader's) comprehension of discourse. According to Johnson-Laird (1981b: 139):

a major function of language is to enable one person to have another's experience of the world by proxy: instead of a direct apprehension of a state of affairs, the listener constructs a model of them based on a speaker's remarks.

As a simple example, Johnson-Laird & Garnham (1979) point out that the interpretation of a definite description is not determined by uniqueness in the world, but uniqueness in the local model constructed for the particular discourse. If a speaker says:

(38)   The man who lives next door drives to work.

the hearer may have a model of a particular state of affairs in which there is an individual (neighbour of speaker, has a car, has a job, etc.), but the hearer is unlikely to assume that the speaker has only one neighbour.

The proposal that understanding takes place via the construction of mental models leads Johnson-Laird to a view of comprehension and inference which is quite different from those we have already investigated. In this view, there is a level of comprehension which is based on the construction of an initial mental model which, as we noted with example (36), need not result from any elaborate consideration of the text encountered. There are, however, other levels of comprehension which result from the manipulation of the mental model constructed and which can lead to the abandonment of the initial model and the construction of another. In this process of manipulation, there are no rules of inference, there are only procedures for testing the constructed mental model to find out if it fits the state of affairs described by the text. As an illustration of this process, Johnson-Laird (1980) takes an example (39) of the type used in discussions of syllogistic inference.

(39)   All of the singers are professors.
         All of the poets are professors.

Given the pair of premises in (39), we can construct a model with, for instance, six individuals in a room and assign the roles of singer, poet and professor to those individuals in a way that fits the state of affairs described by the two sentences in (39). One model which immediately comes to mind is that, for all six individuals, the following representation (40) is true:

(40)   singer = professor = poet

According to this model, the conclusion that *all of the singers are poets* or *all of the poets are singers* is justified. Johnson-Laird & Steedman (1978) report that, for many people, this conclusion is the natural one. It is possible to test the model in (40) against the state of affairs described in (39) and find that it is not necessarily a correct representation. By manipulating the model, it is possible to arrive at a representation (41) in which *a* is true for three individuals and *b* is true for the other three.

(41)   a. singer = professor

         b. poet = professor

On the basis of (41), one might conclude that *none of the singers are poets*. On further manipulation, one might arrive at a model (42) in which *a* is true for four individuals, *b* is true for one, and *c* is true for the other one.

(42)   a. singer = professor = poet

         b. singer = professor

         c. poet = professor

So, one could conclude that *some of the singers are poets*.

It should be clear that the sentences in (39) can give rise to several different versions of a mental model involving the six individuals with different identities. The process of manipulation of the model which has just been described is characterised by Johnson-Laird (1980: 81) as 'testing your mental model to destruction'. The discourse analyst may not be as interested as the logician in carrying out the 'testing' procedure to its extreme, but he must acknowledge that Johnson-Laird's notion of understanding via the construction and manipulation of mental models provides a useful metaphor for the way a piece of text can be 'understood' at different levels. It also accommodates that aspect of discourse understanding (which we have argued for already in section 6.2) which allows interpretations in different receivers' minds to differ from the interpretation intended by the discourse producer. The individual hearer's mental model of the discourse can differ from the speaker's, and there is no suggestion that *the text* is, in any sense, *the model*.

It should be apparent from the consideration of the sentences in (39) how Johnson-Laird intends us to understand his claim that, in the mental model approach to understanding, there are no rules of inference. Whereas the formulae in (40), (41) and (42) are normally considered inferences from (39), in Johnson-Laird's analysis they are different versions of a mental model for the text. That is, what we normally describe as a process of inferring one state of affairs on the basis of another is presented in this alternative view as building a model of one state of affairs, or building another model from another state of affairs. From a discourse analyst's point of view, this distinction is of little practical significance.

Johnson-Laird's view of discourse understanding via mental models is never described in terms of the sets of stereotypical elements found in 'frames' or the sets of characteristic events of a narrative 'schema'. Possibly for this reason, the practical details of mental models remain elusive. They seem to represent a way of thinking about how we understand discourse rather than a way of doing analysis of discourse. Yet the problem we have frequently noted with other methods of representing discourse processing and understanding – that of fixing the constraints on what knowledge we use – must also exist for mental models. When we construct a mental model for a piece of discourse, we use some of our pre-existing knowledge and experience to get a 'picture' of the state of affairs described by the discourse. How is it that we do not use *all* of our pre-existing knowledge? Putting this question in more specific terms, will a mental model theory predict that, in asking subjects to recall a sentence like *The fish attacked the swimmer*, not only is *shark* a better cue than *fish*, but that *blood* or *teeth* or *ocean* or *bite* or *splash* are also better? At the moment, we have no answers to these questions.

As it is presently described, the theory of mental models actually predicts massively detailed mental representations of any event encountered, whether in life or via text. Admittedly, one of the advantages of the concept of a mental model is that it allows for a richer representation than the rather bare outlines of the stereotypic versions found in scripts and scenarios. The scenario example, quoted earlier as (32), to demonstrate the 'In court – the lawyer' connection, seems to describe a strangely empty and non-detailed court-scene which is at odds with the experience of most people. However, the unconstrained potential of the mental model concept takes us to the other extreme. It would lead to a pathological inability to process text at all. A well-documented case-history of an individual whose 'mental models' were unconstrained is presented in Luria (1969). The incapacitating effects of this lack of constraints can be detected in the following account:

Last year I was read an assignment having to do with a merchant who had sold so many meters of fabric . . . As soon as I heard the words *merchant* and *sold*, I saw both the shop and the storekeeper, who was standing behind the counter with only the upper part of his body visible to me. He was dealing with a factory representative. Standing at the door of the shop I could see the buyer, whose back was toward me. When he moved off a little to the left, I saw not only the factory but also some account books – details that had nothing to do with the assignment. So I couldn't get the gist of the story.

(Luria, 1969: 66)

The outstanding problem for Luria's patient, and also for the discourse analyst who wishes to represent the interaction between previous knowledge / experience and the comprehension of the discourse at hand, is to reach a working compromise. In this compromise representation, there should be enough richness of detail to capture the potential complexity of our pre-existing knowledge / experience, but there should also be a constraint on how much of this richness of detail we actually use in our processing of the discourse we encounter.

7.7 Determining the inferences to be made

Much of the data presented in this chapter is of the type that has generally been treated as requiring **inferences** on the reader's part to arrive at an interpretation. The rather general notion of inference appealed to is used to describe that process which the reader (hearer) must go through to get from the literal meaning of what is written (or said) to what the writer (speaker) intended to convey. For example, the general view of the interpretation of an utterance such as (43) – used to convey an indirect request – is that the hearer works from the literal meaning to a meaning like (43a) via inference(s) of what the speaker intended to convey.

(43)   It's really cold in here with that window open.

(43a)   Please close the window.

In other words, utterance (43) does not 'mean' (43a). Rather, the hearer, on receiving (43) in a particular context, must infer that the speaker intended it to convey (43a). As evidence that some inferential process is required in the interpretation of indirect requests, Clark & Lucy (1975) demonstrated that, across a wide range of indirect versus direct forms, readers performing a verification task consistently took longer with the indirect forms. The additional time taken, Clark (1978) claims, is required by the reader's inferential processing of the indirect request.

Very similar evidence is presented by Haviland & Clark (1974) to show that 'identifying referents for definite noun phrases is a highly inferential activity' (Clark, 1978: 313). Haviland & Clark found that determining the referent for *the beer* in (45b) took readers significantly longer than in (44b).

(44)   a. Mary got some beer out of the car.
         b. The beer was warm.

(45)   a. Mary got some picnic supplies out of the car.
         b. The beer was warm.

This finding is explained in terms of a particular aspect of the inferential process described as forming a **bridging assumption**. The bridging assumption required between (45a) and (45b) is that shown in (45c).

(45)   c. The picnic supplies mentioned include some beer.

Forming this type of bridging assumption takes time and so the difference in comprehension times noted between (44b) and (45b) is accounted for. The implication from this type of research finding is that inferences take time.

7.8   Inferences as missing links

The information in (45c) can be seen, in formal terms, as the **missing link** which is required to make an explicit connection between (45a) and (45b). Is it possible, then, to think of an inference as a process of filling in the missing link(s) between two utterances? This seems to be implicit in the research of Clark and his co-authors and also seems to be the basis of Prince's (1981) category of 'inferrable', described already in section 5.3.2. Indeed, there are many examples in the literature concerning definite descriptions which we could treat in terms of the 'missing link' phenomenon. Let us consider some of these examples, which we will present with the *a* and *b* sentences ('the text') as *linked* via the information in the *c* sentence ('the missing link').

(46)   a. I bought a bicycle yesterday.
       b. The frame is extra large.

       (Chafe, 1972)

       c. *The bicycle has a frame.*

(47)   a. I looked into the room.
       b. The ceiling was very high.

       (Clark, 1977)

       c. *The room has a ceiling.*

(48)   a. This afternoon a strange man came to my office.
       b. His nose was nearly purple.

       (van Dijk, 1977)

       c. *The man has a nose.*

(49)   a. I got on a bus yesterday
       b. and the driver was drunk.

       (Prince, 1981)

       c. *The bus has a driver.*

In each of these examples, the missing link expresses a type of generally true relationship which might take the form of a universally quantified proposition such as *Every X has a Y*. In fact, each of the four *c* sentences in (46) – (49) expresses information which we might expect to be represented in one of the stereotypic knowledge formats (e.g. frames, schemata) discussed already in section 7.6. The same could be said for the relationship (*Every X is a Y*) expressed in the *c* sentences of the following two examples.

(50) a. A bus came roaring round the corner.
    b. The vehicle nearly flattened a pedestrian.
              (Garrod & Sanford, 1977)
    c. The bus is a vehicle.

(51) a. Draw a diameter in black.
    b. The line is about three inches.
                (Yule, 1981)
    c. The diameter is a line.

These types of 'generally true' missing links are also presented in terms of a connection between the verb of one sentence or clause, and the definite noun phrase of another, as in the following examples.

(52) a. She decided to sell the cow
    b. and buy a shop with the money
               (Chafe, 1972)
    c. Selling involves money.

(53) a. It was dark and stormy the night the millionaire was murdered. .
    b. The killer left no clues for the police to trace.
            (Carpenter & Just, 1977b)
    c. Murdering involves a killer.

(54) a. Mary dressed the baby.
    b. The clothes were made of pink wool.
            (Sanford & Garrod 1981)
    c. Dressing involves clothes.

This last example (54) was used in a controlled experiment by Sanford & Garrod to test whether the type of missing link involved required the additional processing time which Haviland & Clark

(1974) noted in connection with the *picnic supplies–beer* example, quoted earlier in this chapter as (45). When the times taken to understand the *b* sentence in (54) were compared with those for the *b* sentence in (55), no significant differences was found.

(55) a. Mary put the baby's clothes on.
      b. The clothes were made of pink wool.

In other words, despite the fact that we can point to a missing link in (54c), the experimental subjects did not behave as if that missing link required additional processing time to work out. Does this result nullify the finding of Haviland & Clark (1974) that the existence of a missing link creates additional processing requirements? Sanford & Garrod do not think so. They suggest that when the missing link is already part of the knowledge representation (e.g. frame, schema) activated by one part of the text, no additional processing is required to understand subsequent reference to another element in that knowledge representation. They claim that because *dressing* activates *clothes* in our representation of the first part of the text (54a), subsequent mention of *the clothes* is understood as quickly as it would be if *the clothes* had already been explicitly mentioned, as in (55a). However, since *picnic supplies* did not automatically activate beer in the knowledge representations of Haviland & Clark's subjects, they had to make a bridging assumption and so took additional processing time.

It seems, then, that we have (at least) two categories of missing link. One kind is automatically made and does not result in additional processing time and the other is not automatic, but is the result of a bridging assumption and leads to additional processing time. If we wish to maintain, as was suggested earlier, that inferences take time, then it should follow that those missing links which are automatically made (and do not take additional processing time) are not to be described as inferences. This would be the natural conclusion of any researcher who, working on an empirical basis, finds no evidence for the existence of a hypothesised process. Let us assume, then, that 'missing links' are formally identifiable sentences which can be shown to provide a connection, in formal cohesive terms, between text sentences. Providing missing links may be part of an exercise in text-representation, but that is not the same as providing a representation of what people are doing in comprehending text. We could then draw a distinction between inferences and missing links in the following terms: texts may have formal missing links, but it is readers and hearers who make inferences. Identifying missing links is not the same as identifying inferences.

7.9 Inferences as non-automatic connections

Sanford & Garrod's proposal that automatic connections are made between elements in a text via pre-existing knowledge representations could be used as a basis for deciding which missing links are, and which are not, likely to be inferences. That is, all the *c* sentences in (46)–(54) are automatic connections, and consequently should not count as inferences, but the connection between *picnic supplies* and *beer* in (45) is non-automatic and ought, therefore, to be treated as an inference. Such a proposal appears to be in line with de Beaugrande's suggestion that there is a process, in our understanding of what we read and hear, of 'spreading activation' which 'results naturally from concept activation in ideation and comprehension without specifically directed impulses' (1980: 229). Those 'specifically directed impulses', on the other hand, are expressly aimed towards overcoming discontinuities or gaps in the reader's (hearer's) understanding of what he reads (hears) and are more properly treated as inferences. This distinction allows us to think of non-automatic connections (inferences) as requiring *more interpretive work* on the reader's (hearer's) part than automatic connections made via pre-existing knowledge.

The idea of 'automatic connections' can also be usefully applied to an aspect of text understanding which has been discussed in terms of 'informational inferences' (Warren et al., 1979). Since the type of 'information' described appears to involve automatic connections across text sentences, it may be that the phenomenon has been inappropriately characterised as an example of 'inference'. Warren et al. (1979) claim that, in our understanding of a text, we continually need to know the answers to a set of *who, what, where* and *when* questions. Arriving at the answers to these questions, at a particular point in a text, is accomplished, they suggest, by making 'informational inferences'. Thus, on encountering the final sentence, *he tied her shoelaces together*, in the text shown here as (56), the reader has to infer who is doing what to whom, where and when.

(56)   It was Friday afternoon.
         Carol was drawing a picture in the classroom.
         David felt mischievous.
         David decided to tease Carol.
         When Carol was not looking,
         he tied her shoelaces together.

                                    (Warren et al., 1979: 24)

It may be particularly unfortunate that Warren et al., choose to
discuss 'informational inferences' in relation to our understanding
of such a simple piece of text. Given the principles of analogy and
local interpretation which we described in Chapter 2, there is a
fairly automatic understanding of who is doing what to whom,
when and where, in the final sentence of this text. Since there is no
competition between different times, different locations or different
referents, the reader has very little interpretive 'work' to carry out
in understanding the final sentence. Let us assume that the reader's
understanding that *David tied Carol's shoelaces together in the
classroom on Friday afternoon* is a result of making fairly automatic
connections and is not the product of any inference-making at all.

There are, however, some texts which, for some readers, will
pose more substantial comprehension problems of the *who, what,
where* and *when* variety than the simple text in (56). We shall
consider this issue in relation to examples (61) and (62) later.

Warren et al. continue the text of (56) with the sentence shown in
(56a). They suggest that a 'logical inference' has to be made to
connect the final sentence of (56) with the sentence in (56a).

(56a)   Carol tripped and fell down.

This type of 'logical inference', alternatively described as an
'enabling inference' by Hildyard & Olson (1978), is typically
supplied by readers to make a connection in terms of action A
causing action B. Interestingly, Warren et al. describe the 'causation' relationship in their example in terms of a 'specific prediction'
(1979: 26) which the reader of (56) is likely to make. If a 'logical
inference' of this type can be based on a prediction, then it is clearly
in the category of automatic connections. Presumably the know-
ledge-base used in making such predictions is concerned with
general cause and effect relationships. This type of knowledge will
lead the reader not to derive a 'logical inference' to connect the first
two sentences of (56). That is, the fact that it was *Friday afternoon*

did not cause *Carol* to start *drawing a picture*. In the simple text under consideration, the notion of 'logical inference' seems to lead to automatic connections. However, there are texts in which a causation relation may, in fact, be far from automatically made. This is because the reader may have to ask a *why* or *how* question with regard to some action or event described in a text. Such questions also give rise to what Warren et al. wish to describe as 'elaborative' and 'evaluative' inferences. At this point, the categories of the inference types proposed in the taxonomy begin to merge into one another. We shall try to illustrate 'elaborative' and 'evaluative' inferences in the discussion of extract (61) later in this chapter.

For the moment, we shall concentrate on the implications of an approach which maintains that automatic connections made in text comprehension should not be treated as inferences.

One of the simplifying assumptions made in many psycholinguistic investigations of text understanding is that the experimental subjects are a representative sample of a population which has fairly homogeneous background knowledge and experience. Another assumption is that the two-sentence text, specially constructed and decontextualised, is a representative sample of the linguistic material encountered by the language-user as naturally occurring discourse. On the basis of these two assumptions, it is possible to draw a distinction between the processing of texts which contain automatic connections (*dressing the baby – the clothes*) and those which contain non-automatic connections (*picnic supplies – the beer*). We can then suggest that only the latter type should be treated as an example of inference, because we have evidence (additional time taken) that the reader has had to undertake some additional interpretive 'work' in his processing of the text. This is basically a useful distinction and may provide a general heuristic for predictions about which texts will probably be more difficult to process than others.

The danger of this approach, however, is that it tends to identify inferences with specific text-connections and to base those text-connections on the words in the text. Consider again the idea that, if an element is activated because it is necessarily part of the reader's (hearer's) pre-existing knowledge representation, then it receives 'direct interpretation' (Sanford & Garrod, 1981: 105), and does not require additional processing time. Now consider Haviland & Clark presenting their *beer – beer* (44) and *picnic supplies – beer* (45) examples to a group of real ale enthusiasts who often indulge their enthusiasm on picnics at the local park. By Sanford & Garrod's prediction, there should not be, for this group, any differences in processing time under the two conditions. This would also be predicted by Anderson et al.'s (1977) concept of schema, described already in connection with extract (34). What this means is that the identification of a connection as 'automatic' or 'non-automatic' cannot be made independently of the person(s) considering the text. For some people, *beer* is an automatic component of *picnic supplies*, for others it has to be included on a particular occasion because understanding the text at hand requires its inclusion.

A second problem arises in connection with determining exactly which elements will be automatically activated via the reader's (hearer's) pre-existing knowledge representations. Given the following sentence (57), we presumably should be ready to make a 'direct interpretation' of the elements referred to by some of the definite expressions in the sentences listed under (58).

(57)   Socrates is a lovely striker of the ball.

(58)   a. His height gives him a great advantage.
         b. His father was in love with Greek culture.
         c. The Brazilian midfield man is interested in playing in
            Europe.
         d. The goalkeeper didn't even have time to move.
         e. The nail on the index finger of his left hand is broken.

The first point to be made is that, for many reasons, some of these potential co-text sentences in (58) may not be interpretable at all without the general context of (57). If that is the case, then knowledge-activation is clearly context-dependent for naturally occurring texts. Example (57) is quoted from a commentary on a soccer match during the World Cup Finals in Spain, in June 1982. The sentence which actually follows (57) in the commentary is (58d). The definite expression *the goalkeeper* may, of course, be quite automatically interpreted given the hearer's activated knowledge of elements in his soccer match 'frame'. Notice that this 'automatic' connection is not made across the two-sentence text formed by (57) and (58d) alone. Sentences (58a–c) are taken from other parts of the commentary, but all have definite expressions which depend, for their interpretation, on a connection to the 'Socrates' of sentence (57). Perhaps the most obvious connection is from 'Socrates' to 'his height', but even this connection is hardly automatic in this text without some additional connections which make Socrates a soccer player who hits the ball with his head, on occasion, hence the advantage of 'his height'. The connection between 'Socrates' and 'his father' might seem relatively simple, since every person has a father. Yet, in this text, the mention of his father is embedded in what seems to be an explanation for this particular soccer player having the name he does. The connection between 'Socrates' and 'his father', in this text, may require the reader to 'fill in' several other connections, none of which is necessarily derived from the activated soccer match 'frame'. The connection between (57) and (58c) is of a type which is frequently made in sports and news reports, and we have discussed this role-related aspect of reference already in Chapter 6. Whether this type of connection is automatic or not clearly depends on very localised knowledge, because it is not of the same generality as the 'every bus is a vehicle' type noted in example (50) earlier. Finally, sentence (58e), which is not taken from the commentary, but is a constructed sentence, is presented as an example of a definite expression used to refer to an element which is a necessary part of any person. Every person has a 'nail on the index finger of his left hand', but would we really expect this information to be automatically activated by the mention of a person's name in a preceding co-text sentence? If the answer to this question is 'yes', then what human feature is not activated? The problem is very similar to those noted with the representation of context in Chapter 2 and with representing background knowledge in section 7.6 – how do we set the boundaries on these representations? The example in (58e) is presented as part of what could be described as a *reductio* argument against the unconstrained nature of the knowledge representations which are claimed to provide automatic connections within texts. Maratsos (1971) makes a similar type of argument regarding the use of definite noun phrases. Some connections appear to be automatic, as exemplified in examples (46)–(54), yet others, though clearly filled in via aspects of our knowledge representations, as between (57) and (58a–e), are not automatic for the majority of readers (hearers).

A third problem with the automatic connection via background-knowledge view is the assumption that the connection can be described in terms of a decomposition of lexical meaning. Chafe (1972: 61) suggests that this may be a reasonable approach and Sanford & Garrod make the point in processing terms: 'when a verb like *dress* is encountered, this will evoke from memory a representation which contains slots for a variety of entities implied in the meaning of the verb, such as *clothing*' (1981: 108). If this really were the case, then there would be an extremely large, and massively redundant, representation which would be unlikely to lead to the automatic connection type of processing indicated in their experimental findings. Why would *clothing*, for example, enter into the representation of our understanding the following two constructed texts?

(59)   a. Mary dressed the baby's arm.
        b. The bandage was made of white cotton.

(60)   a. Mary dressed the turkey.
        b. The entrails spilled out into the bowl.

It is clearly not the lexical item *dress* alone which is the source of the activated knowledge representations we use in the comprehension of two-sentence texts such as (59), (60) and (54).

Given these problems, it may be that the discourse analyst can make only very limited use of the results of psycholinguistic experiments on the nature of inference. The two-sentence text, specially constructed and presented in isolation from communicative context, is not generally what the discourse analyst encounters as data, nor what the language-user encounters as a linguistic message. The controlled experiment offers insight into some aspects of our processing of sentences, but it can be misleading to take discourse processing as generally occurring in this concentrated and narrowly delimited way.

7.10. Inferences as filling in gaps or discontinuities in interpretation

We have argued against equating inferences with any form of connection between sentences in a *text*. We have emphasised that inferences are connections people make when attempting to reach an interpretation of what they read or hear. We have also suggested that the more interpretive 'work' the reader (hearer) has to undertake in arriving at a reasonable interpretation of what the writer (speaker) intended to convey, the more likely it is that there are inferences being made. The problem with this view is that it leaves 'inferencing' as a process which is context-dependent, text-specific and located in the individual reader (hearer).

While we believe that this is a correct view and that it is, in principle, impossible to predict the *actual* inferences a reader will make in arriving at an interpretation of a text, we may be able to make predictions regarding particular aspects of individual texts which readers will generally have to interpret on the basis of inference. Such predictions will be closely related to some concept of 'depth of processing'. Clearly, the reader who casually skims across the news article presented below as (61) while sitting in the dentist's waiting room, is likely to be 'reading' the text in a qualitatively different way from the reader who is anticipating being asked comprehension questions after he has finished the text. Since the type of 'understanding' normally discussed in discourse analysis, in psycholinguistics, and in computational modelling, tends to be of the latter type, let us consider the text in terms of a set of comprehension questions which might be asked of the reader. If answering some of these questions appears to involve the reader in additional 'work' such as filling in gaps or discontinuities in his interpretation, then we may find a basis for predicting what kind of inferences will be required.

(61) 1. The agents of the Public Security Bureau seemed intent on terrorizing their victim, and they succeeded.
2. It was 1 a.m. when they marched into Peking's sprawling Friendship Hotel where many foreigners working in China live.
3. The police told room clerks to awaken American teacher Lisa Wichser, 29, and tell her that an urgent telegram had arrived for her.
4. When the petite, sandy-haired and somewhat sleepy Wichser appeared to claim it, she was handcuffed and hustled without explanation into a police car.
5. Technically, at least, the graduate student from Noblesville, Ind., had not been arrested.

(*Time*, 14 June 1982)

If we first try to answer the set of *who, what, where* and *when* questions, proposed by Warren et al. (1979), we should arrive at a partial representation of what we understand about the persons and events described in this text. The first thing we may note is that there isn't the simple proper name–pronoun connection throughout, as there was in (56). Instead, there is an array of different definite descriptions. We are not explicitly told that *the agents of the Public Security Bureau* are the same people as *the police* and that they *handcuffed* an individual. Nor are we explicitly informed that the expressions *their victim, American teacher Lisa Wichser, 29, the petite, sandy-haired and somewhat sleepy Wichser* and *the graduate student from Noblesville, Ind.* are all being used to refer to this particular individual. Unless the reader has some previous, specialised knowledge about this news item, he most likely has to 'work out' that *the police* in line 3 are the same individuals, more or less, as *the agents* in line 1. Some comparable interpretive 'work' has to be involved in equating *their victim* with *Lisa Wichser* and then with *the graduate student*. The interesting thing about this last expression is that it is a definite expression apparently being used to refer to an individual already introduced into the discourse domain and so a candidate for 'given' status. However, the information carried by the expression is 'new', in the discourse. It is, as we have noted in Chapter 5, a 'given' entity in a 'new' role. We suggest that, unless the reader has specialised knowledge about the entity in the mentioned role, this type of expression will create a potential discontinuity in the reader's interpretation and require inferencing.

Perhaps this last point can be more forcefully made by considering a brief text in which highly specialised knowledge is assumed and within which totally mistaken connections could be inferred by the uninformed reader.

(62)   As bullion levels dropped below the psychological $300 barrier, putting most high-cost mines into loss, kaffirs fell sharply, with 'the heavies' closing $1 to $4 down.

(*The Guardian*, 22 June 1982)

One might, on reading (62), infer that *kaffirs* are *bullion levels* or *high-cost mines*, or that *'the heavies'* are *high-cost mines* or 'bullion dealers' or some types of metals. We have been reliably informed that none of these inferences is justified, in fact.

Returning to extract (61), we can note that the *when* and *where* of the described events are only mentioned explicitly in sentence 2, but that we can operate with the 'no-spatio-temporal-change-unless-indicated' principle, expounded in Chapter 2, to place the events described in the other sentences in the same spatio-temporal location. However, in order to answer the question – *where was Lisa Wichser sleeping?* – some readers may feel that they have to perform some interpretive 'work'. Other readers may answer the question without hesitation and feel that no inferences have to be made. Clearly, it is not stated explicitly in the text that *Lisa Wichser* is even living in the *Friendship Hotel*. In order to answer the question, we would tentatively suggest, the reader would probably have to fill in the discontinuity existing in his interpretation. Such a conclusion, however, is intended largely as a hypothesis which might be tested in some experimental investigation with 'real' data such as the text in (61). At the moment, we can only suggest likely points at which inferences may be required.

Once one goes beyond the strictly factual considerations of *who, what, where* and *when* questions, the need for inference becomes very obvious. If *how* and *why* questions are asked, we immediately have to make what Warren et al. (1979) describe as 'elaborative' and 'evaluative' inferences. An elaborative inference would involve, for example, deciding how *Lisa Wichser* was probably dressed when she appeared to receive her *telegram*. An evaluative inference might involve deciding whether the police behaviour was justified or whether *the telegram* actually existed. It might be made in response to a question about why *Lisa Wichser* was *handcuffed* and taken away. A large part of our comprehension of what we read and hear (and see, no doubt) is, after all, a product of our making sense of the motivations, goals, plans and reasons of participants in de-scribed or witnessed events. Evaluative inferences must clearly be based on more than the reader's interpretation of the literal description of events in the text. They might be based on such diverse beliefs that, on the one hand, all Americans in China are CIA agents or, alternatively, that the Chinese continually harass foreigners for no reason. Such inferences will readily be made by a reader to try to account for behaviour which is described, but not explained, in a text. They represent the open-ended aspect of 'filling gaps' in text-described events which a reader may perform in arriving at his or her 'comprehension' of a text.

Given this 'open-ended' feature of inferencing, it is extremely difficult to provide, for any naturally occurring text, the single set of inferences which an individual reader has made in arriving at an interpretation. One might say, as Clark (1977) does, that there is a set of *necessary* inferences which every reader must make to arrive at an interpretation. However, those necessary inferences appear to be exactly the type which, on existing experimental evidence, do not require additional processing time. The fact that the *room clerks*, mentioned in sentence 3 of (61), must work in the *Hotel*, mentioned in sentence 2, would have to be treated as an automatic connection and likely to produce no evidence (in empirical terms) of processing via inference. The discourse analyst may consequently find himself in the confusing position that the so-called 'necessary' inferences may not justifiably be described as inferences at all, and the 'elaborative' and 'evaluative' inferences may be, in principle, undeterminable. In other words, the analyst may be left with no secure basis for talking, in analytic as opposed to intuitive terms, about the inferences involved in the comprehension of texts.

This rather bleak conclusion is not intended as a suggestion that the nature of inference is beyond description. Rather, it is an attempt to state the existing problem quite specifically. The illusion that we can determine the nature of inference by inventing a taxonomy and illustrating each type with a constructed set of sentences, as in Warren et al. (1979) and Clark (1977), is exposed whenever a naturally occurring piece of text is encountered (see van Dijk (1981) for a criticism of this taxonomic approach). The fact is that, until we can develop experimental techniques which allow us to draw conclusions about how people process naturally occurring discourse in 'real-life' contexts, we shall continue to underdetermine human understanding and overindulge our simplistic analytic metaphors. This applies not only to the nature of inference, but to the more general concept of comprehension itself.

At the present time, the most we can say is that a highly cohesive text which has few 'missing links' will require a lot of space to convey very little information, but will not demand a lot of interpretive 'work', via inference, on the part of the reader. However, it is typically the case that the texts which a reader will normally encounter will show a minimal amount of formal cohesion, assume massive amounts of existing background knowledge, and normally require the reader to make whatever inferences he feels willing to work for in order to reach an understanding of what is being conveyed. As an extreme example of this latter type of text, we leave the reader with extract (63) and ask him / her to try to write out even a few of the connections (one might say 'inferences') which have to be made in order to produce a coherent interpretation for what the reader thinks the text-producer intended to convey.

(63)   *Swap a child this summer: Family Centre Special Education Centre*

When 'O' or 'A' levels loom, there aren't many subjects in which parents can give direct help: except languages. The only satisfactory way to learn a language is to be immersed in it for a while. And since just on the other side of the water, a European teenager is in the same position with his English as yours with his French or German, a swap seems obvious. Three weeks or so in each other's family and the candidates surely will have that part of the G.C.E. or *bac* safely buttoned up. It's a simple idea and often it works very well but many mistakes are made by attempting it too soon. However, a well-adjusted child of 14+ should be able to cope.

(*Good Housekeeping Magazine*, 14 April 1976)

7.11 Conclusion

In this book we have tried to assemble some of the ingredients which would be required to construct an account of how people use language to communicate with each other. We have paid particular attention to ingredients which are dominant in the literature. We have tried to show that, at the present time, workers in discourse analysis have only a partial understanding of even the most-studied ingredients. There is a dangerous tendency, among established scholars as among students, to hope that a particular line of approach will yield 'the truth' about a problem. It is very easy to make claims which are too general and too strong. We have tried to show that some of the established wisdom in the area of discourse analysis may illuminate some aspects of discourse processing and of language use, but that all approaches open up yet more gaps in our understanding.

We have only discussed some of the relevant questions. We have largely ignored many aspects of the language of discourse which receives attention in mainstream linguistics. We have concentrated on questions relating to reference and to the general issues of coherence and relevance. We have left virtually untouched several areas which occupy scholars working on the interaction of semantics and syntax – questions of aspect, tense, modality, quantification, negation, adverbial modification and so on, as well as relevant issues like the influence of metaphor in the interpretation of discourse.

Such an approach obviously has pitfalls. We hope that the losses, in terms of the occasional simplified explication, will be outweighed by the gains in terms of accessibility. Above all, we hope that the analysis of discourse, undertaken in the manner presented in this book, will not only provide the reader with insights into the workings of his own language, but also encourage him to think afresh about the nature of that complex cognitive and social phenomenon we call 'discourse'.

References

Abelson, R. P. (1976) 'Script processing in attitude formation and decision-making' in (eds.) J. S. Carroll & J. W. Payne *Cognition and Social Behavior* Hillsdale, N. J.: Lawrence Erlbaum

Abercrombie, D. (1964) 'Syllable quantity and enclitics in English' in (eds) D. Abercrombie, D. B. Fry, P. A. D. MacCarthy, N. C. Scott, J. L. M. Trim *In Honour of Daniel Jones* London: Longman

Abercrombie, D. (1968) 'Paralanguage' *British Journal of Disorders of Communication* 3: 55–9

Allerton, D. J. (1975) 'Deletion and pro-form reduction' *Journal of Linguistics* 11: 213–37

Allwood, J., Andersson, L-G & Dahl, Ö. (1977) *Logic in Linguistics* Cambridge University Press

Anderson, R. C. (1977) 'The Notion of schemata and the educational enterprise' in (eds.) R. C. Anderson, R. J. Spiro & W. E. Montague

Anderson, R. C. & Ortony, A. (1975) 'On putting apples into bottles: a problem of polysemy' *Cognitive Psychology* 7: 167–80

Anderson, R. C., Pichert, J. W., Goetz, E. T., Schallert, D. L., Stevens, K. V. & Trollip, S. R. (1976) 'Instantiation of general terms' *Journal of Verbal Learning and Verbal Behaviour* 15: 667–79

Anderson, R. C., Reynolds, R. E., Schallert, D. L. & Goetz, E. T. (1977) 'Frameworks for comprehending discourse' *American Educational Research Journal* 14: 367–81

Anderson, R. C., Spiro, R. J. & Montague, W. E. (eds.) (1977) *Schooling and the Acquisition of Knowledge* Hillsdale, N. J.: Lawrence Erlbaum

Argyle, M. (ed.) (1969) *Social Encounters* Harmondsworth, Middx: Penguin Books

Austin, J. L. (1962) *How to do Things with Words* Oxford: Clarendon Press

Bar-Hillel, Y. (1970) *Aspects of Language* The Hebrew University, Jerusalem: The Magnes Press

Bartlett, F. C. (1932) *Remembering* Cambridge University Press

Becker, A. L. (1980) 'Text-building epistemology, and aesthetics in Javenese Shadow Theatre' in (eds.) A. Becker & A. Yengoyan *The Imagination of Reality* Norwood, N. J.: Ablex

Bennett, J. (1976) *Linguistic Behaviour* Cambridge University Press

Berry, M. (1975) *An Introduction to Systemic Linguistics 1: Structures and Systems* London: Batsford

Bobrow, D. & Fraser, B. (1969) 'An augmented state transition network analysis procedure' Paper presented at the *First International Joint Conference on Artificial Intelligence*

Bobrow· D. G., Kaplan R. M., Kay M., Norman D. A., Thompson H., & Winograd T. (1977) 'GUS, a frame-driven dialog system' *Artificial Intelligence* 8: 155–73

Bolinger, D. L. (1970) 'Relative height' reprinted in Bolinger (ed.) (1972) *Intonation* Harmondsworth, Middx: Penguin Books

Bower, G. H. (1978) 'Experiments on story comprehension and recall' *Discourse Processes* 1: 211–31

Bower, G. H., Black, J. B. & Turner, T. J. (1979) 'Scripts in memory for text' *Cognitive Psychology* 11: 177–220

Bransford, J., Barclay, R. & Franks, J. (1972) 'Sentence memory: a constructive versus interpretive approach' *Cognitive Psychology* 3: 193–209

Bransford, J. & Franks, J. (1971) 'The abstraction of linguistic ideas' *Cognitive Psychology* 2: 331–50

Bransford, J. D. & Johnson, M. K. (1973) 'Considerations of some problems of comprehension' in (ed.) W. G. Chase *Visual Information Processing* New York: Academic Press

Brewer, W. F. & Treyens, J. C. (1981) 'Role of schemata in memory for places' *Cognitive Psychology* 13: 207–30

Brown, E. K. & Miller, J. E. (1980) *Syntax: a Linguistic Introduction to Sentence Structure* London: Hutchinson

Brown, G. (1977) *Listening to Spoken English* London: Longman

Brown, G. (1983) 'Intonation, the categories given/new and other sorts of knowledge' in (eds.) A. Cutler & R. Ladd *Prosodic Function and Prosodic Representation* Cambridge University Press

Brown, G., Currie, K. L. & Kenworthy, J. (1980) *Questions of Intonation* London: Croom Helm

Brown, P. & Levinson, S. C. (1978) 'Universals in language usage: politeness phenomena' in (ed.) E. N. Goody

Bühler, K. (1934) *Sprachtheorie* Gustav Fischer: Jena

Butterworth, B. (ed.) (1980) *Language Production Volume 1: Speech and Talk* New York: Academic Press

Caramazza, A., Grober, E., Garvey, C. & Yates, J. (1977) 'Comprehension of anaphoric pronouns' *Journal of Verbal Learning and Verbal Behavior* 16: 601–9

Carpenter, P. A. & Just, M. A. (1977a) 'Integrative processes in comprehension' in (eds.) D. Laberge & S. J. Samuels

Carpenter, P. A. & Just M. A. (1977b) 'Reading comprehension as eyes see it' in (eds.) M. A. Just & P.A. Carpenter *Cognitive Processes in Comprehension* Hillsdale, N. J.: Lawrence Erlbaum

Chafe, W. L. (1970) *Meaning and the Structure of Language* University of Chicago Press

Chafe, W. L. (1972) 'Discourse structure and human knowledge' in (eds.) J. B. Carroll & R. O. Freedle *Language Comprehension and the Acquisition of Knowledge* Washington: Wiley

Chafe, W. L. (1974) 'Language and consciousness' *Language* 50

Chafe, W. L. (1976) 'Givenness, contrastiveness, definiteness, subjects, topics, and point of view' in (ed.) C. N. Li

Chafe, W. L. (1977a) 'The recall and verbalization of past experience' in (ed.) R. W. Cole *Current Issues in Linguistic Theory* Bloomington: Indiana University Press

Chafe, W. L. (1977b) 'Creativity in verbalization and its implication for the nature of stored knowledge' in (ed.) R. O. Freedle (1977)

Chafe, W. L. (1979) 'The flow of thought and the flow of language' in (ed.) T. Givón

Chafe, W. L. (ed.) (1980) *The Pear Stories: Cognitive, Cultural and Linguistic Aspects of Narrative Production* Norwood, N. J.: Ablex

Charniak, E. (1975) 'Organization and inference in a frame-like system of common-sense knowledge' in (eds.) R. C. Schank & B. L. Nash-Webber

Charniak, E. (1979) 'Ms. Malaprop, a language comprehension program' in (ed.) D. Metzing

References

Chastain, C. (1975) 'Reference and context' in (ed.) K. Gunderson *Language, Mind and Knowledge* Minnesota Studies in the Philosophy of Science Vol VII

Chiesi, H. L., Spilich, G. J. & Voss, J. F. (1979) 'Acquisition of domain-related information in relation to high and low domain knowledge' *Journal of Verbal Learning and Verbal Behavior* 18: 257–73

Chomsky, N. (1957) *Syntactic Structures* The Hague: Mouton

Chomsky N. (1965) *Aspects of the Theory of Syntax* Cambridge, Mass.: M.I.T. Press

Chomsky, N. (1968) *Language and Mind* New York: Harcourt, Brace & World

Chomsky, N. (1972) *Studies on Semantics in Generative Grammar* The Hague: Mouton

Christopherson, P. (1939) *The Articles: A Study of their Theory and Use in English* Oxford University Press

Cicourel, A. (1973) *Cognitive Sociology* Harmondsworth, Middx: Penguin Books

Cicourel, A. (1981) 'Language and the structure of belief in medical communication' in (eds.) B. Sigurd and J. Svartvik *Proceedings of AILA 81 Studia Linguistica* 5: 71–85

Clark, H. H. (1977) 'Inferences in comprehension' in (eds.) D. Laberge & S. J. Samuels

Clark, H. H. (1978) 'Inferring what is meant' in (eds.) W. J. M. Levelt & G. B. Flores d'Arcais

Clark, H. H. & Clark, E. V. (1977) *Psychology and Language* New York: Harcourt, Brace, Jovanovich

Clark, H. H. & Lucy, P. (1975) 'Understanding what is meant from what is said: a study in conversationally conveyed requests' *Journal of Verbal Learning and Verbal Behavior* 14: 56–72

Clark, H. H. & Marshall, C. R. (1981) 'Definite reference and mutual knowledge' in (eds.) A. K. Joshi, B. L. Webber & I. A. Sag

Clements, P. (1979) 'The effects of staging on recall from prose' in (ed.) R. O. Freedle (1979)

Cole, P. (ed.) (1978) *Syntax & Semantics 9: Pragmatics* New York: Academic Press

Cole, P. (ed.) (1981) *Radical Pragmatics* New York: Academic Press

Coulthard M. (1977) *An Introduction to Discourse Analysis* London: Longman

Creider C. A. (1979) 'On the explanation of transformations' in (ed.) T. Givón

Crystal D. (1975) *The English Tone of Voice* London: Edward Arnold

Crystal D. (1980) 'Neglected grammatical factors in conversational English' in (eds.) S. Greenbaum, G. Leech and J. Svartvik, *Studies in English Linguistics* London: Longman

Dahl Ö. (1969) *Topic and Comment: A Study in Russian and Transformational Grammar* Slavica Gothoburgensia 4: Göteborg

Dahl, Ö. (1976) 'What is new information?' in (eds.) N. E. Enkvist & V. Kohonen *Reports on Text Linguistics: Approaches to Word Order* Åbo, Finland: Åbo Akademi Foundation

Daneš, F. (1974) 'Functional sentence perspective and the organization of the text' in (ed.) F. Daneš

Daneš, F. (ed.) (1974) *Papers on Functional Sentence Perspective* Prague: Academia

Davidson, A. (1980) 'Peculiar Passives' *Language* 56: 42–67

de Beaugrande, R. (1980) *Text, Discourse and Process* London: Longman

de Beaugrande, R. & Dressler, W. U. (1981) *Introduction to Text Linguistics* London: Longman

Dechert, H. W. & Raupach, M. (eds.) (1980) *Temporal Variables in Speech* The Hague: Mouton

Deese, J. (1980) 'Pauses, prosody and the demands of production in language' in (eds.) H. W. Dechert & M. Raupach

de Long, A. J. (1974) 'Kinesic signals at utterance boundaries in preschool children' *Semiotica* 11: 43–73 de Villiers, J. G. & de Villiers, P. A. (1978) *Language Acquisition* Cambridge, Mass.: Harvard University Press

Donnellan, K. S. (1966) 'Reference and definite descriptions' *Philosophical Review* 75

Donnellan, K. S. (1978) 'Speaker references, descriptions and anaphora' in (ed.) P. Cole (1978)

Dover Wilson, J. (ed.) (1934) *The Manuscripts of Shakespeare's Hamlet and the Problems of its Transmission* Cambridge University Press

Downing, P. (1980) 'Factors influencing lexical choice in narrative' in (ed.) W. L. Chafe

Dresher, B. E. & Hornstein, N. H. (1976) 'On some supposed contributions of artificial intelligence to the scientific study of language' *Cognition* 4: 321–98

Dressler, W. U. (ed.) (1978) *Current Trends in Textlinguistics* Berlin: Walter de Gruyter

Duncan, S. (1973) 'Towards a grammar for dyadic conversation' *Semiotica* 9: 29–46

Duncan, S. (1974) 'On the structure of speaker–auditor interaction during speaking turns' *Language in Society* 3: 161–80

Ekman, P. and Friesen, W. V. (1969) 'Non-verbal leakage and cues to deception' in (ed.) M. Argyle

Enkvist, N. E. (1978) 'Coherence, pseudo-coherence, and non-coherence' in (ed.) J-O. Östman

Enkvist, N. E. (1980) 'Categories of situational context from the perspective of stylistics' *Language Teaching and Linguistics Abstracts* 13: 75–74

Fillmore, C. J. (1968) 'The case for case' in (eds.) E. Bach & R. Harms *Universals in Linguistic Theory* New York: Holt, Rinehart & Winston

Fillmore, C. J. (1975) 'An alternative to checklist theories of meaning' *Proceedings of the First Annual Meeting of the Berkeley Linguistics Society* University of California

Fillmore, C. J. (1977) 'Topics in lexical semantics' in (ed.) R. W. Cole *Current Issues in Linguistic Theory* Bloomington: Indiana University Press

Fillmore, C. J. (1981) 'Pragmatics and the description of discourse' in (ed.) P. Cole

Findler, N. (ed.) (1979) *Associative Networks. The Representation and Use of Knowledge in Computers* New York: Academic Press

Firbas, J. (1974) 'Some aspects of the Czechoslovak approach to the problems of functional sentence perspective' in (ed.) F. Daneš

Firth, J. R. (1957) *Papers in Linguistics* Oxford University Press

Freedle, R. O. (ed.) (1977) *Discourse Production and Comprehension* Norwood, N. J.: Ablex

Freedle, R. O. (ed.) (1979) *New Directions in Discourse Processing* Norwood, N. J.: Ablex

Garnham, A. (1979) 'Instantiation of verbs' *Quarterly Journal of Experimental Psychology* 31: 207–14

Garnham, A., Oakhill, J. & Johnson-Laird, P. (1982) 'Referential continuity and the coherence of discourse' *Cognition* 11: 29–46

Garrod, S. & Sanford, A. J. (1977) 'Interpreting anaphoric relations: the integration of semantic information while reading' *Journal of Verbal Learning and Verbal Behavior* 16: 77–90

Garvey, C., Caramazza, A. & Yates, J. (1975) 'Factors influencing assignment of pronoun antecedents' *Cognition* 3: 227–43

Gazdar, G. (1979) *Pragmatics* New York: Academic Press

Gazdar, C. (1980) 'Pragmatic constraints on linguistic production' in (ed.) B. Butterworth

Gensler, O. (1977) 'Non-syntactic anaphora and frame semantics' *Proceedings of the Third Annual Meeting of the Berkeley Linguistics Society* University of California

Giglioli, P. P. (ed) (1972) *Language and Social Context* Harmondsworth, Middx: Penguin Books

Givón, T. (1976) 'Topic, pronoun and grammatical agreement' in (ed.) C.N. Li

References

Givón, T. (1979a) *On Understanding Grammar* New York: Academic Press

Givón, T. (1979b) 'From discourse to syntax: grammar as a processing strategy' in (ed.) T. Givón

Givón, T. (ed.) (1979) *Syntax and Semantics Volume 12: Discourse and Syntax* New York: Academic Press

Gladwin, T. & Sturtevant, W. C. (1962) *Anthropology and Human Behavior* Anthropological Society of Washington

Goffman, E. (1974) *Frame Analysis* New York: Harper & Row

Goffman, E. (1981) *Forms of talk* Oxford: Basil Blackwell

Gomulicki, B. R. (1956) 'Recall as an abstractive process' *Acta Psychologica* 12: 77–94

Goody, E. N. (ed.) (1978) *Questions and Politeness* Cambridge University Press

Goody, J. (1977) *The Domestication of the Savage Mind* Cambridge University Press

Goody, J. and Watt, I. P. (1963) 'The consequences of literacy' *Comparative Studies in History and Society* 5: 304–45

Graesser, A. C., Higginbotham, J., Robertson, S. P. & Smith, W. R. (1978) 'A natural inquiry into the National Enquirer: Self-induced versus task-induced reading comprehension' *Discourse Processes* 1: 355–72

Grice, H. P. (1957) 'Meaning' *Philosophical Review* 64: 377–88

Grice, H. P. (1975) 'Logic and conversation' in (eds.) P. Cole & J. Morgan *Syntax and Semantics 3: Speech Acts* New York: Academic Press

Grice, H. P. (1981) 'Presupposition and conversational implicature' in (ed.) P. Cole

Grimes, J. E. (1975) *The Thread of Discourse* The Hague: Mouton

Grimes, J. E. (ed.) (1978) *Papers on Discourse* Summer Institute of Linguistics, Dallas, Texas

Grosz, B. (1979) 'Focusing in dialog' *American Journal of Computational Linguistics* Fiche 79: 96–103

Grosz, B. J. (1981) 'Focusing and description in natural language dialogues' in (eds.) A. K. Joshi, B. L. Webber & I. A. Sag

Gumperz, J. J. (1977) 'Sociocultural knowledge in conversational inference' in (ed.) M. Saville-Troike *Georgetown University Round Table on Languages and Linguistics, 1977* Washington: Georgetown University Press

Gutwinski, W. (1976) *Cohesion in Literary Texts* The Hague: Mouton

Halle, M., Bresnan, J. & Miller, G. A. (1978) *Linguistic Theory and Psychological Reality* Cambridge, Mass.: M.I.T. Press

Halliday, M. A. K. (1967) 'Notes on transitivity and theme in English: Part 2' *Journal of Linguistics* 3: 199–244

Halliday, M. A. K. (1970a) *A Course in Spoken English: Intonation* Oxford University Press

Halliday, M. A. K. (1970b) 'Language structure and language function' in (ed.) J. Lyons *New Horizons in Linguistics* Harmondsworth, Middx: Penguin Books

Halliday, M. A. K. (1978) *Language as Social Semiotic* London: Edward Arnold

Halliday, M. A. K. & Hasan, R. (1976) *Cohesion in English* London: Longman

Hankamer, J. & Sag, I. (1976) 'Deep and surface anaphora' *Linguistic Inquiry* 7: 391–426

Hankamer, J. & Sag, I. (1977) 'Syntactically versus pragmatically controlled anaphora' in (eds.) R. W. Fasold & R. W. Shuy *Studies in Language Variation* Washington: Georgetown University Press

Harris, J. (1751) *Hermes: or a Philosophical Inquiry concerning Language and Universal Grammar* Reproduced Facsimile Edition, Menston (1968): Scolar Press

Harweg, R. (1978) 'Substitutional text linguistics' in (ed.) W. Dressler

Haviland, S. & Clark, H. H. (1974) 'What's new? Acquiring new information as a process in comprehension' *Journal of Verbal Learning and Verbal Behavior* 13: 512–21

Hawkins, J. A. (1978) *Definiteness and Indefiniteness* London: Croom Helm

Hayes, P. J. (1979) 'The logic of frames' in (ed.) D. Metzing

Hayes-Roth, B. & Thorndyke, P. W. (1979) 'Integration of knowledge from text' *Journal of Verbal Learning and Verbal Behavior* 18: 91–108

Hildyard, A. & Olson, D. R. (1978) 'Memory and inference in the comprehension of oral and written discourse' *Discourse Processes* 1: 91–117

Hinds, J. (1977) 'Paragraph structure and pronominalization' *Papers in Linguistics* 10: 77–99

Hinds, J. (1979) 'Organizational patterns in discourse' in (ed.) T. Givón

Hockett, C. F. (1958) *A Course in Modern Linguistics* New York: Macmillan

Horn, L. R. (1973) 'Greek Grice: a brief survey of proto-conversational rules in the history of logic' in *Papers from the Ninth Regional Meeting* Chicago Linguistic Society

Hornby, P. A. (1972) 'The psychological subject and predicate' *Cognitive Psychology* 3: 632–42

Hudson, R. A. (1980) *Sociolinguistics* Cambridge University Press

Hymes, D. (1962) 'The ethnography of speaking' in (eds.) T. Gladwin & W. C. Sturtevant

Hymes D. (1964) 'Toward ethnographies of communicative events' in (ed.) P. P. Giglioli

Isard S. (1975) 'Changing the context' in (ed.) E. L. Keenan

Jakobson R. (1960) 'Closing statements: linguistics and poetics' in (ed.) T. A. Sebeok *Style in Language* Cambridge, Mass.; M.I.T. Press

Jefferson G. (1972) 'Side sequences' in (ed.) D. Sudnow

Jefferson, G. (1973) 'A case of precision timing in ordinary conversation: overlapped tag-positioned address terms in closing sequences' *Semiotica* 9: 47–96

Johnson-Laird, P. N. (1980) 'Mental models in cognitive science' *Cognitive Science* 4: 71–115

Johnson-Laird, P. N. (1981a) 'Mental models of meaning' in (eds.) A. K. Joshi, B. L. Webber & I. A. Sag

Johnson-Laird, P. N. (1981b) 'Comprehension as the construction of mental models' in *The Psychological Mechanisms of Language* Philosophical Transactions of the Royal Society of London: The Royal Society and The British Academy

Johnson-Laird, P. N. & Garnham, A. (1979) 'Descriptions and discourse models' *Linguistics and Philosophy* 3: 371–393

Johnson-Laird, P. N. & Steedman, M. (1978) 'The psychology of syllogisms' *Cognitive Psychology* 10: 64–99

Jones, L. K. (1977) *Theme in English Expository Discourse* Jupiter Press

Joshi, A. K., Webber, B. L. & Sag, I. A. (eds.) (1981) *Elements of Discourse Understanding* Cambridge University Press

Källgren, G. (1978) 'Can a deep case model be used for text analysis?' in (ed.) K. Gregerson *Papers from the Fourth Scandinavian Conference of Linguistices* Odense University Press

Källgren, G. (1979) 'Some types of textual cohesion and their effects on texts' in (eds.) N. E. Enkvist & J. Wiksell *Papers from the Fifth Scandinavian Conference of Linguistics* Stockholm

Kaplan, S. J. (1981) 'Appropriate responses to inappropriate questions' in (eds.) A. K. Joshi, B. L. Webber & I. A. Sag

Karttunen, L. (1974) 'Presupposition and linguistic context' *Theoretical Linguistics* 1: 181–94

Karttunen, L. & Peters, S. (1979) 'Conventional implicature' in (eds.) C.-K. Oh & D. A. Dineen

Katz, J. (1980) 'Chomsky on meaning' *Language* 56: 1–42

Katz, J. J. & Fodor, J. A. (1963) 'The structure of a semantic theory' *Language* 39: 170–210

Keenan, E. L. (1971) 'Two kinds of presupposition in natural language' in (eds.) C. J. Fillmore & D. T. Langendoen *Studies in Linguistic Semantics* New York: Holt, Rinehart & Winston

References

Keenan, E. L. (ed.) (1975) *Formal Semantics of Natural Language* Cambridge University Press

Keehan, E. O. & Schieffelin, B. (1976) 'Topic as a discourse notion' in ed.) C. N. Li

Kempson, R. (1975) *Presupposition and the Delimitation of Semantics* Cambridge University Press

Kendon, A. (1967) 'Some functions of gaze direction in social interaction' *Acta Psychologica* 26: 22–63

Kintsch, W. (1974) *The Representation of Meaning in Memory* Hillsdale, N. J.: Lawrence Erlbaum

Kintsch, W. & Keenan, J. (1973) 'Reading rate and retention as a function of the number of propositions in the base structure of sentences' *Cognitive Psychology* 5: 257–74

Kuno, S. (1976) 'Subject, theme and the speaker's empathy' in (ed.) C.N. Li

Kuno, S. & Kaburaki, E. (1977) 'Empathy and syntax' *Linguistic Inquiry* 8: 627–72

Laberge, D. & Samuels, S. J. (eds.) (1977) *Basic Process in Reading: Perception and Comprehension* Hillsdale, N. J.: Lawrence Erlbaum

Labov, W. (1966) 'On the grammaticality of everyday speech' Paper presented at the LSA Annual Meeting, New York

Labov, W. (1970) 'The study of language in its social context' *Studium Generale* 23: 30–87 reprinted in Labov (1972a)

Labov, W. (1972a) *Sociolinguistic Patterns* Philadelphia: University of Pennsylvania Press

Labov, W. (1972b) 'Rules for ritual insults' in (ed.) D. Sudnow

Lacey, A. R. (1976) *A Dictionary of Philosophy* London: Routledge & Kegan Paul

Laffal, J. (1965) *Pathological and Normal Language* New York: Atherton Press

Lakoff, R. (1973) 'The logic of politeness; or minding your P's and Q's' in (ed.) C. Corum et al. *Papers from the Ninth Regional Meeting,* Chicago Linguistic Society

Laver, J. D. (1980) *The Phonetic Description of Voice Quality* Cambridge University Press

Lehiste, I. (1970) *Suprasegmentals* Cambridge, Mass.: M.I.T. Press

Levelt, W. J. M. (1981) 'The speaker's linearisation problem' in *The Psychological Mechanisms of Language* The Royal Society and The British Academy

Levelt, W. J. M. & Flores d'Arcais, G. B. (eds.) (1978) *Studies in the Perception of Language* New York: Wiley

Levinson, S. C. (1980) 'Speech Act theory: the state of the art' *Language Teaching and Linguistics: Abstracts* 13: 5–24

Levinson, S. C. (forthcoming) *Pragmatics* Cambridge University Press

Levy, D. M. (1979) 'Communicative goals and strategies: between discourse and syntax', in (ed.) T. Givón

Lewis, D. (1969) *Convention* Cambridge, Mass., Harvard University Press

Lewis, D. (1972) 'General Semantics' in (eds.) D. Davidson & G. H. Harman *Semantics of Natural Language* Dordrecht: Reidel

Li, C. N. (ed.) (1976) *Subject and Topic* New York: Academic Press

Linde, C. & Labov, W. (1975) 'Spatial networks as a site for the study of language and thought' *Language* 51: 924–40

Loftus, E. (1975) 'Leading questions and the eyewitness report' *Cognitive Psychology* 7: 560–72

Loftus, E. & Zanni, G. (1975) 'Eyewitness testimony' *Bulletin of the Psychonomic Society* 5: 86–8

Longacre, R. E. (1979) 'The paragraph as a grammatical unit' in (ed.) T. Givón

Luria, A. R. (1969) *The Mind of a Mnemonist* London: Jonathan Cape

Lyons, J. (1968) *Introduction to Theoretical Linguistics* Cambridge University Press

Lyons, J. (1977) *Semantics* Cambridge University Press

Lyons, J. (1979) 'Deixis and anaphora' in (ed.) T. Myers *The Development of Conversation and Discourse* Edinburgh University Press

McCawley, J. D. (1979) 'Presupposition & discourse structure' in (eds.) C.-K. Oh & D. Dinneen *Syntax & Semantics, Vol 11: Presupposition* New York: Academic Press

McKay, D. G. & Fulkerson, D. C. (1979) 'On the comprehension and production of pronouns' *Journal of Verbal Learning and Verbal Behavior* 18: 662–73

Malinowski, B. (1935) *Coral Gardens and their Magic, Volume 2* London: Allen & Unwin

Mandler, J. & Johnson, N. (1977) 'Remembrance of things parsed: story structure and recall' *Cognitive Psychology* 9: 111–51

Maratsos, M. (1971) 'A note on NPs made definite by entailment' *Linguistic Inquiry* 2: 254

Mathesius, V. (1942) 'From comparative word order studies' *Časopis pro Moderní Filoligii* 28

Matthews, P. H. (1981) *Syntax* Cambridge University Press

Maynard, D. W. (1980) 'Placement of topic changes in conversation' *Semiotica* 30: 263–90

Metzing, D. (ed.) (1979) *Frame Conceptions and Text Understanding* Berlin: de Gruyter

Meyer, B. J. F. (1975) *The Organisation of Prose and its Effects on Memory* Amsterdam: North Holland

Meyer, B. J. F. (1977) 'What is remembered from prose: a function of passage structure' in (ed.) R. O. Freedle (1977)

Minsky, M. (1975) 'A framework for representing knowledge' in (ed.) Winston, P. H. *The Psychology of Computer Vision* New York: McGraw-Hill

Mitchell, T. F. (1957) 'The language of buying and selling in Cyrenaica: a situational statement' *Hesperis* 44: 31–71

Morgan, J. L. (1975) 'Some remarks on the nature of sentences' in *Papers from the Parasession on Functionalism* Chicago Linguistic Society

Morgan, J. L. (1979) 'Toward a rational model of discourse comprehension' *American Journal of Computational Linguistics* Fiche 79

Morris, C. W. (1938) 'Foundations of the theory of signs' reprinted in Morris, C. W. (1971) *Writings on the General Theory of Signs* The Hague: Mouton

Nunberg, G. D. (1978) 'The pragmatics of reference' Indiana University Linguistics Club, Bloomington

Nunberg, G. D. (1979) 'The non-uniqueness of semantic solutions: polysemy' *Linguistics and Philosophy* 3: 143–84

Ochs, E. (1979) 'Planned and unplanned discourse' in (ed.) T. Givón

Oh, C.-K. & Dineen, D. A. (eds.) (1979) *Syntax and Semantics Volume 11 : Presupposition* New York: Academic Press

Omanson, R. C., Warren, W. H. & Trabasso, T. (1978) 'Goals, inferential comprehension and recall of stories by children' *Discourse Processes* 1: 337–54

Östman J.-O. (1978) 'Text, cohesion, and coherence' in (ed.) J.-O. Östman

Östman J.-O. (ed.) (1978) *Cohesion and Semantics* Åbo, Finland: Åbo Akademi Foundation

Paivio, A. (1971) *Imagery and Verbal Processes* New York: Holt, Rinehart & Winston

Partee, B. H. (1978) 'Bound variables and other anaphors' *American Journal of Computational Linguistics* Fiche 78

Partee, B. H. (ed.) (1976) *Montague Grammar* Academic Press

Pellowe, J. & Jones, V. (1979) 'Establishing intonationally variable systems in a multi-dimensional linguistic space' *Language & Speech* 22: 97–116

Perfetti, C. A. & Goldman, S. R. (1974) 'Thematization and sentence retrieval' *Journal of Verbal Learning and Verbal Behavior* 13: 70–9

Petöfi, J. S. (ed.) (1978) *Texts vs Sentence. Basic Questions of Textlinguistics* Hamburg: Buske Verlag

Petöfi, J. S. & Rieser, H. (eds.) (1974) *Studies in Text Grammar* Dordrecht: Reidel

References

Pirsig, R. M. (1976) *Zen and the Art of Motor-cycle Maintenance* London: Corgi Books

Popper, K. R. (1963) *Conjectures and Refutations* London: Routledge & Kegan Paul

Prince, E. F. (1978) 'A comparison of WH-clefts and it-clefts in discourse' *Language* 54: 883–907

Prince, E. F. (1981) 'Toward a taxonomy of given – new information' in (ed.) P. Cole *Radical Pragmatics* New York: Academic Press

Quine, W. V. (1960) *Word and Object* Cambridge, Mass.: M.I.T. Press

Quine, W. V. (1969) *Ontological Relativity and Other Essays* New York: Columbia University Press

Quirk, R., Greenbaum, S., Leech G. and Svartvik, J. (1972) *A Grammar of Contemporary English* London: Longman

Reder, L. (1979) 'The role of elaborations in memory for prose' *Cognitive Psychology* 11: 221–34

Reder, L. & Anderson, J. (1980) 'A comparison of texts and their summaries: memorial consequences' *Journal of Verbal Learning and Verbal Behavior* 19: 121–34

Riesbeck, C. K. (1975) 'Computational understanding' in (eds.) R. C. Schank & B. L. Nash-Webber

Riesbeck, C. K. & Schank, R. C. (1978) 'Comprehension by computer: expectation-based analysis of sentences in context' in (eds.) W. J. M. Levelt & G. B. Flores d'Arcais

Rochester, S. R. & Martin J. R. (1977) 'The art of referring: the speaker's use of noun phrases to instruct the listener' in (ed.) R. O. Freedle (1977)

Rochester, S. & Martin, J. R. (1979) *Crazy Talk: A Study of the Discourse of Schizophrenic Speakers* New York: Plenum Press

Rommetveit R. (1974) *On Message Structure: A Framework for the Study of Language and Communication* New York: Wiley

Rosch, E. (1973) 'Natural categories' *Cognitive Psychology* 4: 328–50

Rosch, E. (1977) 'Classification of real-world objects: origins and representations in cognition' in (eds.) P. Johnson-Laird & P. C. Wason *Thinking: Readings in Cognitive Science* Cambridge University Press

Rosch, E., Mervis, C. B., Gray, W. D., Johnson, D. M. & Boyes-Braem, P. (1976) 'Basic objects in natural categories' *Cognitive Psychology* 8: 382–439

Ross, R. N. (1975) 'Ellipsis and the structure of expectation' *San Jose State Occasional Papers in Linguistics* 1: 183–91

Rumelhart, D. (1975) 'Notes on a schema for stories' in (eds.) D. Bobrow & A. Collins *Representation and Understanding: Studies in Cognitive Science* New York: Academic Press

Rumelhart, D. E. (1977) 'Understanding and summarizing brief stories' in (eds.) D. Laberge & S. J. Samuels

Rumelhart, D. E. & Ortony, A. (1977) 'The representation of knowledge in memory' in (eds.) R. C. Anderson, R. J. Spiro & W. E. Montague

Sacks, H. (1971) 'Mimeo lecture notes' Quoted in Coulthard (1977)

Sacks, H. (1972) 'An initial investigation of the usability of conversational data for doing sociology' in (ed.) D. Sudnow

Sacks, H., Schegloff E. A. & Jefferson G. (1974) 'A simplest systematics for the organisation of turn-taking for conversation' *Language* 50: 696–735. Reprinted in (ed.) J. Schenkein (1978)

Sadock, J. M. (1978) 'On testing for conversational implicature' in (ed.) P. Cole

Sampson, G. (1980) *Schools of Linguistics* London: Hutchinson

Sanford, A. J. & Garrod, S. C. (1981) *Understanding Written Language* Chichester: Wiley

Sapir, E. (1933) 'Language' in (ed.) D. G. Mandelbaum (1962) *Edward Sapir: Culture Language and Personality* University of California Press

Schank, R. C. (1972) 'Conceptual dependency: a theory of natural language understanding' *Cognitive Psychology* 3: 552–631

Schank, R. C. (1973) 'Identification of conceptualizatons underlying natural language' in (ed.) R. C. Schank & K. M. Colby *Computer Models of Thought and Language* San Francisco: Freeman

Schank, R. C. (1977) 'Rules and topics in conversation' *Cognitive Science* 1: 421–42

Schank, R. C. (1979) 'Some prerequisites for a computational pragmatics' in (ed.) J. L. Moy *Pragmalinguistics* The Hague: Mouton

Schank, R. C. & Abelson, R. (1977) *Scripts, Plans, Goals and Understanding* Hillsdale, N. J.: Lawrence Erlbaum

Schank, R. C. & Nash-Webber, B. L. (eds.) (1975) *Theoretical Issues in Natural Language Processing* Cambridge, Mass.: Bolt, Beranek & Newman

Schegloff, E. A. (1968) 'Sequencing in conversational openings' *American Anthropologist* 70: 1075–95

Schegloff, E. A. (1972) 'Notes on conversational practice: formulating place' in (ed.) D. Sudnow

Schegloff, E. A. & Sacks, H. (1973) 'Opening up closings' *Semiotica* 8: 289–327

Schenkein, J. (ed.) (1978) *Studies in the Organization of Conversational Interaction* New York: Academic Press

Schiffer, S. R. (1972) *Meaning* Oxford: Clarendon Press

Schmerling, S. (1974) 'A re-examination of "normal stress"' *Language* 50: 66–73

Schustack, M. W. & Anderson, J. R. (1979) 'Effects of analogy to prior knowledge on memory for new information' *Journal of Verbal Learning and Verbal Behavior* 18: 565–83

Schutz, A. (1953) 'Common-sense and scientific interpretation of human action' *Philosophy and Phenomenological Research* 14: 1–38

Searle, J. R. (1969) *Speech Acts* Cambridge University Press

Searle, J. R. (1975) 'Indirect speech acts' in (eds.) P. Cole & J. L. Morgan *Syntax and Semantics 3: Speech Acts* New York: Academic Press

Searle, J. R. (1979) *Expression and Meaning* Cambridge University Press

Searle, J. R., Kiefer, F. & Bierwisch, M. (eds.) (1980) *Speech Act Theory and Pragmatics* Dordecht: Reidel

Sgall, P. (1980) 'Towards a pragmatically based theory of meaning' in (eds.) J. R. Searle, F. Kiefer & M. Bierwisch

Sgall, P., Hajičová E. & Benečová E. (1973) *Topic, Focus and Generative Semantics* Kronberg: Scriptor Verlag

Sinclair, J.McH. & Coulthard, R. M. (1975) *Towards an Analysis of Discourse* Oxford University Press

Smith, N. & Wilson, D. (1979) *Modern Linguistics* Harmondsworth, Middx: Penguin Books

Spiro, R. J. (1977) 'Remembering information from text: the "state of schema" approach' in (eds.) R. C. Anderson, R. J. Spiro & W. E. Montague

Stalnaker R. C. (1978) 'Assertion' in (ed.) P. Cole

Steedman, M. J. & Johnson-Laird, P. N. (1980) 'The production of sentences, utterances and speech acts: Have computers anything to say?' in (ed.) B. Butterworth

Stein, N. & Glenn, C. (1979) 'An analysis of story comprehension in elementary school children' in (ed.) R. O. Freedle (1979)

Stein, N. & Nezworski, T. (1978) 'The effects of organization and instructional set on story memory' *Discourse Processes* 1: 177–94

Stenning, K. (1978) 'Anaphora as an approach to pragmatics' in (eds.) M. Halle et al.

Strawson, P. F. (1950) 'On referring' *Mind* 54

References

Sudnow, D. (ed.) (1972) *Studies in Social Interaction* NewYork: The Free Press

Tannen, D. (1979) 'What's in a frame? Surface evidence for underlying expectations' in (ed.) R. O. Freedle (1979)

Tannen, D. (1980) 'A comparative analysis of oral narrative strategies: Athenian Greek and American English' in (ed.) W. L. Chafe

Thomason, R. (ed.) (1974) *Formal Philosophy. Selected Papers of Richard Montague* New Haven, Conn.: Yale University Press

Thompson, H. S. (1980) 'Stress and salience in English' Palo Alto Research Centre: Xerox

Thorndyke, P. W. (1977) 'Cognitive structures in comprehension and memory of narrative discourse' *Cognitive Psychology* 9: 77–110

Thorne, J., Bratley, P. & Dewar, H. (1968) 'The syntactic analysis of English by machine' in (ed.) D. Michie *Machine Intelligence 3* University of Edinburgh Press

Trudgill, P. (1974) *Sociolinguistics: an introduction* Harmondsworth, Middx: Penguin Books

Tyler, S. A. (1978) *The Said and the Unsaid* New York: Academic Press

Vachek, J. (1966) *The Linguistic School of Prague* Bloomington: Indiana University Press

Venneman, T. (1975) 'Topic, sentence accent, and ellipsis: a proposal for their formal treatment' in (ed.) E. L. Keenan

van der Auwera, J. (ed.) (1980) *The Semantics of Determiners* London: Croom Helm

van Dijk, T. A. (1972) *Some Aspects of Text Grammars* The Hague: Mouton

van Dijk, T. A. (1973) 'Text grammar and text logic' in (eds.) J. Petöfi & H. Rieser *Studies in Text Grammars* Dordrecht: Reidel

van Dijk, T. A. (1977) *Text and Context* London: Longman

van Dijk, T. A. (1981) 'Review of R. O. Freedle (ed.) 1979' *Journal of Linguistics* 17: 140–8

van Dijk, T. A., Ihwe J., Petöfi J. & Rieser H. (1972) *Zur Bestimmung Narrativer Strukturen auf der Grundlage von Textgrammatiken* Hamburg: Buske Verlag

Vygotsky, L. A. (1962) *Thought and Language* trans. E. Haufmann and G. Vakar Cambridge, Mass.: M.I.T. Press

Warren, W. H., Nicholas, D. W. & Trabasso, T. (1979) 'Event chains and inferences in understanding narratives' in (ed.) R. O. Freedle (1979)

Webber, B. L. (1978) *A Formal Approach to Discourse Anaphora* Report No. 3761 Cambridge, Mass.: Bot, Beranek & Newman

Webber, B. L. (1981) 'Discourse model synthesis: preliminaries to reference' in (eds.) A. K. Joshi, B. L. Webber & I. A. Sag

Widdowson, H. G. (1978) *Teaching Language as Communication* Oxford University Press

Widdowson, H. G. (1979a) *Explorations in Applied Linguistics* Oxford University Press

Widdowson, H. G. (1979b) 'Rules and procedures in discourse analysis' in (ed.) T. Myers *The Development of Conversation and Discourse* Edinburgh University Press

Wilks, Y. (1977) 'Natural language understanding systems within the AI paradigm: a survey' in (ed.) A. Zampolli *Linguistic Structures Processing* Amsterdam: North Holland

Wilks, Y. (1979) 'Frames, semantics and novelty' in (ed.) D. Metzing

Winograd, T. (1972) *Understanding Natural Language* New York: Academic Press

Winston, P. (1977) *Artificial Intelligence* Rowley, Mass.: Addison-Wesley

Wittgenstein, L. J. J. (1953) *Philosophical Investigations* Oxford: Basil Blackwell

Woods, W. (1970) 'Transition network grammars for natural language analysis' *Communications of the Association for Computing Machinery* 13: 591–606

Wootton, A. (1975) *Dilemmas of Discourse* London: Allen & Unwin

Yekovich, F. R. & Thorndyke, P. W. (1981) 'An evaluation of alternative functional models of narrative schemata' *Journal of Verbal Learning and Verbal Behavior* 20: 454–69

Yule, G. (1979) 'Pragmatically controlled anaphora' *Lingua* 49: 127–35

Yule, G. (1980) 'The functions of phonological prominence' *Archivum Linguisticum* XI: 31–46

Yule G. (1981) 'New, current and displaced entity reference' *Lingua* 55: 41–52

SUBJECT INDEX

AUTHOR INDEX

Author index

文库索引

Semantics 语义学

Lyons, J.	*Linguistic Semantics: An Introduction*
	语义学引论
Saeed, J. I.	*Semantics*
	语义学

Pragmatics 语用学

Peccei, J. S.	*Pragmatics*
	语用学
Verschueren, J.	*Understanding Pragmatics*
	语用学新解

Discourse Analysis 话语分析

Brown, G. et al.	*Discourse Analysis*
	话语分析
Gee, J. P.	*An Introduction to Discourse Analysis: Theory & Method*
	话语分析入门：理论与方法

Lexicography 词典学

Hartmann, R. R. K. et al.	*Dictionary of Lexicography*
	词典学词典

Stylistics 文体学

Thornborrow, J. et al.	*Stylistics for Students of Language and Literature*
	语言模式：文体学入门
Wright, L. et al.	*Stylistics: A Practical Coursebook*
	实用文体学教程

Typology 语言类型学

Croft, W.	*Typology and Universals*
	语言类型学与普遍语法特征

Sociolinguistics 社会语言学

Fasold, R.	*The Sociolinguistics of Language*
	社会语言学
Hudson, R. A.	*Sociolinguistics* Second edition
	社会语言学教程

290

Wardhaugh, R.　　　　　*Introduction to Sociolinguistics* Third edition
　　　　　　　　　　　社会语言学引论

Psycholinguistics 心理语言学

Aitchison, J.　　　　　*The Articulate Mammal*: *An Introduction to Psycholinguistics* Fourth edition
　　　　　　　　　　　会说话的哺乳动物：心理语言学入门

Carroll, D. W.　　　　 *Psychology of Language* Third edition
　　　　　　　　　　　语言心理学

Functional Linguistics 功能语言学

Halliday, M. A. K.　　　*An Introduction to Functional Grammar* Second edition
　　　　　　　　　　　功能语法导论

Thompson, G.　　　　　*Introducing Functional Grammar*
　　　　　　　　　　　功能语法入门

Historical Linguistics 历史语言学

Trask, R. L.　　　　　 *Historical Linguistics*
　　　　　　　　　　　历史语言学

Corpus Linguistics 语料库语言学

Biber, D. et al.　　　　*Corpus Linguistics*
　　　　　　　　　　　语料库语言学

Kennedy, G.　　　　　 *An Introduction to Corpus Linguistics*
　　　　　　　　　　　语料库语言学入门

History of the English Language 英语史

Freeborn, D.　　　　　*From Old English to Standard English* Second edition
　　　　　　　　　　　英语史：从古代英语到标准英语

Intercultural Communication 跨文化交际

Samovar, L. A. et al.　　*Communication Between Cultures* Second edition
　　　　　　　　　　　跨文化交际

Scollon, R. et al.　　　 *Intercultural Communication*: *A Discourse Analysis*
　　　　　　　　　　　跨文化交际：语篇分析法

Translatology 翻译学

Baker, M.	*In Other Words : A Coursebook on Translation*
	换言之：翻译教程

Statistics in Linguistics 语言统计学

Woods, A. et al.	*Statistics in Language Studies*
	语言研究中的统计学

First Language Acquisition 第一语言习得

Goodluck, H.	*Language Acquisition : A Linguistic Introduction*
	从语言学的角度看语言习得
Peccei, J. S.	*Child Language* New edition
	儿童语言

Second Language Acquisition 第二语言习得

Cohen, A. D.	*Strategies in Learning and Using a Second Language*
	学习和运用第二语言的策略
Cook, V.	*Linguistics and Second Language Acquisition*
	语言学和第二语言习得
Cook, V.	*Second Language Learning and Language Teaching*
	Second edition
	第二语言学习与教学
Larsen-Freeman, D. et al.	*An Introduction to Second Language Acquisition*
	Research
	第二语言习得研究概况

Course Design 课程设计

Yalden, J.	*Principles of Course Design for Language Teaching*
	语言教学课程设计原理

Methodology 教学法

Harmer, J.	*How to Teach English*
	怎样教英语
Richards, J. et al.	*Approaches and Methods in Language Teaching*
	语言教学的流派
Trudgill, P. et al.	*International English* Third edition
	英语：国际通用语

Ur, P.   *A Course in Language Teaching*: *Practice and Theory*
                                    语言教学教程:实践与理论

Testing 测试学
Alderson, J.C. et al.   *Language Test Construction and Evaluation*
                                    语言测试的设计与评估
Heaton, J.B.   *Writing English Language Tests* New edition
                                    英语测试

Research Method 研究方法
McDonough, J. et al.   *Research Methods for English Language Teachers*
                                    英语教学科研方法
Slade, C.   *Form and Style*: *Research Papers*, *Reports*, *Theses*
                                    Tenth edition
                                    如何写研究论文与学术报告

Academic Writing 学术写作
Roberts, W.H. et al.   *About Language*: *A Reader for Writers* Fifth edition
                                    谈语言：写作读本

English Grammar 英语语法
Biber,D. et al.   *Longman Grammar of Spoken and Written English*
                                    朗文英语口语和笔语语法

Dictionary 辞典
Bussmann, H.   *Routledge Dictionary of Language and Linguistics*
                                    语言与语言学词典
Richards, J.C. et al.   *Longman Dictionary of Language Teaching &*
                                    Applied Linguistics
                                    朗文语言教学及应用语言学辞典(英英·英汉双解)